...may 7 2005

Presented to the

All party and multifaith Committee
on Religious-Cultural Harmony
with gratitude
for the significant contribution
being made through its efforts
to promote religious and cultural
harmony

Susanne Tauras —
on behalf of
the Bahá'í Community of Canada

The Bahá'í World
2002–2003

159 OF THE BAHÁ'Í ERA

THE BAHÁ'Í WORLD

2002-2003

AN INTERNATIONAL RECORD

BAHÁ'Í WORLD CENTRE
HAIFA

Order department:
Bahá'í Distribution Service
4703 Fulton Industrial Blvd.
Atlanta, GA 30336-2017
USA
E-mail: bds@usbnc.org

Senior editor: Ann Boyles
Assistant editor: Alex McGee

Photo credits: p. 63, Ryan Lash; p. 64, Helen Kontos; pp. 46, 52, originally appeared on the Bahá'í World News Service; p. 83, originally appeared in *One Country*. All others courtesy of the Audio-Visual Department of the Bahá'í World Centre. Map on p. 180, copyright UNAIDS. Graph on p. 181, copyright Basia Zaba, published in the UNAIDS Global Report 2000.

ISBN 0-85398-973-7

CONTENTS

Essays, Statements, and Profiles

Statements by the Bahá'í International Community

Statements by National Spiritual Assemblies

Information and Resources

Introduction to the Bahá'í Community

G iving a paper on the theme of "Prosperity" to an audience of some 100 people in the UK, a 13-year-old girl asserts that humanity will not reach its highest level of attainment until the equality of women and men is fully established. A new radio station is launched in the Philippines, and the staff dedicate themselves to providing programs that lead not only to social and economic development but also to the development of the moral, spiritual, and human resources of the 2.3 million-member listening audience. In Zambia, some 300 people from 17 countries gather to celebrate a special "golden jubilee." Educators in Tonga inaugurate two new buildings on the campus of a school that aims to create graduates dedicated to the service of humanity. A museum in Charleston, South Carolina, in the US, is dedicated to the memory of a black lawyer who, in the early years of the twentieth century, was a pioneer in promoting race unity. The originators of a tutorial learning program that started in Colombia and has spread throughout Latin America are honored for their work by the Club of Budapest. A youth group in Australia receives a grant from the government to promote harmony in diversity in schools, using the arts. In Kosovo, a nongovernmental organization is asked to host moral leadership seminars to promote better understanding among ethnic groups. And organizers are over-whelmed by the huge turnout at a children's festival in Cambodia, open to children and youth of all social classes.

Although they come from diverse backgrounds and far-flung areas of the planet, these people all share a united view of the world, its future, and their role in shaping it. They are Bahá'ís.

The Bahá'í International Community, comprising members of the Bahá'í Faith from all over the globe, now numbers more than five million souls. Its members represent 2,112 ethnic and tribal groups who live in more than 100,000 localities in 191 independent countries and 46 dependent territories. What was once regarded by some as a small, obscure sect was reported by the *Britannica Book of the Year 2002* to be the second-most widely spread independent religion in the world, after Christianity. Its membership cuts across all bound-aries of class and race, governing itself through the establishment of local and national elected bodies known as Spiritual Assemblies. Its international center and the seat of its world governing council, known as the Universal House of Justice, are located in the Holy Land, in Haifa, Israel.

This article offers a brief introduction to the Bahá'í community, its history, its spiritual teachings, and its aims and objectives.

Origins

In 1844, a young Persian merchant named Siyyid 'Alí-Muḥammad declared Himself to be the Promised Qá'im awaited by Shia Muslims. He adopted the title "the Báb," which means "the Gate," and His teachings quickly attracted a large following. Alarmed by the grow-ing numbers of "Bábís," as His followers were known, the Muslim clergy allied themselves with ministers of the Shah in an effort to destroy the infant Faith. Many thousands of Bábís were persecuted, tortured, and killed in the following years, but the growth of the new religion continued even after the Báb Himself was imprisoned and later executed in July 1850. The horrific treatment of the Bábís at the hands of the secular and religious authorities was recorded by a number of Western diplomats, scholars, and travelers, who expressed their admiration for the character and fortitude of the victims.

The Bábí religion sprang from Islam in much the same manner that Christianity sprang from Judaism or Buddhism did from Hinduism. That is to say, it was apparent early in the Báb's ministry that the religion established by Him was not merely a sect or a movement within Islam but an independent Faith. Furthermore, one of the main tenets of Bábí belief was the Báb's statement that He had been sent by God to prepare the way for One greater than Himself, Who would inaugurate an era of peace and righteousness throughout the world, representing the culmination of all past religious dispensations.

Mírzá Husayn-'Alí was one of the leading adherents of the Bábí Faith Who was arrested and imprisoned during the tumultuous years of the Báb's brief ministry. Because of pressure on the Persian Shah from European diplomats, He was spared from execution but was banished from Persia to Baghdad, Constantinople, Adrianople, and finally the penal colony of Acre in Palestine. Thus, the Persian government, which had secured the support of the rulers of the rival Ottoman Empire in suppressing the new movement, expected that His sphere of influence would be severely limited.

During His initial imprisonment, Mírzá Husayn-'Alí had received the first divine intimations that He was the Promised One of Whom the Báb had spoken. He adopted the title "Bahá'u'lláh," which means "Glory of God," and publicly declared His mission on the eve of His exile from Baghdad, in April 1863.

Bahá'u'lláh was still nominally a prisoner when He passed away near Acre in May 1892, although the authorities had gradually loosened their restrictions as they became acquainted with Him and the nature of His teachings. During the long years of His exile Bahá'u'lláh revealed the equivalent of more than 100 volumes of writings, consisting of the laws and ordinances of His dispensation, letters to the kings and rulers of the East and the West, mystical teachings, and other divinely inspired writings.

In His Will and Testament, Bahá'u'lláh appointed His eldest son, 'Abbás Effendi, Who adopted the title "'Abdu'l-Bahá" ("Servant of Bahá"), as His successor and the sole authoritative interpreter of His teachings. 'Abdu'l-Bahá had shared His Father's long exile and imprisonment and was freed only after a new regime was installed by the "Young Turk" movement in 1908. Shortly thereafter, at an advanced age, He embarked on an arduous journey to Europe and America where, from 1911 to 1913, He proclaimed Bahá'u'lláh's message of universal brotherhood and peace to large audiences, consolidated fledgling Bahá'í communities, and warned of the potential catastrophe looming on Europe's darkening horizon. By the outbreak of World War I in 1914, 'Abdu'l-Bahá had returned to His home in Haifa, just across the bay from Acre, and devoted Himself to caring for the local people, fending off famine by feeding them from stores of grain He had safeguarded for such an emergency. 'Abdu'l-Bahá's humanitarian services and His promotion of intercultural harmony were recognized by the British government, which, at the end of the war, conferred upon Him knighthood—a title He acknowledged but declined to use. He passed away in 1921 and is buried on Mount Carmel in a vault near the spot where He had interred the remains of the Báb some years before.

Among the legacies that 'Abdu'l-Bahá bequeathed to history is a series of letters called the Tablets of the Divine Plan, which He had addressed to the Bahá'ís of North America during the years of World War I. These 14 letters directed the recipients to scatter to countries on all continents and share with their populations the teachings of Bahá'u'lláh—a mandate that led to the global expansion of the Bahá'í community.

Another legacy of 'Abdu'l-Bahá is His Will and Testament, which Bahá'ís regard as the charter of the administrative order conceived by Bahá'u'lláh. This document appointed 'Abdu'l-Bahá's eldest grandson, Shoghi Effendi, as Guardian of the Bahá'í Faith and authorized interpreter of its teachings. Successorship to the Founders of the Bahá'í Faith would be shared by the Guardian and an elected Universal House of Justice, whose complementary role would be to create legislation supplementing the Faith's scriptures.

During the period of his Guardianship, from 1921 to 1957, Shoghi Effendi concentrated on four main areas: the development of the Bahá'í World Centre in the environs of Haifa; the translation and interpretation of the Bahá'í sacred writings; the rise and consolidation of the institutions of the Bahá'í administrative order; and the implementation of 'Abdu'l-Bahá's plan for the propagation of the Bahá'í Faith around the world.

At the Bahá'í World Centre, Shoghi Effendi effected the construction of a superstructure for the mausoleum containing the remains of the Báb, which had been brought secretly from Persia and interred by 'Abdu'l-Bahá in a spot designated by Bahá'u'lláh on Mount Carmel. Shoghi Effendi beautified and expanded the simple native stone structure, which is today a site of pilgrimage for Bahá'ís from all over the world. He enhanced the Bahá'í properties and initiated construction of the International Bahá'í Archives building to house the original Bahá'í scriptures and artifacts from the early days of the Bahá'í Faith. This building, the first on the arc-shaped path on the site designated as the world administrative center of the Bahá'í community, was completed in 1957. Shoghi Effendi's actions laid the foundations, literally and figuratively, for the further development of the Bahá'í World Centre.

Shoghi Effendi was also instrumental in interpreting the writings of Bahá'u'lláh and 'Abdu'l-Bahá and in translating them from the original Persian and Arabic into English. The Guardian had served as secretary to 'Abdu'l-Bahá for a number of years and was a student at Oxford University at the time of his Grandfather's passing. Shoghi Effendi's mastery of Persian, Arabic, and English, coupled with the authority conferred upon him as the appointed interpreter of the Bahá'í writings, made him uniquely qualified to undertake their translation. He also translated *The Dawn-Breakers*, a history of the Bábí Faith; authored *God Passes By*, a history of the first century of the Bahá'í Faith; and wrote thousands of letters to communities and individuals around the world, elucidating passages from the writings and giving direction and impetus to Bahá'í communities.

Development of the Administrative Order

Shoghi Effendi's work in developing the Bahá'í administrative order is one of the most dramatic legacies of his years as Guardian. The first step in this development was to encourage the organized, planned expansion of Bahá'í communities in places where local and national Bahá'í councils, known as Spiritual Assemblies, would eventually be established. The Guardian effected this global expansion of Bahá'í communities through a series of international plans of varying duration, during which 12 National Spiritual Assemblies were elected.

At the time of Shoghi Effendi's sudden passing in 1957, the Bahá'í community was in the middle of a global plan of expansion and consolidation called the Ten Year Crusade. During this period, which concluded in 1963—the centenary of Bahá'u'lláh's declaration of His mission in the Garden of Riḍván in Baghdad—the goal was to open 132 new countries and major territories to the Faith and to expand existing communities in 120 countries and territories that had previously been opened. These ambitious targets were in certain instances actually exceeded by the end of the plan, in spite of the difficulties posed by the Guardian's death.

'Abdu'l-Bahá, in His Will and Testament, had authorized the continuation of the Guardianship through the appointment by the Guardian of a successor from among his own sons, should he have them, or other direct descendants of Bahá'u'lláh. Such a designation was dependent upon the decision of Shoghi Effendi as to whether an individual could be named who met the demanding spiritual qualifications specified by 'Abdu'l-Bahá. Shoghi Effendi had no children and died without designating such a Guardian to follow him. He had, however, taken steps towards the election of the Universal House of Justice, the supreme governing body of the Bahá'í Faith. He had also appointed a number of individual Bahá'ís to an auxiliary institution of the Guardianship called Hands of the Cause of God. These individuals had been charged with protecting the unity of the Faith and collaborating with National Spiritual Assemblies around the world to ensure that the goals of the Ten Year Crusade were won. Upon Shoghi Effendi's passing, these men and women guided the Bahá'í community to complete the plan initiated by the Guardian and to hold the first election of the Universal House of Justice in 1963.

Conceived by Bahá'u'lláh Himself, the institution of the Universal House of Justice is established on principles laid down in the Bahá'í sacred writings. Its initial election, by the members of the 56 National Spiritual Assemblies that existed in April 1963, clearly demonstrated the principle of unity so central to the Bahá'í Faith, with the nine members coming from four continents and representing a variety of religious and ethnic backgrounds.

Based on the authority conferred on it by the Founder of the Faith, the Universal House of Justice is now elected every five years. It stands as the acknowledged central authority in the worldwide Bahá'í community and has, during the past 39 years, launched eight global plans for the advancement of the Faith. From a worldwide population of 408,000 in 1963, the Bahá'í community has grown to more than five million members; the number of National and Regional Spiritual Assemblies has grown from 56 to 182; and the number of Local Spiritual Assemblies has increased from 3,555 to 10,344.

Spiritual and Moral Teachings and Bahá'í Community Life

The force that unites this diverse body of people is the vision achieved through their belief in Bahá'u'lláh as a Manifestation of God, in the social and administrative structures He established, and in the spiritual and moral teachings He propagated. Central to these spiritual teachings is the concept that there is only one God and that the world's great religions have been established by Messengers or Manifestations of this Divine Reality—Abraham, Krishna, Moses, Buddha, Zoroaster, Jesus, and Muhammad—Who have been sent throughout history to deliver a divine message commensurate with humanity's stage of development. Though the religions' social teachings change through this process of progressive revelation, the spiritual essence of all the major religions remains the same: humanity has been created to know and to worship God. The Bahá'í perspective sees the cumulative benefits of progressively revealed religions as fundamental to an "ever-advancing civilization." What divides various religious communities, Bahá'ís believe, comes not from God but from humanity and its accretions to the essential religious teachings brought by the divine Messengers.

At this stage of humanity's development, the unity of the human race must be recognized, the equality of women and men must be established, the extremes of wealth and poverty must be eliminated, and the age-old promise of universal peace must be realized. Likening the development of the human race to that of an individual, the Bahá'í writings say that we have passed through stages analogous to infancy and childhood and are now in the midst of a tumultuous adolescence, standing on the threshold of maturity. Bahá'u'lláh taught that humanity is destined to come of age, but the course it takes to achieve that goal is entirely in its own hands.

To promote the development of a society in which Bahá'í ideals can be fully realized, Bahá'u'lláh established laws and moral teachings that are binding on Bahá'ís. Central to these is daily obligatory prayer. Study of and meditation upon the Bahá'í sacred writings each morning and evening is also enjoined. Bahá'ís between the ages of 15 and 70, with certain exceptions, observe an annual 19-day, dawn-to-dusk fast. Bahá'u'lláh referred to prayer and fasting as the "twin pillars" of faith, an indication of their importance and the benefits to be gained from them. He also raised work to the level of worship. The main repository of Bahá'u'lláh's laws is a volume entitled the Kitáb-i-Aqdas, or the "Most Holy Book."

There are no dietary restrictions in the Bahá'í Faith, but the consumption of alcohol and the use of narcotic and hallucinogenic drugs are forbidden, as they affect the mind and interfere with spiritual growth. Bahá'u'lláh counseled Bahá'ís to be honest and trustworthy, to render service to humanity with an abundance of deeds rather than mere words, to be chaste, and to avoid gossip and backbiting. He forbade lying, stealing, adultery, homosexual acts, and promiscuity. The importance of the family is central to Bahá'í community life, as is the moral and spiritual education of children.

Bahá'ís often gather together in their communities to study the sacred writings of their Faith and to pray, but a central feature in Bahá'í community life is a meeting called the Nineteen Day Feast, at which all members join in worship, consult about community affairs, and socialize. Pending the further development of Bahá'í communities, these meetings often occur in rented facilities, people's homes, or in local Bahá'í centers. The Bahá'í writings call for the erection in each community of a beautifully designed House of Worship, surrounded by gardens and functioning as a spiritual center of activity. A variety of social and humanitarian institutions are also to be established around it. Seven Bahá'í Houses of Worship presently exist, in Australia, Germany, India, Panama, Uganda, the United States, and Western Samoa. Plans have been launched for the construction of an eighth House of Worship in Chile, and sites have been purchased around the world for the erection of many more. The Houses of Worship are open to people of all faiths—or those professing no particular faith—for prayer and meditation. Services are nondenominational. There are no sermons, only readings and prayers from the Bahá'í writings and scriptures of other faiths with music by an *a capella* choir. This preserves the sacredness of the experience of hearing and meditating upon the Holy Word without the interference of man-made concepts.

Aims, Objectives, and Activities

As the Universal House of Justice stated in a message addressed to the peoples of the world written in October 1985, coinciding with the United Nations International Year of Peace, "Acceptance of the oneness of mankind is the first fundamental prerequisite for the reorganization and administration of the world as one country, the home of humankind." The ultimate aim of the Bahá'í Faith is to establish unity among all the peoples of the world, and it is because of its orientation towards unity on an international scale that the Bahá'í community has been active at the United Nations since that organization's inception. Today the Bahá'í International Community, a nongovernmental organization (NGO) that represents the collective voice of national Bahá'í communities around the world, enjoys special status with the Economic and Social Council (ECO-SOC). It is particularly involved in addressing human rights issues, the needs of women and children, and environmental concerns, as well as pursuing sound, sustainable development policies. To coordinate its international efforts in these areas, the Bahá'í International Community's United Nations Office and Office of Public Information, as well as the Office of the Environment and the Office for the Advancement of Women, collaborate with National Spiritual Assemblies around the world. The Bahá'í International Community's activities at the United Nations have earned it a reputation as one of the most effective religious NGOs in the UN system. Its national and international representatives have taken active roles in the major world summits and NGO forums sponsored by the United Nations during the past decades.

Bahá'ís look towards a day when a new international order will be established, a commonwealth to which all the nations of the world will belong. As Shoghi Effendi wrote in 1936:

The unity of the human race, as envisaged by Bahá'u'lláh, implies the establishment of a world commonwealth in which all nations, races, creeds, and classes are closely and permanently united, and in which the autonomy of its state members and the personal freedom and initiative of the individuals that compose them are definitely and completely safeguarded. This commonwealth must, as far as we can visualize it, consist of a world legislature, whose members will, as the trustees of the whole of mankind, ultimately control the entire resources of all the component nations, and will enact such laws as shall be required to regulate the life, satisfy the needs, and adjust the relationships of all races and peoples. A world executive, backed by an international Force, will carry out the decisions arrived at, and apply the laws enacted by, this world legislature, and will safeguard the organic unity of the whole commonwealth. A world tribunal will adjudicate and deliver its compulsory and final verdict in all and any disputes that may arise between the various elements constituting this universal system.[1]

Shoghi Effendi went on to describe the tremendous benefits to humanity resulting from such a world order:

The enormous energy dissipated and wasted on war, whether economic or political, will be consecrated to such ends as will extend the range of human inventions and technical development, to the increase of the productivity of mankind, to the extermination of disease, to the extension of scientific research, to the raising of the standard of physical health, to the sharpening and refinement of the human brain, to the exploitation of the unused and unsuspected resources of the planet, to the prolongation of human life, and to the furtherance of any other agency that can stimulate the intellectual, the moral, and spiritual life of the entire human race.[2]

[1] Shoghi Effendi, *The World Order of Bahá'u'lláh: Selected Letters*, 2nd rev. ed. (Wilmette, IL: Bahá'í Publishing Trust, 1993), p. 203.
[2] Ibid., p. 204.

To make its aims and objectives widely known and to promote its perspective on various issues, the Bahá'í International Community not only collaborates with like-minded organizations within and outside of the United Nations, but it engages in public information efforts to bring the spiritual and social principles of the Faith to the attention of people everywhere. The persecution of the Bahá'ís in Iran since the 1979 Iranian revolution has prompted wide dissemination of information about the Bahá'í Faith in the international news media. More than 200 members of the Faith have been executed for their belief, which is considered as heresy by the regime, and thousands more have been imprisoned, fired from their jobs, or had their homes confiscated or their pensions cut off as a result of government orders. Bahá'ís around the world have responded in unity to this ongoing persecution in Iran—the land in which their religion was born—by petitioning their governments to take action against this injustice. It is, to some degree, as a result of these efforts that the persecutions have not been more extreme, although Iran's Bahá'ís still face the possibility of arbitrary imprisonment and execution, and are still denied fundamental rights and freedoms.[3]

The Bahá'í community has also taken a proactive approach to promulgating its views. The statement on peace issued by the Universal House of Justice in 1985, entitled *The Promise of World Peace*, sparked a worldwide campaign of presentations and public awareness programs throughout the International Year of Peace and since, aimed at government figures, leaders of thought, and the general population. The centenary of Bahá'u'lláh's passing in 1992 was commemorated, in part, with the publication of a statement detailing His life, teachings, and mission, designed to increase knowledge of the Bahá'í Faith among members of the public. A statement presenting the Bahá'í perspective on social development, *The Prosperity of Humankind*, was disseminated at the World Summit for Social Development in Copenhagen in March 1995, and later that year a statement entitled *Turning Point for All Nations* was released as a contribution to discussions on the future of the United Nations during its 50th anniversary. In 1999, the Bahá'í International

---

[3] See pp. 139–44 and 247–53 for further information on the continuing persecution of Iran's Bahá'í community.

Community released *Who Is Writing the Future? Reflections on the Twentieth Century*.

The Bahá'í community has also been continually engaged in a series of international teaching plans. It has seen rapid expansion in different parts of the world, perhaps most notably in Eastern Europe and the former Soviet Union, where national Bahá'í communities have been established in recent years following the collapse of long-standing political barriers. New national governing bodies are also being formed elsewhere, as the Universal House of Justice deems communities to have reached a sufficient level of maturity.

The existence and growth of the Bahá'í community offers irrefutable evidence that humanity, in all its diversity, can learn to live and work together in harmony. While Bahá'ís are not unaware of the turmoil in the world surrounding them, their view is succinctly depicted in the following words, taken from *The Prosperity of Humankind*:

> A world is passing away and a new one is struggling to be born. The habits, attitudes, and institutions that have accumulated over the centuries are being subjected to tests that are as necessary to human development as they are inescapable. What is required of the peoples of the world is a measure of faith and resolve to match the enormous energies with which the Creator of all things has endowed this spiritual springtime of the race.[4]

The source of this faith and resolve is the message offered by the teachings of Bahá'u'lláh, a message that deserves the thoughtful consideration of all those who yearn for peace and justice in the world.

---

[4] Bahá'í International Community's Office of Public Information, *The Prosperity of Humankind* (1995). See *The Bahá'í World 1994–95*, pp. 273–96, for the complete text of this statement.

WRITINGS
AND MESSAGES

Sacred Writings

From the Writings of Bahá'u'lláh

All men have been created to carry forward an ever-advancing civilization. The Almighty beareth Me witness: To act like the beasts of the field is unworthy of man. Those virtues that befit his dignity are forbearance, mercy, compassion, and loving-kindness towards all the peoples and kindreds of the earth.

ॐ

It is incumbent upon everyone to firmly adhere to and observe that which hath streamed forth from Our Most Exalted Pen. God, the True One, beareth Me witness, and every atom in existence is moved to testify that such means as lead to the elevation, the advancement, the education, the protection, and the regeneration of the peoples of the earth have been clearly set forth by Us and are revealed in the Holy Books and Tablets by the Pen of Glory.

ॐ

O Friends! You must all be so ablaze in this day with the fire of the love of God that the heat thereof may be manifest in all your veins, your limbs and members of your body, and the peoples of the world may be ignited by this heat and turn to the horizon of the Beloved.

꙳

The third Ṭaráz concerneth good character. A good character is, verily, the best mantle for men from God. With it He adorneth the temples of His loved ones. By My life! The light of a good character surpasseth the light of the sun and the radiance thereof. Whoso attaineth unto it is accounted as a jewel among men. The glory and the upliftment of the world must needs depend upon it.

꙳

It is incumbent upon every man of insight and understanding to strive to translate that which hath been written into reality and action.… That one indeed is a man who, today, dedicateth himself to the service of the entire human race. The Great Being saith: Blessed and happy is he that ariseth to promote the best interests of the peoples and kindreds of the earth. In another passage He hath proclaimed: It is not for him to pride himself who loveth his own country, but rather for him who loveth the whole world.

꙳

God hath prescribed unto everyone the duty of teaching His Cause. Whoever ariseth to discharge this duty, must needs, ere he proclaimeth His Message, adorn himself with the ornament of an upright and praiseworthy character, so that his words may attract the hearts of such as are receptive to his call. Without it, he can never hope to influence his hearers. Thus doth God instruct you. He, verily, is the Ever-Forgiving, the Most Compassionate.…

Say: We have ordained that our Cause be taught through the power of utterance. Beware lest ye dispute idly with anyone. Whoso ariseth wholly for the sake of his Lord to teach His Cause, the Holy Spirit shall strengthen him and inspire him with that which will illumine the heart of the world, how much more the hearts of those who seek Him. O people of Bahá! Subdue the citadels of men's hearts with the swords of wisdom and of utterance.

꙳

Strive that ye may be enabled to manifest to the peoples of the earth the signs of God, and to mirror forth His commandments. Let your acts be a guide unto all mankind, for the professions of most men, be they high or low, differ from their conduct. It is through your deeds that ye can distinguish yourselves from others. Through them the brightness of your light can be shed upon the whole earth. Happy is the man that heedeth My counsel, and keepeth the precepts prescribed by Him Who is the All-Knowing, the All-Wise.

༉

Be generous in prosperity, and thankful in adversity. Be worthy of the trust of thy neighbor, and look upon him with a bright and friendly face. Be a treasure to the poor, an admonisher to the rich, an answerer of the cry of the needy, a preserver of the sanctity of thy pledge. Be fair in thy judgment, and guarded in thy speech. Be unjust to no man, and show all meekness to all men. Be as a lamp unto them that walk in darkness, a joy to the sorrowful, a sea for the thirsty, a haven for the distressed, an upholder and defender of the victim of oppression. Let integrity and uprightness distinguish all thine acts. Be a home for the stranger, a balm to the suffering, a tower of strength for the fugitive. Be eyes to the blind, and a guiding light unto the feet of the erring. Be an ornament to the countenance of truth, a crown to the brow of fidelity, a pillar of the temple of righteousness, a breath of life to the body of mankind, an ensign of the hosts of justice, a luminary above the horizon of virtue, a dew to the soil of the human heart, an ark on the ocean of knowledge, a sun in the heaven of bounty, a gem on the diadem of wisdom, a shining light in the firmament of thy generation, a fruit upon the tree of humility.

༉

Great care should be exercised that whatever is written in these days doth not cause dissension, and invite the objection of the people. Whatever the friends of the one true God say in these days is listened to by the people of the world.... Whatever is written should not transgress the bounds of tact and wisdom, and in the words used there should lie hid the property of milk, so that the children of the world may be nurtured therewith, and attain maturity. We have said in the past that one word hath the influence of spring and causeth hearts to become fresh and verdant, while another is like unto blight which causeth the blossoms and flowers to wither. God grant that authors among the friends will write in such a way as would be acceptable to fair-minded souls, and not lead to caviling by the people.

From the Writings and Utterances of 'Abdu'l-Bahá

God has created man lofty and noble, made him a dominant factor in creation. He has specialized man with supreme bestowals, conferred upon him mind, perception, memory, abstraction, and the powers of the senses. These gifts of God to man were intended to make him the manifestation of divine virtues, a radiant light in the world of creation, a source of life and the agency of constructiveness in the infinite fields of existence.

❧

God has given man the eye of investigation by which he may see and recognize truth. He has endowed man with ears that he may hear the message of reality and conferred upon him the gift of reason by which he may discover things for himself. This is his endowment and equipment for the investigation of reality. Man is not intended to see through the eyes of another, hear through another's ears, nor comprehend with another's brain. Each human creature has individual endowment, power, and responsibility in the creative plan of God. Therefore, depend upon your own reason and judgment and adhere to the outcome of your own investigation; otherwise, you will be utterly submerged in the sea of ignorance and deprived of all the bounties of God. Turn to God, supplicate humbly at His threshold, seeking assistance and confirmation, that God may rend asunder the veils that obscure your vision. Then will your eyes be filled with illumination, face to face you will behold the reality of God, and your heart become completely purified from the dross of ignorance, reflecting the glories and bounties of the Kingdom.

Holy souls are like soil which has been plowed and tilled with much earnest labor, the thorns and thistles cast aside and all weeds uprooted. Such soil is most fruitful, and the harvest from it will prove full and plenteous. In this same way man must free himself from the weeds of ignorance, thorns of superstitions, and thistles of imitations that he may discover reality in the harvests of true knowledge. Otherwise, the discovery of reality is impossible, contention and divergence of religious belief will always remain, and mankind, like ferocious wolves, will rage and attack each other in hatred and antagonism.... Man is a child of God, most noble, lofty, and beloved by God, his Creator. Therefore, he must ever strive that the divine bounties and virtues bestowed upon him may prevail and control him. Just now the soil of human hearts seems like black earth, but in the innermost substance of this dark soil there are thousands of fragrant flowers latent. We must endeavor to cultivate and awaken these potentialities, discover the secret treasure in this very mine and depository of God, bring forth these resplendent powers long hidden in human hearts. Then will the glories of both worlds be blended and increased and the quintessence of human existence be made manifest.

❧

Ye should strive to widen the circle of those with whom ye enjoy friendly relations, and to establish the closest contact with those benevolent souls whose only thought is to do good, who are laboring in the cause of universal peace, and who cherish no desire but to witness the unification of the world of humanity. Ye should seek out the company of such people as these, that ye may imbue them with an awareness of the heavenly Kingdom, for albeit their motives are of the finest, yet they do not realize that all the powers of the earth are impotent either to establish universal peace or to promote the oneness of the human world. Nothing short of the power of the Word of God and the breaths of the Holy Spirit can ever succeed.

❧

If a soul of his own accord advances toward God he will be accepted at the Threshold of Oneness, for such a one is free of personal considerations, of greed and selfish interests, and he has taken refuge within the sheltering protection of his Lord. He will become known among men as trustworthy and truthful, temperate and scrupulous, high-minded and loyal, incorruptible and God-fearing. In this way the primary purpose in revealing the Divine Law—which is to bring about happiness in the after life and civilization and the refinement of character in this—will be realized. As for the sword, it will only produce a man who is outwardly a believer, and inwardly a traitor and apostate.

❧

Bahá'u'lláh … stated that God, through His Prophets and Chosen Ones, explained that the heart of man is His home; it should be sanctified for His entry, and that his spirit is His place of Revelation; it should be cleansed so that it may become His abode. We, therefore, understand that nearness to God is possible through setting our faces towards Him. Nearness to God is through entrance into the Kingdom of God. Nearness to God is made possible through service to humanity. Nearness to God is possible through the unity of all peoples and religions. Nearness to God is dependent upon kindness to all mankind. Nearness to God is made possible through investigation of the Truth. Nearness to God is through the acquisition of knowledge and praiseworthy virtues. Nearness to God is possible through service to universal peace. Nearness to God is dependent upon purity and sanctity. Nearness to God is dependent upon self-sacrifice, self-abnegation, and the giving up of one's glory and position for Him.

❧

O ye friends of God! Because, in this most momentous of ages, the Sun of Truth hath risen at the highest point of the spring equinox, and cast its rays on every clime, it shall kindle such tremulous excitement, it shall release such vibrations in the world of being, it shall stimulate such growth and development, it shall stream out with such a glory of light, and clouds of grace shall pour down such plentiful waters, and fields and plains shall teem with such a galaxy of sweet-smelling plants and blooms, that this lowly earth will become the Abhá Kingdom, and this nether world the world above.…

Wherefore, O loved ones of God! Make ye a mighty effort till you yourselves betoken this advancement and all these confirmations, and become focal centers of God's blessings, dayprings of the light of His unity, promoters of the gifts and graces of civilized life. Be ye in that land vanguards of the perfections of humankind; carry forward the various branches of knowledge, be active and progressive in the field of inventions and the arts. Endeavor to rectify the conduct of men, and seek to excel the whole world in moral character. While the children are yet in their infancy feed them from the breast of heavenly grace, foster them in the cradle of all excellence, rear them in the embrace of bounty. Give them the advantage of every useful kind of knowledge. Let them share in every new and rare and wondrous craft and art. Bring them up to work and strive, and accustom them to hardship. Teach them to dedicate their lives to matters of great import, and inspire them to undertake studies that will benefit mankind.

⚭

Act in accordance with the counsels of the Lord: that is, rise up in such wise, and with such qualities, as to endow the body of this world with a living soul, and to bring this young child, humanity, to the stage of adulthood. So far as ye are able, ignite a candle of love in every meeting, and with tenderness rejoice and cheer ye every heart. Care for the stranger as for one of your own; show to alien souls the same loving kindness ye bestow upon your faithful friends. Should any come to blows with you, seek to be friends with him; should any stab you to the heart, be ye a healing salve unto his sores; should any taunt and mock at you, meet him with love. Should any heap his blame upon you, praise ye him; should he offer you a deadly poison, give him the choicest honey in exchange; and should he threaten your life, grant him a remedy that will heal him evermore. Should he be pain itself, be ye his medicine; should he be thorns, be ye his roses and sweet herbs. Perchance such ways and words from you will make this darksome world turn bright at last; will make this dusty earth turn heavenly, this devilish prison place become a royal palace of the Lord—so that war and strife will pass and be no more, and love and trust will pitch their tents on the summits of the world.

⚭

Let the loved ones of God, whether young or old, whether male or female, each according to his capabilities, bestir themselves and spare no efforts to acquire the various current branches of knowledge, both spiritual and secular, and of the arts. Whensoever they gather in their meetings let their conversation be confined to learned subjects and to information on the knowledge of the day.

If they do thus, they will flood the world with the Manifest Light, and change this dusty earth into gardens of the Realm of Glory.

∞

Again, is there any deed in the world that would be nobler than service to the common good? Is there any greater blessing conceivable for a man, than that he should become the cause of the education, the development, the prosperity and honor of his fellow-creatures? No, by the Lord God! The highest righteousness of all is for blessed souls to take hold of the hands of the helpless and deliver them out of their ignorance and abasement and poverty, and with pure motives, and only for the sake of God, to arise and energetically devote themselves to the service of the masses, forgetting their own worldly advantage and working only to serve the general good….

Glory be to God! What an extraordinary situation now obtains, when no one, hearing a claim advanced, asks himself what the speaker's real motive might be, and what selfish purpose he might not have hidden behind the mask of words. You find, for example, that an individual seeking to further his own petty and personal concerns, will block the advancement of an entire people. To turn his own water mill, he will let the farms and fields of all the others parch and wither. To maintain his own leadership, he will everlastingly direct the masses toward that prejudice and fanaticism which subvert the very base of civilization….

O People of Persia! Open your eyes! Pay heed! Release yourselves from this blind following of the bigots, this senseless imitation which is the principal reason why men fall away into paths of ignorance and degradation. See the true state of things. Rise up; seize hold of such means as will bring you life and happiness and greatness and glory among all the nations of the world.

∞

The world of politics is like the world of man; he is seed at first, and then passes by degrees to the condition of embryo and foetus, acquiring a bone structure, being clothed with flesh, taking on his own special form, until at last he reaches the plane where he can

befittingly fulfill the words: "the most excellent of Makers."[1] Just as
this is a requirement of creation and is based on the universal Wisdom, the political world in the same way cannot instantaneously
evolve from the nadir of defectiveness to the zenith of rightness and
perfection. Rather, qualified individuals must strive by day and by
night, using all those means which will conduce to progress, until
the government and the people develop along every line from day
to day and even from moment to moment.

❧

You have written on the question of how the friends should proceed in their business dealings with one another. This is a question
of the greatest importance and a matter that deserveth the liveliest
concern. In relations of this kind, the friends of God should act with
the utmost trustworthiness and integrity. To be remiss in this area
would be to turn one's face away from the counsels of the Blessed
Beauty and the holy precepts of God. If a man in his own home
doth not treat his relations and friends with entire trustworthiness
and integrity, his dealings with the outside world—no matter how
much trustworthiness and honesty he may bring to them—will prove
barren and unproductive. First one should order one's own domestic
affairs, then attend to one's business with the public.

❧

O ye lovers of God! The world is even as a human being who is dis-
eased and impotent, whose eyes can see no longer, whose ears have
gone deaf, all of whose powers are corroded and used up. Wherefore
must the friends of God be competent physicians who, following
the holy Teachings, will nurse this patient back to health. Perhaps,
God willing, the world will mend, and become permanently whole,
and its exhausted faculties will be restored, and its person will take
on such vigor, freshness, and verdancy that it will shine out with
comeliness and grace.

❧

---

[1] Qur'an 23:14: "Blessed therefore be God, the most excellent of Makers."

The first remedy of all is to guide the people aright, so that they will turn themselves unto God, and listen to His counselings, and go forth with hearing ears and seeing eyes. Once this speedily effective draught is given them, then, in accordance with the Teachings, they must be led to acquire the characteristics and the behavior of the Concourse on high, and encouraged to seek out all the bounties of the Abhá Realm. They must cleanse their hearts from even the slightest trace of hatred and spite, and they must set about being truthful and honest, conciliatory and loving to all humankind—so that East and West will, even as two lovers, hold each other close; that hatred and hostility will perish from the earth, and universal peace be firmly rooted in their place....

Indulge not your bodies with rest, but work with all your souls, and with all your hearts cry out and beg of God to grant you His succor and grace. Thus may ye make this world the Abhá Paradise, and this globe of earth the parade ground of the realm on high. If only ye exert the effort, it is certain that these splendors will shine out, these clouds of mercy will shed down their rain, these life-giving winds will rise and blow, this sweet-smelling musk will be scattered far and wide.

☙

[I]t is evident that the Prophets of God have come to unite the children of men and not to disperse them, to establish the law of love and not enmity. Consequently, we must lay aside all prejudice—whether it be religious, racial, political, or patriotic; we must become the cause of the unification of the human race. Strive for universal peace, seek the means of love, and destroy the basis of disagreement so that this material world may become divine, the world of matter become the realm of the Kingdom, and humanity attain to the world of perfection.

☙

Now the new age is here and creation is reborn. Humanity hath taken on new life. The autumn hath gone by, and the reviving spring is here. All things are now made new. Arts and industries have been reborn, there are new discoveries in science, and there are new inventions; even the details of human affairs, such as dress and personal effects—even weapons—all these have likewise been renewed. The laws and procedures of every government have been revised. Renewal is the order of the day.

And all this newness hath its source in the fresh outpourings of wondrous grace and favor from the Lord of the Kingdom, which have renewed the world. The people, therefore, must be set completely free from their old patterns of thought, that all their attention may be focused upon these new principles, for these are the light of this time and the very spirit of this age.

Unless these Teachings are effectively spread among the people, until the old ways, the old concepts, are gone and forgotten, this world of being will find no peace, nor will it reflect the perfections of the Heavenly Kingdom.

❧

Let all your striving be for this, to become the source of life and immortality, and peace and comfort and joy, to every human soul, whether one known to you or a stranger, one opposed to you or on your side. Look ye not upon the purity or impurity of his nature: look ye upon the all-embracing mercy of the Lord, the light of Whose grace hath embosomed the whole earth and all who dwell thereon, and in the plenitude of Whose bounty are immersed both the wise and the ignorant. Stranger and friend alike are seated at the table of His favor. Even as the believer, the denier who turneth away from God doth at the same time cup his hands and drink from the sea of His bestowals.

It behooveth the loved ones of the Lord to be the signs and tokens of His universal mercy and the embodiments of His own excelling grace. Like the sun, let them cast their rays upon garden and rubbish heap alike, and even as clouds in spring, let them shed down their rain upon flower and thorn. Let them seek but love and faithfulness, let them not follow the ways of unkindness, let their talk be confined to the secrets of friendship and of peace.

❧

Make every effort to acquire the advanced knowledge of the day, and strain every nerve to carry forward the divine civilization. Establish schools that are well organized, and promote the fundamentals of instruction in the various branches of knowledge through teachers who are pure and sanctified, distinguished for their high standards of conduct and general excellence, and strong in faith—scholars and educators with a thorough knowledge of sciences and arts.

❧

In the Bahá'í Cause arts, sciences, and all crafts are [counted as] worship. The man who makes a piece of notepaper to the best of his ability, conscientiously, concentrating all his forces on perfecting it, is giving praise to God. Briefly, all effort and exertion put forth by man from the fullness of his heart is worship, if it is prompted by the highest motives and the will to do service to humanity. This is worship: to serve mankind and to minister to the needs of the people. Service is prayer. A physician ministering to the sick, gently, tenderly, free from prejudice and believing in the solidarity of the human race, he is giving praise.

❧

In this enlightened world of the West, woman has advanced an immeasurable degree beyond the women of the Orient. And let it be known once more that until woman and man recognize and realize equality, social and political progress here or anywhere will not be possible. For the world of humanity consists of two parts or members: one is woman; the other is man. Until these two members are equal in strength, the oneness of humanity cannot be established, and the happiness and felicity of mankind will not be a reality.

Highlights of Messages
from the Universal House of Justice

The Universal House of Justice, the international governing
body of the Bahá'í Faith, derives its authority from the
explicit text of Bahá'u'lláh, as revealed in His book of laws,
the Kitáb-i-Aqdas, which is also known to Bahá'ís as "the Most
Holy Book." Its primary role is "to ensure the continuity of that
divinely appointed authority which flows from the Source of the
Faith, to safeguard the unity of its followers, and to maintain the
integrity and flexibility of its teachings."[1] It is the sole institution
in the Bahá'í Faith that is empowered to enact further application
of the laws of Bahá'u'lláh. Through its communications to Bahá'í
institutions and individuals, the Universal House of Justice coordinates the worldwide community's activities and provides it with
both vision and direction. In its communications with the wider
community, the Universal House of Justice sets forward the Bahá'í
perspective on issues that are of particular concern to the well-being
of the peoples of the world with the goal of inspiring constructive
action in relation to them.

---

[1] The Universal House of Justice, *The Constitution of the Universal House of
Justice* (Haifa: Bahá'í World Centre, 1972), p. 4.

During the period from Riḍván 2002 to Riḍván 2003 the Universal House of Justice addressed a significant message to the leaders of the world's religions as well as a number of major letters to the Bahá'í community. The full text of its letter to the religious and spiritual leaders of the world appears on pp. 89–98 of this volume.

Riḍván 159 BE Message

Each year during the period of the Riḍván Festival, known also as "the King of Festivals," which marks the anniversary of Bahá'u'lláh's declaration of His mission, the Universal House of Justice addresses a message to the Bahá'ís of the world, reviewing the events of the past year, assessing present conditions, and looking ahead to the coming period. In its Riḍván 2002 message, 159 BE, the Universal House of Justice first looked back to the inaugural events that took place in Haifa in May 2001 as "the latest evidences in the tangible unfolding of the Tablet of Carmel," a writing of Bahá'u'lláh that serves as a charter for the development of the Faith's World Centre. The House of Justice commented on the historical importance of these events and the fact that they received "the most extensive media coverage ever accorded a Bahá'í occasion." From there, the message reviewed and analyzed the "internal processes" that propelled the community forward throughout the previous year.

The period from April 2001 to April 2002 marked the first year of the Five Year Plan, a worldwide process of systematic development of human resources in which the Bahá'í community is currently engaged to effect its consolidation and expansion. To facilitate this, the Universal House of Justice noted in its Riḍván message, national communities around the world held planning sessions with Continental Counsellors, mapping their countries and sectioning them into "clusters," with each "of a composition and size consonant with a scale of activities for growth and development that is manageable." This mapping, as reported by some 150 countries, has created "a perspective, or vision, of systematic growth that can be sustained from cluster to cluster across an entire country" with the involvement of "the three constituent components of the Plan: the individual, the institutions, and the community." Progress was also seen in "the training institute process," which promotes "three core activities—study circles, devotional meetings, and children's classes" —as a means of development both for believers and for members of the public who wish to participate in them. "By combining study circles, devotional meetings and children's classes within the frame- work of clusters, a model of coherence in lines of action has been put in place," the House of Justice noted, looking forward to "worldwide application of this model." Further focus on this process of systematic growth was also given through the sponsorship by the International Teaching Centre of 16 "regional orientation conferences" for the 990 Auxiliary Board members around the world at the beginning of their five-year term of service.

In contrast to this community, which is "so richly endowed, so experienced, so focused on a divinely-inspired plan of action," the House of Justice noted that the world is sinking "more deeply into a slough of multiple disorders." "And yet," it continued, "it is pre- cisely under these seemingly inhospitable conditions that the Cause is meant to advance, and will thrive." In such a climate,

> *The Summons of the Lord of Hosts*, the newly released volume containing English translations of the full texts of Bahá'u'lláh's Tablets to the kings and rulers of the world, has come as a propi- tious reminder of the dire consequences of ignoring His warnings against injustice, tyranny, and corruption.[2] The violent shocks being inflicted on the consciousness of people everywhere em- phasize the urgency of the remedy He has prescribed.

The House of Justice concluded that the Bahá'ís' task is "to ex- ploit the current turmoil, without fear or hesitation, for the purpose of spreading and demonstrating the transformational virtue of the one Message that can secure the peace of the world."

The Evolution of a "Culture of Learning"

On 17 January 2003, the Universal House of Justice addressed another letter to the Bahá'ís of the world to review the insights gained and to clarify issues relating to the "culture of learning" being established

---

[2] For more information on this book, see pp. 99–103.

throughout the world in the two years since the community took its impetus from another seminal letter of the Universal House of Justice written on 9 January 2001. Again, the House of Justice reviewed the establishment of almost 17,000 clusters worldwide as well as the categorization of each as "a way of evaluating its capacity for growth, in order that an approach compatible with its evolving development can be adopted." In evaluating clusters, the House of Justice noted, two criteria are "especially important." These are "the strength of the human resources raised up by the training institute for the expansion and consolidation of the Faith in the cluster, and the ability of the institutions to mobilize these resources in the field of service." Communities around the world are now focused on moving the most promising clusters "from their current stage of growth to the next." The participation of increasing numbers of Bahá'ís in courses offered by the institute in their area has been found to be a key element in this process. The House noted that there is "a growing sense of initiative and resourcefulness," along with "courage and audacity," "consecration, zeal, confidence, and tenacity" among the Bahá'ís around the world. The development of such qualities has empowered individuals to arise to settle in clusters where there were previously no Bahá'ís.

In the words of the House of Justice, "a systematic approach to training has created a way for Bahá'ís to reach out to the surrounding society, share Bahá'u'lláh's message with friends, family, neighbors, and coworkers, and expose them to the richness of His teachings." The letter continued, "This outward-looking orientation is one of the finest fruits of the grassroots learning taking place."

Now some Bahá'í clusters are ready to move to the next stage of growth, in which "carefully designed projects are being added to the existing pattern of growth to reach receptive populations and lift the rate of expansion to a higher level." The challenge to existing institutions is "to utilize the energies and talents of the swelling human resources available in their respective areas of jurisdiction both to create a vibrant community life and to begin influencing the society around them." Many clusters have found that the holding of periodic consultative meetings enables them to "reflect on experience gained, share insights, explore approaches, and acquire a better understanding of how each can contribute to achieving the aim of the Plan," leading to a mode of "learning in action" framed by individual and collective short-term goals. The next stage of growth, the House of Justice concluded, will call for "an intensity of effort yet to be achieved."

The Release of *Gems of Divine Mysteries*

In pursuance of one of the goals of the Five Year Plan—"the development of the Centre for the Study of the Texts, with special emphasis on the translation of the Holy Writings"—the Universal House of Justice announced, on 26 June 2002, the publication of the English translation of Javáhiru'l-Asrár, or *Gems of Divine Mysteries*. This brief work of Bahá'u'lláh was revealed during His exile in Baghdad and "contains an exposition of the stages in the path of the spiritual wayfarer which complements that of the Seven Valleys and sets forth some of the doctrinal themes which would later be central to the Book of Certitude."[3]

Preparations for the Election
of the Universal House of Justice

On 11 November 2002, the Universal House of Justice advised all National Spiritual Assemblies that it had regretfully accepted the resignations of Hushmand Fatheazam and 'Alí Nakhjavání, long-time members of the international governing body. The House of Justice remarked on the "highly valued services" rendered by both men and noted that they had agreed to remain in office until the next international election in April 2003.

While the election of the Universal House of Justice would proceed uninterrupted, on 4 April 2003 the Universal House of Justice wrote to all National Spiritual Assemblies announcing that "current conditions" in the world had compelled the cancellation of the Ninth International Convention, which had been scheduled to be held at the Bahá'í World Centre in Haifa from 29 April to 2 May 2003. Under a provision of its constitution empowering it to decide how

---

[3] For more information on this book, see pp. 103–04.

the election should take place should the holding of an International Convention be considered "impracticable or unwise," the Universal House of Justice arranged for all ballots to be mailed in and for the 19 delegates chosen as tellers to travel to the Holy Land to count the votes.

The Institution of Ḥuqúqu'lláh

On 12 January 2003, the Universal House of Justice wrote a letter to the Deputies and Representatives of the institution of Ḥuqúqu'lláh, or "Right of God," reviewing its accomplishments in the 10 years since the universal application of the law of Ḥuqúqu'lláh. The House of Justice remarked upon the "wise and loving guidance" provided by the Trustee of Ḥuqúqu'lláh, Hand of the Cause of God 'Alí-Muḥammad Varqá, and the network established around the world to provide coordination and direction to the work of the institution in educating the Bahá'ís regarding the significance of this important law. In concluding, the Universal House of Justice noted,

> The institution of Ḥuqúqu'lláh will, during the course of this Dispensation, contribute to the spiritualization of humanity through the promotion of a new attitude to the acquisition and use of material resources. It will provide the material resources necessary for great collective enterprises designed to improve all aspects of life, and will be a powerful element in the growth of a world civilization.

EVENTS
2002–2003

Bahá'ís in Kigali, Rwanda, participate in a Ruhi study group in September 2002.

The Year in Review

O f the imprisonments and indignities Bahá'u'lláh unjustly suffered during His life, perhaps none was more terrible than confinement in the Síyáh-Chál, the "black pit." Describing the conditions, Bahá'u'lláh wrote, "No pen can depict that place, nor any tongue describe its loathsome smell. Most of these men had neither clothes nor bedding to lie on. God alone knoweth what befell Us in that most foul-smelling and gloomy place!"[1]

History was made in that prison, despite those inhuman conditions, as Bahá'u'lláh received the intimations of His divine mission. Shoghi Effendi wrote, "Bahá'u'lláh lay wrapped in the gloom of the Síyáh-Chál of Tehran, His feet in stocks, His neck freighted with chains, and surrounded by vile and wretched criminals," but it was there that the "most glorious and momentous stage in the Heroic Age of the greatest religious Dispensation in the spiritual history of mankind" was ushered in.[2]

---

[1] Bahá'u'lláh, *Epistle to the Son of the Wolf* (Wilmette, IL: Bahá'í Publishing Trust, 1995), p. 21.

[2] Shoghi Effendi, *Messages to America: Selected Letters and Cablegrams Addressed to the Bahá'ís of North America, 1932–1946* (Wilmette, IL: Bahá'í Publishing Committee, 1947), pp. 99–100.

In October 2002, US Congressman Mark Steven Kirk recalled the 150th anniversary of Bahá'u'lláh's imprisonment in the Síyáh-Chál with a statement to Congress that recalled not only His sufferings, but also the triumphs that resulted from it:

> On the 150th anniversary of Bahá'u'lláh's imprisonment and the founding of the Bahá'í Faith, we salute along with the American Bahá'í community the ideals of universal brotherhood, peace, cooperation, and understanding espoused by Bahá'u'lláh. These are Bahá'í values, they are American values, and they are universal values. I also would like to recognize the immense sacrifices that many around the world have made striving to ensure that true liberty and justice for all becomes not just an American dream, but also a global reality.[3]

That global reality is being actualized by the Faith's more than five million members, spread throughout nearly every country in the world.

Throughout the history of the Faith, crisis and victory have been intertwined, with the persecutions and sufferings of the community matched by its advancement. Neither imprisonment nor tragedy has been able to extinguish the flame of Bahá'u'lláh's Cause. Instead, it has ignited growing and vibrant communities. Whether through establishing educational programs, contributing to social and economic development, or advancing processes of unity, the Bahá'ís are actively engaged in creating a better, more prosperous world for all humanity. Though the scope and sheer number of activities makes a complete record impossible, this article offers a brief survey of some highlights of the activities in the past year.

Advancement of Women

Despite the advances made in recent decades, sexual inequality remains a problem in all nations. The energy wasted keeping women from their rightful place in society has had the effect not only of depriving them of the opportunity to contribute fully to society,

---

[3] Congressman Mark Steven Kirk, 16 October 2002, to the 107th Cong., 2nd session, *Congressional Record: Extensions of Remarks*, pp. E1906–07.

but also of retarding the progress of all people. 'Abdu'l-Bahá made this clear in His statement, "Until the reality of equality between man and woman is fully established and attained, the highest social development of mankind is not possible."[4]

In the United Kingdom, a 13-year-old Bahá'í, Anisa Fadei, used that quotation in her presentation to the annual "Girls Speak Up" conference, held on 7 December 2002 at the Cranfield Management Development Centre in Bedfordshire. More than 100 people from around the United Kingdom attended the conference, which was organized by the British Association of Bahá'í Women.

Miss Fadei's paper, titled "Prosperity," reflected one of the central themes identified by conference organizers. Other young Bahá'í women speakers offered papers that elucidated the key themes, including talks titled "Citizenship," "Partnership," and "Information Technology." Workshops and panels on related themes gave participants an opportunity to explore the topics further, with each participant requested to put forward action points that could be presented to decision makers in the country.

Expert presenters offered responses to panel discussions, and among the responders were Soroptimist member Valerie Evans, CBE, a former elected chair of the Women's National Commission and current chair of the UK Gender Statistics Users Group; Roz Ozborne of the Royal College of Nurses and a member of the Women's National Commission Steering Group; and Dr. Val Singh, Senior Research Fellow in organizational behavior and a lecturer associated with the School of Management at the University of Cranfield.

Additional presentations at the event were made by the Bahá'í Office of Social and Economic Development and the Bahá'í Agency for Social and Economic Development-UK, Soroptimist International of Bedford, and the YWCA (Young Women's Christian Association). Artistic elements included paintings by women artists displayed at the art gallery and entertainment by two young Indian dancers. Support for the conference was given by the United Nations Development Fund for Women (UNIFEM), the Bedford County Council,

---

[4] 'Abdu'l-Bahá, *The Promulgation of Universal Peace: Talks Delivered by 'Abdu'l-Bahá during His Visit to the United States and Canada in 1912*, rev. ed. (Wilmette, IL: Bahá'í Publishing Trust, 1995), p. 76.

and the Cranfield Centre for Women Business Leaders; Jordans Cereals and the Marks and Spencer's national chain store provided sponsorship.

In Cyprus, Bahá'í Suha Vakil Fanaiean took part in a televised two-hour debate as part of activities for United Nation's Women's Day on 8 March 2003. Mrs. Fanaiean shared Bahá'í perspectives on the station of women and the value of the family during the live show. Other local Bahá'í women attended forums and panel discussions organized for the day. They also supported other activities of like-minded organizations and received an invitation from the newly formed nongovernmental organization (NGO) Urban Women to offer workshops at two distant villages.

Women of all ages were attracted to the workshops, which used stories, visual aids, symbolic elements, and music to portray the purpose of life as an individual woman and as a member of both a family and a world community. One village project drew more than 55 people, many of whom stayed for several hours asking questions and sharing their experiences, and in another village a similar response came from the 45 attendees there. National television in Cyprus reported on the workshops, and participants said they were deeply affected by the programs because of their appeal to the heart and the soul.

Bahá'ís in Zimbabwe also participated in International Women's Day, taking part in an event that drew more than 2,000 people to Harare's International Convention Center. A Bahá'í banner proclaiming "Bahá'í Faith fosters Equality of Man and Woman: Without Equality the Bird of Humanity Cannot Fly" hung at the entrance to the main hall. The event opened with Bahá'í and Christian prayers. Bahá'ís also distributed 300 copies of the Bahá'í International Community's pamphlet entitled "HIV/AIDS and Gender Equality," a topic of particular relevance in Africa and one of the themes of the celebration's discussions.

During the program the organizing committee, which included the Bahá'í representative Flora Teckie, was introduced to the gathering. The group sang a song and was asked to offer support and good wishes to the gathering. Mrs. Teckie explained that the equality of women and men is a prerequisite to world peace and wished the participants peace and prosperity on behalf of the Bahá'ís of Harare.

Women at the Barli Institute in Indore, India, learn practical skills, such as dressmaking, that help them to gain self-esteem, become financially independent, and aid their village communities.

The principle of equality between women and men animates many Bahá'í social and economic development efforts, and when the Bahá'í community in the United Kingdom was invited to present a project highlighting its contributions to the environment, it chose one that has offered training and empowerment to more than 1,300 women. The Barli Development Institute for Rural Women (BDIRW), based in Indore, India, focuses on giving poor young women literacy training, practical knowledge of health, nutrition and sanitation, skills for income generation, and an awareness of village-level environmental conservation.[5]

The BDIRW works to enable women to become agents for social change and "pillars" of their families and communities through a holistic approach to education that provides each trainee with leadership training courses in such subjects as literacy, tailoring, agriculture, environmental awareness, and self-esteem. Its spiritually oriented curriculum empowers women as they examine caste, tribal, and

[5] For a report on the BDIRW, see *The Bahá'í World 2000–2001*, pp. 219–27.

class prejudices in the light of Bahá'í principles such as the oneness of humanity, equality of women and men, respect for diversity, and service to the community.

The presentation was part of a special gathering held in honor of the Golden Jubilee of Queen Elizabeth II. Organized by the Alliance of Religions and Conservation (ARC), the event sought to explore the religions' understanding of the place of humanity in creation. Bahá'í representatives joined with leaders of Buddhism, Christianity, Hinduism, Islam, Jainism, Judaism, Sikhism, Taoism, and Zoroastrianism to celebrate the significant role that religions can play in caring for the environment. Held 13 November 2002 in London's historic Banqueting House in Whitehall and titled "Our Place in Creation," the event featured the presentation of a series of environmental projects to Her Majesty, as well as a program of sacred artistic, musical, and dance performances by representatives of each religion.

In Istanbul, Turkey, three Bahá'í women, including two members of the National Spiritual Assembly, were invited to attend the Women Parliamentarians Conference on "World Peace and Cooperation," held from 17 to 19 October 2002. It was the fourth

The Tondod Public High School Dance Troupe performs at the opening of the new Bahá'í radio station in Bulac, Philippines, on 26 November 2002.

annual international conference organized by the Marmara Group Foundation, a prominent Turkish NGO supported by the First Lady of the Turkish Republic, Semra Sezer. The invited speakers and attendees came from a variety of backgrounds and included women parliamentarians, academics, Turkish and foreign office members of embassies, and many representatives of NGOs from neighboring countries such as Albania, Azerbaijan, Cyprus, Georgia, Hungary, Israel, Romania, Russia, and Turkmenistan. The Bahá'í women, who were acknowledged for the excellence of their presentations, particularly highlighted the importance of the education of children in achieving peace.

Social and Economic Development

The contributions of Bahá'í communities to social and economic development differ both in their nature and character. Their efforts, though, are united by their aim to uplift not only the social and material circumstances of people but also their spiritual condition. Ultimately, they reflect the fundamental purpose of religion, "to effect a transformation in the whole character of mankind, a transformation that shall manifest itself both outwardly and inwardly, that shall affect both its inner life and external conditions."[6]

In Bulac, Philippines, more than 300 people, including local officials and nearby residents, attended the inauguration ceremony for the Bahá'í radio station, which will feature programs designed to promote social and economic development in the community at large. The 26 November 2002 event featured speeches by visiting Bahá'í dignitaries and local officials, as well as performances by children and youth from nearby schools.

The station currently has a full-time staff of four, and as volunteer personnel gain experience the station will increase its offerings, with the goal of including short-term courses, seminars, and workshops in its broadcasts.

Local government officials praised the establishment of the station, which is located in a rural district about 30 kilometers from

---

[6] Bahá'u'lláh, The Kitáb-i-Íqán (Wilmette, IL: Bahá'í Publishing Trust, 1993), p. 240.

the city of San Jose on the main island of Luzon. It will provide programming designed not only to assist in social and economic development but also to promote moral, spiritual, and human resource development in Bahá'í communities by aiding in the organization of spiritual activities. Specifically, the station will help to encourage the holding of study circles, devotional meetings, and children's classes.

Due to the flat topography of the region, the new Philippines station is able to reach a wide area, encompassing the entire province of Nueva Ecija and a portion of the Tarlac and Pangasinan provinces—a potential listenership of more than 2.3 million people. Six other Bahá'í radio projects operate similar stations in Bolivia, Chile, Ecuador, Panama, Peru, and the United States.

Development efforts are not always the result of projects and plans, however—sometimes they are an immediate response to an immediate need. When the Mt. Pago volcano in Papua New Guinea erupted in August 2002, the local government of Kimbe turned to the Bahá'í community for assistance in housing some 200 people from Galilo village who were displaced by the disaster. The large Bahá'í center in Kimbe provided shelter to many of them, and the local Bahá'ís tried to make their stay as pleasant as possible by providing food, tents, and other necessities. Bahá'ís from neighboring communities in Garu and Kambili also contributed food.

The hospitality of the Bahá'ís also included inviting the displaced villagers to Bahá'í functions held at the center. For most of them, it was their first encounter with the Faith. As a result of the experience, several of them became Bahá'ís.

After the Provincial Disaster Committee declared it safe for people to return to their homes, it requested a "farewell night" with the Bahá'ís of Kimbe to be held on 21 November to show its appreciation and gratitude. William Hosea, a government representative and member of the Provincial Disaster Committee, conveyed his gratitude on behalf of the government and thanked the Bahá'í community for its support and sacrifices.

Most long-term Bahá'í projects are focused on creating sustainable practices, and therefore ensuring protection of the environment and natural resources. At an interreligious conference in Germany, three representatives of the Bahá'í community offered their perspectives

Students in the fifth grade at the Puka Puka village school, a Bahá'í-run educational initiative in rural Bolivia.

on the contribution of religion to environmental protection. The goal of the meeting, held 6–7 May 2002 under the auspices of the German Federal Environment Ministry, was to widen the dialogue on environmental issues between the government and various religions in Germany.

Gottfried Orth, director of the Ernst Lange Institute for Ecumenical Studies, chaired the meeting, and other participants included three representatives of the Catholic and Protestant churches; the general secretary of the Central Muslim Council and a Muslim scientific advisor; and a member of the council of the Buddhist Union and two other Buddhists. Also present were observers from the World Conference of Religions for Peace and a group representing the Earth Charter. The dialogue was designed as a follow-up to a meeting of G-8 environment ministers and religious leaders in Trieste in March 2001, at which religious leaders appealed for governments to give environmental concerns a higher priority.

The final memorandum, jointly drafted by the participants and accepted at the end of the conference, established the common ground between them on the issues of nature and the environment and the need for a common responsibility for action. The joint memorandum identified elements such as love, justice, and ethics as a foundation for sustainable development.

The memorandum expresses the commitment to continue the dialogue locally, regionally, and at the European level, and the religious communities pledged to continue the process of discussing environmental issues both inside and outside their own communities. A book containing the statements of the various religious communities was also prepared.

In the United Kingdom, "Tranquility Zones" have been growing in popularity since they were first conceived by the Bahá'í community in Swindon. They are spaces created for prayer, meditation, and reflection and have been provided as a service for police, hospitals, and businesses as well as for the general public. Recently they have been used in youth empowerment projects, and in 2002 a Tranquility Zone was introduced as part of a pilot program run by the Trowbridge Probation Service in an effort to reduce reoffending. The program also includes group and one-on-one counseling, medical attention, literacy lessons, storytelling, and art and color therapy.

Each week, a Bahá'í member of the Probation Team sets up a Tranquility Zone room, which is prepared with cushions, flowers,

Bahá'ís in Finland offer literature at a booth during a multiethnic festival in Helsinki in May 2002.

and candles. The 20 young offenders, joined by the other staff, are encouraged to view themselves in terms of their spiritual capacities. Gentle music is played throughout the session and the overall atmosphere aids in taking the youth on a meditative journey with music, stories, and quotations from the Bahá'í sacred writings.

Introducing the spiritual component of prayer and meditation into the rehabilitation process has been praised by participants, staff, and local government for its effectiveness. In addition to expanding the number of clients who use the room, the Probation Service plans to use it for a 10-minute meditation session at the end of each day.

Children participate in a Bahá'í class at the Mushuk Pakari Center for Integral Education of Indigenous People in Santa Rosa, Ecuador.

Racial Unity

The Bahá'í Faith represents one of the most diverse collections of people on the planet. Though they come from more than 2,000 ethnic and tribal backgrounds, their difference of color and culture is not a cause for separation, but rather a rich and diverse heritage of humanity to be celebrated. Both within Bahá'í communities and in the world around them, Bahá'ís strive to create a society free from

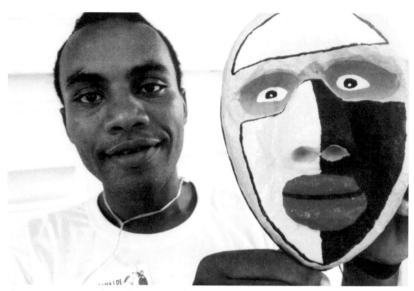

A participant at the Afro-Descendants Gathering, held in Brazil in 2003, displays a mask he made during the African mask workshop.

racial prejudice where "humanity is one kind, one race and progeny, inhabiting the same globe."[7]

From 31 January to 2 February 2003, more than 170 Brazilian Bahá'ís came together to foster personal transformation and promote the principle of the oneness of humanity. Deepening unity, increasing self-esteem, and enhancing spiritual understanding were the themes of the "Afro-Descendants Gathering," held in the regional Bahá'í center in Salvador, Brazil.

In order to better understand racial prejudice and how it operates in today's society, the participants spoke in a session about their personal experiences of day-to-day discrimination. Then they examined the contributions made by "Afro-descendants" to technological and scientific development in both ancient and modern times. Participants also studied selected Bahá'í principles such as the oneness of the human family and the need for unity in diversity.

This was the seventh such gathering in Brazil since 1996, and similar initiatives in the United States—the Black Men's Gathering and the more recent Black Women's Gathering—shared the

---

[7] 'Abdu'l-Bahá, *Promulgation of Universal Peace*, p. 118.

Participants at a training institute campaign for indigenous peoples held in Wakpala, South Dakota, United States, in 2002.

objectives of the Brazilian meeting. Nearly 100 attended the 16th annual Black Men's Gathering, held at the Green Acre Bahá'í School in Eliot, Maine. The week-long conference, held the last week of July 2002, included participants from Kenya, the Gambia, and Suriname.

The fourth annual Black Women's Gathering was held at Louhelen Bahá'í School in Davison, Michigan, from 27 to 29 September 2002. Fifteen women participated in the weekend, which was filled with prayers, singing, music, fellowship, and consultation.

Discussions at both gatherings included sharing experiences common to people of African ancestry and learning new ways to progress beyond feelings of victimization. Also expressed was the desire to include more forms of African-American culture in Bahá'í events and the need to attract more people of African descent to the Bahá'í Faith.

The Black Men's Gathering ended with a procession and memorial program presented at the graveside of Hand of the Cause of God Louis Gregory and his wife Louisa Gregory.

Louis Gregory, an early American Bahá'í who was a leader in promoting racial harmony, was also honored by the local Bahá'í community of Charleston, South Carolina, through the creation of a museum in his former home.

Born in 1874, Mr. Gregory was a successful lawyer and rising star among early black intellectuals who grappled with issues of race relations in the United States at the turn of the century. In 1909, he embraced the Bahá'í Faith and turned his energies towards promoting unity among the races. He was posthumously given the title Hand of the Cause of God in 1951 as a result of his efforts in promoting the aims of the Faith.

The Louis G. Gregory Bahá'í Museum was dedicated in a two-day celebration in February 2003, which was attended by more than 300 people. Dedication program highlights included a multicultural arts presentation, two workshops on race relations, a tour of the museum and nearby sites important to Mr. Gregory, and a devotional gathering. The museum, which resides in a two-story house in the heart of the Charleston peninsula, is the first museum in the city dedicated to a single person.

In Bosnia and Herzegovina, a country whose short history has been marred by constant ethnic tensions, Landegg International University's Education for Peace program (EFP) is creating bonds among the different groups. The program has been running for more than two years and now involves more than 6,000 students, 10,000 parents, and 400 teachers. It offers training in conflict resolution, democracy, ethics, and leadership, and aims to create mutual respect and understanding among the country's people. Operating within the school system, it is integrated into the curriculum and is designed to assist in reconciling the rifts among the country's main ethnic and religious groups—Catholic Croats, Orthodox Serbs, and Muslim Serbs.

Parents, teachers, administrators, support staff, and students are all crucial to the project, as they strive to create an atmosphere of peace and mutual understanding. Lessons are consolidated through artistic expression, and participants go on to educate the wider community through creative presentations that include poetry and dance. Some of the teachers involved with the project have started to write a curriculum acceptable to members of all three ethnic groups. At present, each has its own curriculum, and education is strictly segregated.

The government of Bosnia and Herzegovina has been so impressed with the project's efficacy that it issued a statement on the
Education for Peace program to the heads of state and heads of
delegations at the United Nations Special Session on Children, held
in New York 8–10 May 2002. Within six years, the program will be
introduced into all schools in Bosnia and Herzegovina, eventually
reaching over a million participants. It will also be offered to many
French- and English-speaking African countries in the coming year
and is being started in two private US schools.

Another country where the Bahá'ís are helping to address long-
standing racial and cultural issues is Australia, where events held in
conjunction with National Reconciliation Week, from 27 May to
3 June 2002, included a special service dedicated to reconciliation
between indigenous and other Australians.[8] Bahá'ís, members of
the Manly Pittwater Warringah Aboriginal Support Group, and the
public joined together in the service, held at the Bahá'í House of
Worship near Sydney, Australia, on 26 May. Featured were readings
from the scriptures of the major world religions and a performance
by the Bahá'í Temple Choir. The reception included reading of the
prayer distributed for National Sorry Day by the Aboriginal and
Islander Commission of the National Council of Churches.

The service was preceded by a reception at which Ann Thomas,
a native woman of the Biripi tribe, shared her thoughts on reconciliation. "Reconciliation at this time means a lot," she said, "but it can
only be by the spirit." The Bahá'í Faith, she said, offered a means
for all Australians to work together in unity.

Education

The upliftment of humanity begins with its education. Instruction
in the arts and sciences, particularly with attention given to moral
development, is the means by which people understand themselves
and their environment, and create an "ever-advancing civilization."
Bahá'í schools and educational projects are dedicated to uplifting
the minds and spirits and each year expand in both enrollments and

---

[8] For more information about reconciliation efforts by the Bahá'í community
in Australia, see pp. 120–22.

prominence as more people become attracted to the principles and methods that animate Bahá'í education.

At the opening ceremony for two new Internet-ready buildings, the Ocean of Light International School in Tonga earned high praise from Crown Prince Tupouto'a Tupou V for its technological advancement. The school is owned by the Bahá'í community of Tonga and its curriculum, which is dedicated to developing not only intellectual but spiritual potential, is based on Bahá'í principles; it aims to raise up students committed to the service of humanity. The school fosters the spiritual development of its students through classes in spiritual values in the primary school and moral education in the high school.

"The opening of the buildings could not have come at a better time in Tonga's history because for the first time this school is breaking new ground in using the technology to mitigate the negative effects of the economy," Prince Tupouto'a said in a speech at the ceremony on 25 January 2003. The Prince said he would follow the progress of the school with "much interest and great affection."

The official opening of the new buildings was followed by a luncheon and entertainment for the 600 guests, who included Prince

Children take part in a race as part of World Health Day events at the Louis Gregory Memorial Bahá'í School in Tilling, Uganda, in April 2002.

Tupouto'a's brother, the Honorable Maatu, and his wife Alaileula, the granddaughter of His Highness Susuga Malietoa Tanumafili II, the Head of State of Samoa.

Located on the outskirts of Nuku'alofa, the capital city of Tonga, the school opened in 1996 and started its program with only nine students. During its seven years of operation the school has outgrown its rented facilities. Now the two new buildings will provide some 2,000 square meters of space for classrooms, laboratories, and a library. Classes are available for students ranging in age from 3 to 16, but a 12th grade will be added in 2004 and high school diplomas will be awarded to graduates. Currently 250 children are enrolled at the school. About 80 percent are from Tonga, but the student body also includes children from Australia, Canada, Japan, New Zealand, and the United States.

Another long-standing Bahá'í education project, FUNDAEC, was honored by the Club of Budapest with a "Change the World—Best Practice Award" for its achievements in providing high school education and training to more than 50,000 people living in rural areas in Latin America. In a speech at the award ceremony, Peter Spiegel, the Secretary-General of the Club of Budapest, characterized the project

Participants in a Bahá'í study circle in Bahia, Brazil, use training materials developed at the Ruhi Institute in Colombia.

as "the most considerable revolution of education in the twentieth century" because of its efforts to assist people in developing countries to actively engage in the development process.

The project is known as SAT (which stands for Sistema de Aprendizaje Tutorial, or "System for Tutorial Learning"). It is a tutorial learning program based on a series of interactive workbooks that enables trained tutors to offer a high-quality secondary educational program in rural areas with minimal overhead cost. In most cases, even the tutors themselves lack formal education.

SAT is keyed to the realities of rural life and based on the needs of the local residents, aiming to strengthen local economies and communal identity. It offers students a high school education that not only provides them with theoretical knowledge, as most traditional educational curricula do, but also allows them to become economically independent and to serve their communities.

The "Change the World—Best Practice Award" was given to four international educational projects during the awards ceremony, held at the historic St. Paul's Church in Frankfurt, Germany, on 6 October 2002. Some 1,000 people attended, including honorary Club of Budapest members actor Sir Peter Ustinov and author Paulo Coelho, who were granted the Club's Planetary Consciousness Award. Also at the event was Istvan Hiller, personal assistant to the Hungarian Prime Minister Peter Medgyessy, whose presence reinforced the support of the Hungarian government for the Club's efforts in promoting the emergence of planetary consciousness.

Bahá'í education efforts are not solely focused on elementary and high school education. At the University of Bari, the second-largest university in Italy, a permanent course on Bahá'í-inspired ethics and economics was established in March 2003. Giuseppe Robiati was appointed as the coordinator of the course. A member of the Bahá'í community of Italy and the European Bahá'í Business Forum, Mr. Robiati is a businessman with extensive experience in engineering and business management and in the fields of human resources and economics. The course was approved by the Academic Senate and the Rector of the University of Bari in July 2002 and began in March. The "Ethics and Economy: Towards a New World Order" course consists of 10 seminars focused on essential Bahá'í values such as consultation, justice, equality, universal education,

A study circle in Turkey at the Association for the Unity of Mankind in Antalya, June 2002.

and the unity of science and religion as they relate to the world of business and economics.

And in Switzerland, scholars and academics from 10 countries attended the Second International Conference on Modern Religious Movements in Judaism, Christianity, Islam, and the Bábí and Bahá'í Faiths, held at the Landegg International University campus 27–29 November 2002. It was the second in a series of conferences jointly convened by Landegg and the Hebrew University of Jerusalem.[9]

Participants came from Australia, Canada, France, Liechtenstein, Iran, Israel, Spain, Turkey, the United Kingdom, and the United States. Professor Moshe Sharon, holder of the Chair in Bahá'í Studies at the Hebrew University, cochaired the conference with Dr. H.B. Danesh, Landegg's Rector. Professor Sharon opened the conference with an address on "Millennialism: Significance of the Nineteenth Century" and the following day presented his ideas on "The Problem of Ritual."

---

[9] A report on the First International Conference on Modern Religious Movements in Judaism, Christianity, Islam, and the Bábí and Bahá'í Faiths can be found in *The Bahá'í World 2000–2001*, pp. 103–07.

In total, 17 papers were presented on a wide range of topics including "New Forms of Moving towards the Unity between Faith and Reason in the Catholic Church," "Modern 'Hebrew Christians': An 'Imagined Community,'" "Bahá'í Education in Shiite Iran," and "The Silences of God."

In addition to formal presentations, the conference featured musical performances and a banquet. All papers from the conference will be made available on Landegg's Web site, and the dates for the third conference, to be held at the Hebrew University of Jerusalem, are forthcoming.[10]

Arts

'Abdu'l-Bahá eloquently expressed the high station of the arts in His statement that "in this wonderful new age, art is worship. The more thou strivest to perfect it, the closer wilt thou come to God."[11] There is no distinct category of "Bahá'í art"; rather Bahá'í artists, musicians, and performers strive to express aspects of divinity in their work and thereby contribute to the continual growth and maturation of human culture.

In New York City, a week-long Festival of the Arts was held from 26 June to 2 July 2002. The project was an initiative of Global Music, Inc., a Bahá'í-owned company, and other individuals. The highlight was a concert by the Voices of Bahá choir, a 550-voice group composed of Bahá'ís from some 24 countries, at Carnegie Hall. Voices of Bahá has performed in a variety of incarnations at more than 80 concerts in 30 countries over the past 10 years. The entire choir actually consists of more than 1,000 members, but since its first performance at the Second Bahá'í World Congress in 1992, seldom have more than 200 performed together.

The Bahá'í Gospel Singers, also featured at the World Congress, performed in an event at the Manhattan Center, as did well-known Persian performers who showcased an evening of Persian music.

---

[10] Landegg's Web site can be found at http://www.landegg.edu/.

[11] 'Abdu'l-Bahá, in "The Importance of the Arts in Promoting the Faith," *The Compilation of Compilations*, vol. 3 (Ingleside, NSW: Bahá'í Publications Australia, 2000), p. 22.

Choreographer Ben Hatcher's award-winning "Covenant" premiered 24 July 2002 at the Banff Center, in Canada. The work was inspired by the opening of the Terraces of the Shrine of the Báb on Mount Carmel.

Members of the Artworks Visual Arts Theater group in Australia, whose performances are a unique mix of painting, drama, and contemporary dance.

Other events included a theater festival at the 47th Street Theater and a four-day conference on the arts at the Hotel Pennsylvania. The conference on the arts focused on the role of the arts as described in the Bahá'í writings and applied in the Bahá'í community. It included talks, music, drama, dance, and devotions in an attempt to highlight the spiritual and transformative power of creative endeavor. The theater festival showcased the growing theatrical talent that has emerged within the Bahá'í community in recent years.

The effects of the festival even carried over to other countries. After being informed that two Belgian Bahá'ís had performed in the Voices of Bahá choir at Carnegie Hall, a Belgian national radio station, Radio Musique 3, aired four programs on the Faith and Bahá'í choral music. The 20-minute shows concluded on 1 September after being aired four consecutive weeks on the station's "Chorissimo" program, which focuses on Belgian amateur choirs. The shows included information about the Faith and the New York event, interviews with Belgian singers Lorraine Hetu and Concetta Difrancesco, and music by Tom Price, the conductor of Voices of Bahá, and Van Gilmer, the conductor of the Bahá'í Gospel Singers.

Throughout the worldwide Bahá'í community, arts workshops have contributed both to developing identity within the community and to spreading the message of the Faith. One such workshop, Geração Viva, based in Portugal, performed in front of some 500 people in Lugo, Spain, as part of the "World Citizenship" program organized by the Bahá'í community there. The group's performance was part of a festival of dances from around the world that took place during the last week of July. The newspapers *El Progreso* and *La Voz de Galicia* published articles and photographs of the performance.

In July and August, three members of the Geração Viva group visited Brazil to help in training workshops for Brazilian youth. The structure of the training hinged on both physical and spiritual elements, with the participants learning dance steps and dramatic techniques in addition to studying the Bahá'í writings and focusing on generating love, cooperation, and unity within the group. The dances that the participants learned to perform dramatize Bahá'í principles.

Public presentations were held after each training session, with the largest in Bahia, where close to 400 people gathered to watch the youth perform. In all, seven Bahá'í communities in four different Brazilian states benefited from the training workshops. In São Paulo, the training was held at the Soltaniéh Bahá'í Educational Center, where both Bahá'í and non-Bahá'í young people who completed the training were asked to reproduce it in other cities. The newly trained youth were also invited to make a public presentation for 200 people during a conference in Rio de Janeiro held by the United Religions Initiative.

An Australian group, Artworks Visual Arts Theater, Inc., received a grant from the Department of Immigration, Multicultural, and Indigenous Affairs to promote harmony in diversity in schools throughout Western Australia, South Australia, and the Northern Territory. Among the aims of the grant, which is worth approximately AU$50,000, are to aid in the elimination of racism and prejudice and to help build a peaceful future for children.

Artworks is a performing arts and workshop group whose programs are meant to empower young people. Its widely acclaimed techniques are based on a combination of painting, drama, and contemporary dance. Thanks to the grant, the five-year-old group will be traveling to some 60 schools in total, performing shows about harmony and facilitating workshops where students can learn to use the arts to promote understanding and unity. About half of the schools involved also sponsored extended workshops culminating in community arts performances by the students themselves. Part of the project, known as "Harmony in Diversity Project 2003," will focus on Aboriginal schools in the Northern Territory.

Another arts group, Phoenix Theater, organized a tour for its performance of a play about human rights in July 2002 with the encouragement of the National Spiritual Assembly of Greece. The group of 11 youth inaugurated the tour with a performance at a multicultural school in Athens, attended by some 100 people, mostly from the Turkish-speaking minority.

Other performances included shows in Volos, Thessaloniki, Larissa, and Kalamaria, which drew a crowd of close to 170 people. The municipality of Larissa assisted with the preparations for the show there, where more than 100 people attended—despite adverse weather conditions during the outdoor show.

The group's final performance was on 13 July at a gypsy camp in a former military base outside of Thessaloniki. The performance was arranged by Arsis, an organization for the support of disadvantaged youth, as part of an emerging cultural program. A large crowd from the local gypsy community attended, and after the performance the gypsy children and youth mingled with the Phoenix members in a spirit of warmth and friendship.

News coverage of the performances included stories in local newspapers and a large article in the Thessaloniki-based newspaper, the *Sunday Angelioforos*. The national television channel ERT 3 broadcast part of the performance in Thessaloniki and interviews with participants.

Members of the Phoenix Theater group on their tour in Greece in 2003.

Involvement in the Life of Society

Though the Bahá'í Faith is fundamentally nonpolitical in character, its aims embrace the whole of humanity, and work with governmental and civil bodies, collaborating on projects and promoting the Faith's social ideals, is a key aspect of its activities. Involvement with the United Nations and other international organizations, and dialogues with governments and leaders of thought, are means by which Bahá'ís strive to contribute to the discourse of society by elucidating the position of the Bahá'í Faith and demonstrating how the Bahá'í teachings create the basis for a civilization founded on peace, unity, and justice.

In the Solomon Islands, the National Spiritual Assembly met with Prime Minister Sir Allan Kemakeza during the first week of July 2002. The purpose of the meeting was to discuss the nature and status of the Bahá'í community in the Solomon Islands, and to explain the role of the National Assembly in administering the affairs of the community. The Assembly also used the opportunity to present examples of the work of Bahá'ís around the world, including the projects on Mount Carmel at the Bahá'í World Centre and the recent letter of the Universal House of Justice to the world's religious leaders. The Prime Minister expressed his appreciation of the support for peace that the Bahá'í community had shown throughout the recent difficulties in the country, specifically mentioning efforts Bahá'ís had made in villages throughout the islands.

The Bahá'í community in India hosted a visit of the country's President, Dr. Abdul Kalam, to the Bahá'í House of Worship in New Delhi on 18 March 2003. It was the first official visit by an Indian Head of State since the Temple was opened in December 1986. Dr. Kalam was joined by Deputy Prime Minister Lal Krishna Advani and Mrs. Advani, and Defense Minister George Fernandes. During the visit, Dr. Kalam also met briefly with representatives of the National Spiritual Assembly of India and the Continental Board of Counsellors.

Members of the National Spiritual Assembly of the Solomon Islands, during their July 2002 meeting with Prime Minister Sir Allan Kemakeza (back row, third from right).

The President also visited the Temple's recent addition, an information center for visitors that features a visitor's gallery, comprising a main auditorium with a seating capacity for more than 400 people and two 70-seat auditoriums. The gallery focuses on the history of the Bahá'í Faith, its philosophy, and the development activities of Bahá'ís around the world. On display are photographs, text, and films on the history of the Faith, and excerpts from Bahá'í holy writings. The auditoriums screen films on the Temple itself as well as on the Bahá'í Faith.

Annually, more than three and a half million people visit the Temple, making it one of the most visited sites in the world. Other prominent visitors have included the Prime Ministers of Norway and Sri Lanka, the President of Iceland, the Vice-President of Uruguay, and the Dalai Lama.

In Puerto Rico, the Bahá'í community gave support to International Peace Day celebrations held on 1 November 2002. Bahá'ís participated in three events for the day, which is an observance created by the Puerto Rican legislature. The events included a Harmony for Peace celebration at the botanical gardens in San Juan, a Walk for Peace in Rio Piedras, and a Commitment for Peace rally in San Juan's Central Park. The activities were organized by the Coalition against Family Violence, with support from various other civic and humanitarian organizations.

The first event brought together political leaders and young students who called for peace in Puerto Rico and in the world. Among the speakers was Yolanda Zayas, the Secretary of Family Affairs in Puerto Rico, who said that in order to achieve peace, work must begin in the family. She called for reflection on what each individual might contribute to create a world in harmony. The activity ended with an artistic presentation by the choir of the University of Puerto Rico.

The Walk for Peace was a trip by public and private school students along the streets of the Rio Piedras section of San Juan to the Puerto Rico Art Museum, and the celebration of Peace Day ended at San Juan's Central Park with a gathering of religious leaders from many faiths who made a "Commitment for Peace."

In Kosovo, Global Perspectives, a Bahá'í-inspired NGO, was asked to host moral leadership seminars in the region. The invitation came due to the success of Global Perspectives' first seminar, which brought together 35 people from the region's diverse ethnic groups. Although participants in that seminar, who came from groups that are historically antagonistic, started the seminar by avoiding contact, they ended with warm embraces.

The project is subsidized and supported by the United Nations International Children's Fund (UNICEF), the Organization for Security and Cooperation in Europe (OSCE), the Embassies of the United States and Germany, and the Ministry of Education and Culture of Kosovo. It was initiated by the Global Motion Social Dance Theater, a group that aims to raise awareness of social problems and is dedicated to advancing education of its peers through the arts. The group is particularly relevant in Kosovo, where close to 40 percent of the population is under 20. The dance group takes youth between 15 and 18 through a 20-session process of social, moral, and artistic training, to launch them as active agents of personal and social change.

Another ongoing effort in which the Bahá'ís are involved is the newly formed Center for Studies of Holocaust and Religious Minorities in Norway. Although still in the development stages, the center aims to combine studies of the Holocaust with an examination

Bahá'ís cut a ceremonial ribbon at the inauguration of a new devotional center in Guatemala City, Guatemala.

of the role of religious minorities in the modern world. It was formed at the instigation of the Jewish community and the Norwegian government, and founded by the University of Oslo. It will contribute new research, educational and informational activities, exhibitions, and conferences on the topic.

Britt Strandlie Thoresen, a member of the National Spiritual Assembly of the Bahá'ís of Norway, was elected to represent religious minorities on the center's council. Mrs. Thoresen chairs the working group that plans the themes to be discussed and the religious minorities to be presented at the center.

During a study trip by the center's six board members to the United States, the Bahá'í International Community's Office at the United Nations helped arrange a meeting with more than 20 like-minded NGO representatives, and during a trip to England, Bahá'ís there arranged for the representatives to meet with Brian Pearce, leader of the Interfaith Network of Great Britain, Sandra Barath, from the Oxford Interfaith Centre, and representatives of the Beth Shalom Centre near Nottingham. Mrs. Thoresen also told Katusha Otter Nilsen, coordinator of the Norwegian center, about the work of Landegg International University, and in July Mrs. Otter Nilsen attended a course on "Religion and Conflict Resolution" there.

Interfaith Activities

The activities of Bahá'í communities to promote religious understanding are founded on the idea that "There can be no doubt whatever that the peoples of the world, of whatever race or religion, derive their inspiration from one heavenly Source, and are the subjects of one God."[12] It is in this spirit that Bahá'ís around the world recognize a kinship with worshippers from all religions and are involved in dialogues that promote tolerance and unity. Most recently, the need for greater clarity on the relationship among the major religions was the subject of a letter written by the Universal House of Justice addressed to the world's religious leaders.[13]

---

[12] Bahá'u'lláh, *Gleanings from the Writings of Bahá'u'lláh* (Wilmette, IL: Bahá'í Publishing Trust, 1994), p. 217.

[13] For the text of the letter, see pp. 89–98.

Promoting understanding between religions was also the focus of a recent effort by Bahá'ís in Peru. Their cooperation with the Peruvian human rights organization INTERDES has helped to energize an ongoing interfaith collaboration aimed at winning wider governmental recognition for non-Catholic religions. The result has been the creation of a Peruvian Interfaith Council, which will be the official liaison for non-Catholic organizations with the Ministry of Justice. As well, the government has agreed to appoint a National Director of Interfaith Affairs, which will become a parallel position to the Directorate of Catholic Affairs within the Ministry of Justice.

INTERDES, a nongovernmental organization with the full title of Ministerio Internacional de Desarrollo (Ministry of International Development), had been seeking wider freedoms for non-Catholic religions for several years but had worked mainly with evangelical Christian groups. Ultimately, some 15 different non-Catholic religious organizations in Peru, including the Bahá'ís, joined in asking the government, which has traditionally granted favored status only to the Catholic Church, to grant greater religious freedom for all.

World Religion Day, a celebration held annually since 1949, is a forum for religions to join together and celebrate their common ground. Since its inception by the National Spiritual Assembly of the United States, World Religion Day has grown in scope, with the list of countries observing the day in the past year including Albania, Austria, Australia, Bulgaria, Canada, Republic of the Congo, Finland, Germany, Hong Kong, India, Ireland, Italy, Liechtenstein, Lithuania, New Zealand, Norway, Panama, Portugal, Slovakia, Sweden, Switzerland, the United Kingdom, and Vanuatu.

The celebration in the Republic of Mauritius, organized by the Catholic Church at the invitation of the Bahá'í community, was marked by the presence of the nation's President, Karl Offmann, and senior representatives of the Bahá'í, Buddhist, Christian, Hindu, and Muslim faiths. Each of the religious representatives read prayers to the audience of 500 and spoke on the teachings of his or her respective religion, and each emphasized the same theme—that all the religions teach unity and peace.

Another commemoration, United Nations Day on 24 October 2002, created an opportunity for an interfaith discussion on world peace organized by the local Bahá'í community in Buea, Cameroon.

In Cork, Ireland, a state primary school where there are no Bahá'í students celebrated the Bahá'í festival of Riḍván. The Irish-language school, Gaelscoil Goirt Alainn, chose to celebrate the festival as part of a program of multicultural enrichment. Many of the children constructed banners with the words of Bahá'u'lláh in Irish.

Sponsored by the Local Spiritual Assembly of the Bahá'ís of Buea, the discussion featured speakers representing Bahá'í, Christian, Hindu, and Muslim perspectives. Each of the speakers stressed the importance of religion in contributing to peace and put a special emphasis on the need for religious tolerance. The Reverend Father Alosius Ituka Ndifor, secretary to the Bishop of the Catholic Diocese of Buea, said that peace begins with God because God is peace, and this can affect all of mankind if people open their hearts.

The role of religion was also the theme of a multifaith panel discussion in Jena, Germany. More than 100 people gathered at the Friedrich Schiller University in Jena on 12 November 2002 for discussion on the topic of "Jews, Christians, Muslims, and Bahá'ís: The World Religions' Common Responsibility for World Peace." Sponsored by the Intercultural Council of Germany, the panel explored ways religions could take joint responsibility for promoting international peace, both in relation to the world at large and to each other. The Intercultural Council of Germany was founded in 1994 by a group of governmental and nongovernmental organizations with the aim of promoting social integration.

Representatives of the Jewish, Evangelical Lutheran, Muslim, and Bahá'í communities took part, as did Prof. Udo Tworuschka, Chair of Comparative Religious Sciences at the University of Jena; Dr. Nadeem Elyas, President of the Central Muslim Council of Germany; and Christopher Sprung of the National Spiritual Assembly of the Bahá'ís of Germany. Dr. Jürgen Miksch, the Chairman of the Intercultural Council, hosted the panel.

Children and Youth

In a letter written on behalf of Shoghi Effendi, the plight of young people in the modern age is drawn in a dim but succinct light: "Life is not easy for the young people of this generation. They enter life with a heart full of hope, but find before themselves nothing but failures, and see in the future nothing but darkness. What they need is the light manifested by Bahá'u'lláh, for that brightens their soul and stimulates their vigor in facing difficulties."[14] It is the brightness of hope that Bahá'í communities try to bring not only to their own children, but to the whole of the younger generation, in whose hands lies the future of mankind.

More than a thousand people attended a Cambodian Bahá'í festival for children held on 30 March 2003 at the Psar Leur Bahá'í Center in Battambang. The event created an opportunity for children and youth of all social classes to meet each other and also to give provincial authorities an overview of the Bahá'í educational program for children. Children presented stories about 'Abdu'l-Bahá, recited quotations from the Bahá'í writings, made drawings and displayed their art, performed traditional Khmer music and dance, and played games together.

Organizers of the Battambang event coped with the large crowd, though they were surprised at the turnout—they expected closer to the 400 people who had attended the previous year's festival. Several

---

[14] Letter written on behalf of Shoghi Effendi, in "Youth," in *The Compilation of Compilations*, vol. 2 (Ingleside, NSW: Bahá'í Publications Australia, 1991), p. 423.

Teachers and students in a children's class in Madagascar, October 2002.

Participants in a Bahá'í children's class in Belmopan, Belize, in 2002.

senior government officials were invited guests, including the Director of the Battambang Education Department and Battambang's Director of Religious Affairs. Among the Bahá'í guests were four members of the National Spiritual Assembly of the Bahá'ís of Cambodia and two Auxiliary Board members. The festival followed another successful children's festival, held in Saang on 27 March, an event that attracted another 400 participants.

In Australia, Bahá'í education classes in state schools have been running for 15 years and have now grown to an enrollment of more than 4,000 students. The classes began in New South Wales and have since spread to the Northern Territory, Queensland, Victoria, and Western Australia, where they are offered as an option within the religious education program in government schools. The Bahá'í education classes are based on the teachings of Bahá'u'lláh and are designed to contribute to the awakening and development of the spiritual nature of every child attending the classes, complementing the traditional education provided by schools. Teachers of the classes are accredited and go through a standard approval process, which includes fulfillment of state education department requirements.

While the classes were originally started by Bahá'í parents who wanted their children to learn about their own religion, almost 90 percent of the students now attending the classes come from families of other religious backgrounds. The classes are open to all students regardless of their cultural or religious background, subject to parental approval. Many parents choose the classes for their children because they are attracted by the emphasis placed on the oneness of religion. Parents have also noted their appreciation of the focus placed on the development of virtues such as kindness, honesty, and love.

Bahá'í youth conferences offer opportunities for learning, sharing experiences, and gaining inspiration. More than 120 youth attended the national youth conference in Kampala, Uganda, from 23 to 28 December. Participants came from a variety of countries, including Burundi, Ethiopia, Italy, Kenya, the Netherlands, the Philippines, the Seychelles, Rwanda, the United States, and Zambia.

The conference had sessions on topics such as heroes and heroines of the Bahá'í Faith, marriage and chastity, and the Five Year Plan. The evenings were enlivened by celebrations that included music, dance, and dramatic performances. Following the formal sessions, participants dispersed from the conference in an organized effort to spread the Bahá'í teachings in the area.

"Changing Times" was the theme of the European Youth Seminar, held at the Townshend International School in the Czech Republic from 26 December 2002 to 1 January 2003. One hundred and eighty youth from more than 20 countries attended, to discuss topics such as the Bahá'í standard of life and ethics, the situation of the world and solutions from the Bahá'í writings, Bahá'í scholarship and its practical implications, the Five Year Plan, and *Century of Light*, a document prepared by the Universal House of Justice that describes the emergence of the Bahá'í Faith against the background of the turmoil of the twentieth century. Other issues related to topics about living the Bahá'í life, such as Bahá'í marriage, the equality of the sexes, career management, and socioeconomic development, were presented and discussed in various talks and workshops.

Another large youth conference was held in Norway from 17 to 21 April 2003. The Nordic Youth Conference, titled "Learning in Action," gathered 169 participants, with most coming from Denmark, Finland, Norway, and Sweden. Through group consultation and workshops, participants examined such topics as "The Time We Live In," "You and the Minor Plan," and "Youth at the Forefront."

Children at the Tahirih Center for Excellence in Mexico, in October 2002.

Community Development

Unity is the motivating principle of the Bahá'í Faith—a unity that not only binds together individuals but also creates the framework for a new society. Bahá'ís strive to create unity in the world around them and in their own communities; In more than 200 countries and territories and in thousands of localities they are establishing models of unified life based on consultation, learning, and growth.

On 28 and 29 June 2002, the national Bahá'í community in Zambia had cause for celebration as it marked 50 years since the Faith was first introduced to the country. The celebrations were officially opened by the Honorable Lackson Mapushi, Minister of Home Affairs. Bahá'í visitors included Counsellor-member of the International Teaching Centre Dr. Firaydoun Javaheri, Continental Counsellors Enos Makhele and Maina Mkandawire, and Daphne Masetlha, widow of the late William Mmutle Masetlha, a prominent member of the early Bahá'í community in Africa.

More than 300 participants from 28 regions of Zambia and 17 other countries gathered for two days of "golden jubilee" commemorations. Events included personal recollections recounted by many Bahá'ís about the early history of the Faith in Zambia. Special acknowledgement was also given to the unique positions held by Eric Manton and Christopher Mwitumwa in the history of the Faith in Zambia.

The community was inaugurated in 1952, when Eric Manton and his son Terry arrived from the United Kingdom as the first Bahá'ís in what was then known as Northern Rhodesia. Mr. Manton and his son eventually settled in Lusaka, where he became known for his loving manner and his ideals of peace. His closest Zambian companion was Christopher Mwitumwa, who accompanied him to Nyasaland (now Malawi) where they met other Bahá'ís. On their return in late 1954, Mr. Mwitumwa declared his belief in Bahá'u'lláh and thus became the first Zambian to embrace the Bahá'í Faith. The first National Spiritual Assembly formed in 1967, and the country is now home to nearly 15,000 Bahá'ís, with more than 80 Local Spiritual Assemblies.

For Bahá'í communities, particularly in countries where the Faith has only recently been established, becoming legally incorporated

Some of the participants at the 50th anniversary celebration of Zambia's Bahá'í community, held in June 2002.

adds to the prestige and independent character of the Faith and has many advantages for the Bahá'ís in those countries. It increases the influence of the National Spiritual Assembly and allows the body to hold property, enter into contracts, and can lead to the recognition of Bahá'í marriage ceremonies, holy days, and other community matters.

On 12 June 2002, the Estonian Bahá'í communities in Pärnu, Narva, and Tartu were registered as legal bodies by the Estonian Interior Ministry. Registering at least two local communities was a necessary requirement for the incorporation of the national community, whose legal status is as a union of local communities in accordance with Estonian law. The registration of the national community, which has only existed in the years since the collapse of the Soviet Union, followed on 17 June.

Two communities in South America, Peru and Chile, gained legal incorporation in December 2002. The National Spiritual Assembly of Peru was registered as a legally incorporated entity and the Chilean National Spiritual Assembly was officially recognized by the Ministry of Justice under the new Law of Religious Worship.

The national governing body of the Bahá'í community in Chile played a part in another major development in September 2002 when it called for the submission of designs for a new continental Bahá'í House of Worship. The building, to be constructed southeast of Santiago, will be the eighth House of Worship in the world. The call came after an announcement in 2001 by the Universal House of Justice that efforts should begin to build what would be known as the "Mother Temple of South America."

The announcement specified requirements for the design of the building; it must be nine-sided, it should have an auditorium capable of seating at least 500 people, and its primary feature should be a dome 40 to 45 meters tall. Design submissions must also include basic landscaping features, as the surrounding gardens are a key feature of the other Temples. There are currently seven Houses of Worship, and the design of each is unique, with most reflecting the culture of the lands in which they were built.

The Temples themselves are meant to be not only beautiful structures but also places to commune with God in silence and reverence. Their Arabic name, Mashriqu'l-Adhkár, means "dawning place of the mention of God." In the future, each Bahá'í House of Worship will be the central feature in a complex designed to provide a variety of community services such as health care and education, open to use by followers of any religion.

The Bahá'í community of Hungary, having grown from some 70 Bahá'ís in 1990 to more than 1,200, inaugurated its new national

Participants in a Ruhi study circle in Bulgaria.

Bahá'í center designed to accommodate the growth of the community. A reception was held on 27 November 2002 and more than 50 people attended, including two members of the Hungarian Parliament, representatives of the Prime Minister's Office, a representative of the Ministry of the Interior, a pastor from the Unitarian Church, a representative of the Club of Budapest, and several national media personalities.

The celebration opened with the reading of a congratulatory letter from a former President of Hungary, Arpad Goncz, who conveyed his appreciation and support to the community. The guest of honor was Istvan Szalay, State Secretary for Religious Affairs, who remarked that the Bahá'í community is unique in its promotion of harmony and stability among the population. Peter Koczoh, the secretary of the National Spiritual Assembly of Hungary, said that acquiring the new Bahá'í center was "a turning point" in the life of the Hungarian community.

An Appeal for Unity
TO THE WORLD'S RELIGIOUS LEADERS

In April 2002, the Universal House of Justice issued a letter addressed to the world's religious leaders that called for a greater understanding of unity among religions. This article presents highlights of the presentation of that message.

More than a century ago, Bahá'u'lláh counseled the Bahá'ís, "Consort with the followers of all religions in a spirit of friendliness and fellowship."[1] The Bahá'í teachings on religious unity are clear and unambiguous: religion is one, and all religions spring from the same divine source. In 2002, expressing concern over the worldwide rise of religious prejudice, the Universal House of Justice issued an appeal to the world's religious leaders, calling for decisive action to eradicate religious intolerance.

Warning that "[w]ith every day that passes, danger grows that the rising fires of religious prejudice will ignite a worldwide conflagration the consequences of which are unthinkable," the message states: "Tragically, organized religion, whose very reason for being entails service to the cause of brotherhood and peace, behaves all too frequently as one of the most formidable obstacles in the path; to cite a particular painful fact, it has long lent its credibility to fanaticism."[2]

---

[1] Bahá'u'lláh, *Gleanings from the Writings of Bahá'u'lláh* (Wilmette, IL: Bahá'í Publishing Trust, 1994), p. 95.

[2] The full text of this letter appears on pp. 89–98 of this volume.

The letter suggests that increased interfaith dialogue can be an important step in fighting religious prejudice, but to be effective it must become far more vigorous and searching. "Bahá'ís see in the struggle of diverse religions to draw closer together a response to the Divine Will for a human race that is entering on its collective maturity," the letter states. Yet,

> interfaith discourse, if it is to contribute meaningfully to healing the ills that afflict a desperate humanity, must now address honestly and without further evasion the implications of the overarching truth that called the movement into being: that God is one and that, beyond all diversity of cultural expression and human interpretation, religion is likewise one.

The Universal House of Justice offers the assistance of the worldwide Bahá'í community in efforts to foster this dialogue.

The message, which was issued in April, was quickly delivered via the global network of national Bahá'í communities to religious leaders, academics who study religion, and specialists in related fields; within several months, thousands of leaders in more than 80 countries had received it. Translations were made into numerous languages,[3] and local Bahá'í communities began to present the letter to religious leaders in their villages, towns, and cities. Bahá'í delegations reported that they were received with a high level of courtesy and dignity by leaders of all faith communities. This article will offer a few highlights of those presentations.

⚏

"This is the message. This is the moment. We are facing the greatest challenge that God has ever given us and this is the message we need," responded Professor Jonathan Sacks, Chief Rabbi of the United Hebrew Congregations of Great Britain and the Commonwealth, when he was given the message. Similar sentiments were expressed by the Most Reverend Dr. George Carey, then Archbishop of Canterbury of the Church of England, who wrote, "I very much share your view that we all need to address the question of how

---

[3] To access the document in more than 20 languages, visit http://www.bahai.org/article-1-1-0-1.html.

Professor Jonathan Sacks, Chief Rabbi of the United Hebrew Congregations of Great Britain and the Commonwealth (right), receives the message from the Secretary of the National Spiritual Assembly of the UK.

our different faiths can become forces for peace and justice. Much honest discussion between the communities will be required as we pursue this goal, and it is good to learn, from the message which you delivered, of the ways in which the Bahá'í community is seeking to engage with these matters."

Biharilal Keshavji Tanna of the Hindu Council of Tanzania responded, "I have read the document with great interest and feel that it contains a supremely important message not only to the leaders of the faith groups, but to all thinking individuals, who must shoulder the duty and responsibility of breaking down barriers amongst the various groups of the family of mankind." He indicated that he would distribute copies of it to other members of the council.

In Trinidad and Tobago, Muslim leader Imam Nazim Ali received the message saying that he was very pleased with the Bahá'ís' "concern about establishing a common ground for meaningful discussion and solution to the problem of religious controversy among the human race" and further stated, "I have seen a common line in your belief corresponding to the belief in Islam.... These basic beliefs, if pursued with wisdom and understanding, can create

His Supreme Holiness Venerable Thep Vong (left), reads the message presented to him by the Bahá'ís of Cambodia.

a golden world order to defeat this present age of religious ignorance." In Italy, the President of the World Muslim League replied that he would read the message and share it with the Imam of the Mosque.

Patriarch Samdech of the Mahanikaya Sect in Cambodia, His Supreme Holiness Venerable Thep Vong, spoke about the Buddhist attitude of tolerance towards other religions and said that he would take the message to a conference of the Muslim community in Malaysia to which he had been invited.

During a presentation of the message to Cardinal Francis Arinze and Monsignor Michael Fitzgerald at the Vatican, Cardinal Arinze underscored the Roman Catholic Church's commitment to look for the unifying aspects in religions and promised to study the message carefully. The Apostolic Nuncio in Canada also affirmed the Roman Catholic viewpoint on interfaith dialogue and wished the Bahá'ís well, saying, "May our common efforts bear fruit as we continue to work for the dignity of all human beings."

South Africa's Chief Rabbi called the message "an inspiring impetus towards the essential unity which alone will create the sort of world we want to live in," while the President of the Lutherans of Nicaragua said the Bahá'ís were the only group that could bring the churches together, and a retired Anglican Bishop in New Zealand wrote, "the failure of organized religion to give a lead in world peace and understanding is a cause of real sadness. We need more sharing of this concern by people of goodwill across the religious divide. Many thanks for your initiative."

In response to the message, the Assembly of God leader in Kiribati noted that religious prejudice "is really a problem and walls that separate the churches should be put down," while in Belarus, Pyotr Orlov, the Chair of the Old Belief Orthodox Church, gave the message a warm response and spoke positively about the Faith and its influence on people, saying that all different religions should live in peace and friendship.

Among the many Hindu swamis who received the message in India, Swami Ranganathananda, President of Ramakrishna Math and Mission, responded that the ideas it expressed were "very welcome." He mentioned the traditionally tolerant attitude in India, saying, "The very fact that you have a beautiful Bahá'í temple at Delhi is testimony to this attitude.... I convey to you my love and best wishes." India's Islamic leaders, the Cardinal of the Catholic Church and several archbishops, leaders of the Sikhs, the High Priest of the Buddhist community, the Dalai Lama, the Chief Rabbi of India, and heads of the Zoroastrian and Jain communities also received the message.

A delegation of Bahá'ís in Uganda presents the message to Cardinal Emmanuel Wamala (third from right) of the Roman Catholic Church.

Bahá'ís in Botswana present the message to Anglican Bishop Theo Naledi (center) in May 2002.

In Georgia, two Bahá'ís present the message to Dr. Zezva Gugunishvili, the Chairman of the Healthcare and Social Affairs Committee (far left), and Parliamentarian Lado Chipashvili (far right).

Many religious leaders indicated that they planned to provide the message to others in their own organizations. In Liberia, the National Muslim Council requested additional copies for distribution to all mosques in the capital, and the Supreme Sikh Council of Kenya asked that the message be distributed to 30 leaders who had gathered for a symposium on the occasion of the opening of a Sikh temple.

Members of royalty receiving the letter included Her Majesty Queen Elizabeth II, Head of the Church of England, and His Majesty King Harald V of Norway, who has sponsored many interfaith initiatives within the country. In Jamaica, HE Sir Howard Cooke, the Governor-General, thanked the Bahá'ís for the message and indicated that he would speak about the subject in an upcoming address to the members of the diplomatic corps.

On campuses, the message sparked positive reactions. In New Zealand, it was the topic of discussion at a study group convened by the Rev. Alan Creak, a Christian chaplain at Auckland University, who posted the message on a Web site, together with a brief outline and notes.[4] In Brazil, the Dean of the Peace University (UNIPAZ), Professor Pierre Weil, after reading the message, proposed that UNIPAZ invite representatives of the different religions to discuss the contents and then draft a document to be read in places of worship on World Religion Day.

Dr. Gerald Mader, the President of the European Peace University in Austria, invited the Bahá'ís to participate in an interfaith symposium, and presentations to universities in Kenya brought invitations to the Bahá'í community to participate in several national interfaith initiatives there. In the Cayman Islands, the Director of the Institute of Theological Leadership and Development invited the Bahá'ís to send speakers to a class on comparative religion, while the Dean responsible for Values and Moral Development at the Engineering College of the Universidad Javeriana in Colombia expressed wholehearted agreement with the document and said that he wanted to work with the Bahá'ís to develop a program of spiritualization for the professors and students at the college.

---

[4] http://www.cs.auckland.ac.nz/~alan/chaplain/bahai.htm.

The Director-General of Nicaragua's branch of the Buddhist organization Soka Gakkai International (left) is presented with the letter in May 2002.

Dr. Hans Hermann Henrix, Chairman of the Association of the Directors of the Catholic Academies in Germany, commented, "In view of the aggravating conflicts and antagonisms, I consider this Message an important contribution to the efforts of the world religions to appeal to the human capability for peace and to strengthen the power of religions to promote peace." Another response came from Dr. Karl-Josef Kuschel, Professor at the Catholic Theological Department of Tübingen University and Vice President of the Stiftung Weltethos (World Ethics Foundation). "For me as a Christian theologian," he wrote, "pursuing for years the same concern [i.e. as that of the Message], the contribution of your religious community is a valuable confirmation and encouragement.... I welcome your manifesto and I wish for it a lasting effect."

In the United States the message was widely distributed to interfaith organizations, religious academics, and hundreds of leaders of the major faith communities and associations—Jewish, Muslim, Sikh, Hindu, Buddhist, Zoroastrian, Taoist, Jain, and Protestant, Roman Catholic, Orthodox, and Evangelical Christian. In French Polynesia, the Bahá'í community presented the message to leaders of Protestant, Mormon, Seventh Day Adventist, and Pentecostal churches, following which the Mormons invited the Bahá'ís to participate in a large public event attended by dignitaries representing both government and religious groups.

In some regions, the appeal received significant publicity in the news media. In India, for example, the *Times of India* and the *Hindu*, as well as several other newspapers, featured articles on the message. One newspaper in New Delhi, the *Pioneer*, reprinted excerpts of the letter in two installments. In Nicaragua, *La Prensa*, one of the country's two major newspapers, published an article on the document in its Sunday edition. The entirety of the message was published in the *Caymanian Compass*, the only daily newspaper in the Cayman Islands, which generated positive responses in contrast with a prevailing notion that religious freedom would allow other people to "usurp the Christian heritage" of the country. Religion editors and writers of the main print and broadcast media outlets in the United States and Canada were also presented with copies.

To the World's
Religious Leaders

*This letter, issued by the Universal House of
Justice in April 2002, challenges the leaders of the
world's religious communities to reexamine the
issues lying at the heart of interfaith activity.*

The enduring legacy of the twentieth century is that it compelled the peoples of the world to begin seeing themselves as the members of a single human race, and the earth as that race's common homeland. Despite the continuing conflict and violence that darken the horizon, prejudices that once seemed inherent in the nature of the human species are everywhere giving way. Down with them come barriers that long divided the family of man into a Babel of incoherent identities of cultural, ethnic, or national origin. That so fundamental a change could occur in so brief a period—virtually overnight in the perspective of historical time—suggests the magnitude of the possibilities for the future.

Tragically, organized religion, whose very reason for being entails service to the cause of brotherhood and peace, behaves all too frequently as one of the most formidable obstacles in the path; to cite a particular painful fact, it has long lent its credibility to fanaticism. We feel a responsibility, as the governing council of one of the world religions, to urge earnest consideration of the challenge this poses for religious leadership. Both the issue and the circumstances to which it gives rise require that we speak frankly. We trust that common service to the Divine will ensure that what we say will be received in the same spirit of goodwill as it is put forward.

The issue comes sharply into focus when one considers what has been achieved elsewhere. In the past, apart from isolated exceptions, women were regarded as an inferior breed, their nature hedged about by superstitions, denied the opportunity to express the potentialities of the human spirit and relegated to the role of serving the needs of men. Clearly, there are many societies where such conditions persist and are even fanatically defended. At the level of global discourse, however, the concept of the equality of the sexes has, for all practical purposes, now assumed the force of universally accepted principle. It enjoys similar authority in most of the academic community and information media. So basic has been the revisioning that exponents of male supremacy must look for support on the margins of responsible opinion.

The beleaguered battalions of nationalism face a similar fate. With each passing crisis in world affairs, it becomes easier for the citizen to distinguish between a love of country that enriches one's life, and submission to inflammatory rhetoric designed to provoke hatred and fear of others. Even where it is expedient to participate in the familiar nationalistic rites, public response is as often marked by feelings of awkwardness as it is by the strong convictions and ready enthusiasm of earlier times. The effect has been reinforced by the restructuring steadily taking place in the international order. Whatever the shortcomings of the United Nations system in its present form, and however handicapped its ability to take collective military action against aggression, no one can mistake the fact that the fetish of absolute national sovereignty is on its way to extinction.

Racial and ethnic prejudices have been subjected to equally summary treatment by historical processes that have little patience left for such pretensions. Here, rejection of the past has been especially decisive. Racism is now tainted by its association with the horrors of the twentieth century to the degree that it has taken on something of the character of a spiritual disease. While surviving as a social attitude in many parts of the world—and as a blight on the lives of a significant segment of humankind—racial prejudice has become so universally condemned in principle that no body of people can any longer safely allow themselves to be identified with it.

It is not that a dark past has been erased and a new world of light has suddenly been born. Vast numbers of people continue to endure the effects of ingrained prejudices of ethnicity, gender, nation, caste, and class. All the evidence indicates that such injustices will long persist as the institutions and standards that humanity is devising only slowly become empowered to construct a new order of relationships and to bring relief to the oppressed. The point, rather, is that a threshold has been crossed from which there is no credible possibility of return. Fundamental principles have been identified, articulated, accorded broad publicity, and are becoming progressively incarnated in institutions capable of imposing them on public behavior. There is no doubt that, however protracted and painful the struggle, the outcome will be to revolutionize relationships among all peoples, at the grassroots level.

ॐ

As the twentieth century opened, the prejudice that seemed more likely than any other to succumb to the forces of change was that of religion. In the West, scientific advances had already dealt rudely with some of the central pillars of sectarian exclusivity. In the context of the transformation taking place in the human race's conception of itself, the most promising new religious development seemed to be the interfaith movement. In 1893, the World's Columbian Exposition surprised even its ambitious organizers by giving birth to the famed "Parliament of Religions," a vision of spiritual and moral consensus that captured the popular imagination on all continents and managed to eclipse even the scientific, technological, and commercial wonders that the Exposition celebrated.

Briefly, it appeared that ancient walls had fallen. For influential thinkers in the field of religion, the gathering stood unique, "unprecedented in the history of the world." The Parliament had, its distinguished principal organizer said, "emancipated the world from bigotry." An imaginative leadership, it was confidently predicted, would seize the opportunity and awaken in the earth's long-divided religious communities a spirit of brotherhood that could provide the needed moral underpinnings for the new world of prosperity and progress. Thus encouraged, interfaith movements of every kind took root and flourished. A vast literature, available in many languages, introduced an ever wider public, believers and nonbelievers alike, to the teachings of all the major faiths, an interest picked up in due course by radio, television, film, and eventually the Internet. Institutions of higher learning launched degree programs in the study of comparative religion. By the time the century ended, interfaith worship services, unthinkable only a few decades earlier, were becoming commonplace.

Alas, it is clear that these initiatives lack both intellectual coherence and spiritual commitment. In contrast to the processes of unification that are transforming the rest of humanity's social relationships, the suggestion that all of the world's great religions are equally valid in nature and origin is stubbornly resisted by entrenched patterns of sectarian thought. The progress of racial integration is a development that is not merely an expression of sentimentality or strategy but arises from the recognition that the earth's peoples constitute a single species whose many variations do not themselves confer any advantage or impose any handicap on individual members of the race. The emancipation of women, likewise, has entailed the willingness of both society's institutions and popular opinion to acknowledge that there are no acceptable grounds—biological, social, or moral—to justify denying women full equality with men, and girls equal educational opportunities with boys. Nor does appreciation of the contributions that some nations are making to the shaping of an evolving global civilization support the inherited illusion that other nations have little or nothing to bring to the effort.

So fundamental a reorientation religious leadership appears, for the most part, unable to undertake. Other segments of society embrace the implications of the oneness of humankind, not only as the inevitable next step in the advancement of civilization, but as the fulfilment of lesser identities of every kind that our race brings to this critical moment in our collective history. Yet, the greater part of organized religion stands paralyzed at the threshold of the future, gripped in those very dogmas and claims of privileged access to truth that have been responsible for creating some of the most bitter conflicts dividing the earth's inhabitants.

The consequences, in terms of human well-being, have been ruinous. It is surely unnecessary to cite in detail the horrors being visited upon hapless populations today by outbursts of fanaticism that shame the name of religion. Nor is the phenomenon a recent one. To take only one of many examples, Europe's sixteenth century wars of religion cost that continent the lives of some 30 percent of its entire population. One must wonder what has been the longer term harvest of the seeds planted in popular consciousness by the blind forces of sectarian dogmatism that inspired such conflicts.

To this accounting must be added a betrayal of the life of the mind which, more than any other factor, has robbed religion of the capacity it inherently possesses to play a decisive role in the shaping of world affairs. Locked into preoccupation with agendas that disperse and vitiate human energies, religious institutions have too often been the chief agents in discouraging exploration of reality and the exercise of those intellectual faculties that distinguish humankind. Denunciations of materialism or terrorism are of no real assistance in coping with the contemporary moral crisis if they do not begin by addressing candidly the failure of responsibility that has left believing masses exposed and vulnerable to these influences.

Such reflections, however painful, are less an indictment of organized religion than a reminder of the unique power it represents. Religion, as we are all aware, reaches to the roots of motivation. When it has been faithful to the spirit and example of the transcendent Figures who gave the world its great belief systems, it has awakened in whole populations capacities to love, to forgive, to create, to dare greatly, to overcome prejudice, to sacrifice for the common good, and to discipline the impulses of animal instinct. Unquestionably, the seminal force in the civilizing of human nature has been the influence of the succession of these Manifestations of the Divine that extends back to the dawn of recorded history.

This same force, that operated with such effect in ages past, remains an inextinguishable feature of human consciousness. Against all odds, and with little in the way of meaningful encouragement, it continues to sustain the struggle for survival of uncounted millions, and to raise up in all lands heroes and saints whose lives are the most persuasive vindication of the principles contained in the scriptures of their respective faiths. As the course of civilization demonstrates, religion is also capable of profoundly influencing the structure of social relationships. Indeed, it would be difficult to think of any fundamental advance in civilization that did not derive its moral thrust from this perennial source. Is it conceivable, then, that passage to the culminating stage in the millennia-long process of the organization of the planet can be accomplished in a spiritual vacuum? If the perverse ideologies let loose on our world during the century just past contributed nothing else, they demonstrated conclusively that the need cannot be met by alternatives that lie within the power of human invention.

∞

The implications for today are summed up by Bahá'u'lláh in words written over a century ago and widely disseminated in the intervening decades:

> There can be no doubt whatever that the peoples of the world, of whatever race or religion, derive their inspiration from one heavenly Source, and are the subjects of one God. The difference between the ordinances under which they abide should be attributed to the varying requirements and exigencies of the age in which they were revealed. All of them, except a few which are the outcome of human perversity, were ordained of God, and are a reflection of His Will and Purpose. Arise and, armed with the power of faith, shatter to pieces the gods of your vain imaginings, the sowers of dissension amongst you. Cleave unto that which draweth you together and uniteth you.

Such an appeal does not call for abandonment of faith in the fundamental verities of any of the world's great belief systems. Far otherwise. Faith has its own imperative and is its own justification. What others believe—or do not believe—cannot be the authority in any individual conscience worthy of the name. What the above words do unequivocally urge is renunciation of all those claims to exclusivity or finality that, in winding their roots around the life of the spirit, have been the greatest single factor in suffocating impulses to unity and in promoting hatred and violence.

It is to this historic challenge that we believe leaders of religion must respond if religious leadership is to have meaning in the global society emerging from the transformative experiences of the twentieth century. It is evident that growing numbers of people are coming to realize that the truth underlying all religions is in its essence one. This recognition arises not through a resolution of theological disputes, but as an intuitive awareness born from the ever-widening experience of others and from a dawning acceptance of the oneness of the human family itself. Out of the welter of religious doctrines, rituals, and legal codes inherited from vanished worlds, there is emerging a sense that spiritual life, like the oneness manifest in diverse nationalities, races, and cultures, constitutes one unbounded reality equally accessible to everyone. In order for this diffuse and still tentative perception to consolidate itself and contribute effectively to the building of a peaceful world, it must have the wholehearted confirmation of those to whom, even at this late hour, masses of the earth's population look for guidance.

There are certainly wide differences among the world's major religious traditions with respect to social ordinances and forms of worship. Given the thousands of years during which successive revelations of the Divine have addressed the changing needs of a constantly evolving civilization, it could hardly be otherwise. Indeed, an inherent feature of the scriptures of most of the major faiths would appear to be the expression, in some form or other, of the principle of religion's evolutionary nature. What cannot be morally justified is the manipulation of cultural legacies that were intended to enrich spiritual experience, as a means to arouse prejudice and alienation. The primary task of the soul will always be to investigate reality, to live in accordance with the truths of which it becomes persuaded, and to accord full respect to the efforts of others to do the same.

It may be objected that, if all the great religions are to be recognized as equally Divine in origin, the effect will be to encourage, or at least to facilitate, the conversion of numbers of people from one religion to another. Whether or not this is true, it is surely of peripheral importance when set against the opportunity that history has at last opened to those who are conscious of a world that transcends this terrestrial one—and against the responsibility that this awareness imposes. Each of the great faiths can adduce impressive and credible testimony to its efficacy in nurturing moral character. Similarly, no one could convincingly argue that doctrines attached to one particular belief system have been either more or less prolific in generating bigotry and superstition than those attached to any other. In an integrating world, it is natural that patterns of response and association will undergo a continuous process of shifting, and the role of institutions, of whatever kind, is surely to consider how these developments can be managed in a way that promotes unity. The guarantee that the outcome will ultimately be sound—spiritually, morally, and socially—lies in the abiding faith of the unconsulted masses of the earth's inhabitants that the universe is ruled not by human caprice, but by a loving and unfailing Providence.

Together with the crumbling of barriers separating peoples, our age is witnessing the dissolution of the once insuperable wall that the past assumed would forever separate the life of Heaven from the life of Earth. The scriptures of all religions have always taught the believer to see in service to others not only a moral duty, but an avenue for the soul's own approach to God. Today, the progressive restructuring of society gives this familiar teaching new dimensions of meaning. As the age-old promise of a world animated by principles of justice slowly takes on the character of a realistic goal, meeting the needs of the soul and those of society will increasingly be seen as reciprocal aspects of a mature spiritual life.

If religious leadership is to rise to the challenge that this latter perception represents, such response must begin by acknowledging that religion and science are the two indispensable knowledge systems through which the potentialities of consciousness develop. Far from being in conflict with one another, these fundamental modes of the mind's exploration of reality are mutually dependent and have been most productive in those rare but happy periods of history when their complementary nature has been recognized and they have been able to work together. The insights and skills generated by scientific advance will have always to look to the guidance of spiritual and moral commitment to ensure their appropriate application; religious convictions, no matter how cherished they may be, must submit, willingly and gratefully, to impartial testing by scientific methods.

We come finally to an issue that we approach with some diffidence as it touches most directly on conscience. Among the many temptations the world offers, the test that has, not surprisingly, preoccupied religious leaders is that of exercising power in matters of belief. No one who has dedicated long years to earnest meditation and study of the scriptures of one or another of the great religions requires any further reminder of the oft-repeated axiom regarding the potentiality of power to corrupt and to do so increasingly as such power grows. The unheralded inner victories won in this respect by unnumbered clerics all down the ages have no doubt been one of the chief sources of organized religion's creative strength and must rank as one of its highest distinctions. To the same degree, surrender to the lure of worldly power and advantage, on the part of other religious leaders, has cultivated a fertile breeding ground for cynicism, corruption, and despair among all who observe it. The implications for the ability of religious leadership to fulfil its social responsibility at this point in history need no elaboration.

❧

Because it is concerned with the ennobling of character and the harmonizing of relationships, religion has served throughout history as the ultimate authority in giving meaning to life. In every age, it has cultivated the good, reproved the wrong, and held up, to the gaze of all those willing to see, a vision of potentialities as yet unrealized. From its counsels the rational soul has derived encouragement in overcoming limits imposed by the world and in fulfilling itself. As the name implies, religion has simultaneously been the chief force binding diverse peoples together in ever larger and more complex societies through which the individual capacities thus released can find expression. The great advantage of the present age is the perspective that makes it possible for the entire human race to see this civilizing process as a single phenomenon, the ever-recurring encounters of our world with the world of God.

Inspired by this perspective, the Bahá'í community has been a vigorous promoter of interfaith activities from the time of their inception. Apart from cherished associations that these activities create, Bahá'ís see in the struggle of diverse religions to draw closer together a response to the Divine Will for a human race that is entering on its collective maturity. The members of our community will continue to assist in every way we can. We owe it to our partners in this common effort, however, to state clearly our conviction that interfaith discourse, if it is to contribute meaningfully to healing the ills that afflict a desperate humanity, must now address honestly and without further evasion the implications of the overarching truth that called the movement into being: that God is one and that, beyond all diversity of cultural expression and human interpretation, religion is likewise one.

With every day that passes, danger grows that the rising fires of religious prejudice will ignite a worldwide conflagration the consequences of which are unthinkable. Such a danger civil government, unaided, cannot overcome. Nor should we delude ourselves that appeals for mutual tolerance can alone hope to extinguish animosities that claim to possess Divine sanction. The crisis calls on religious leadership for a break with the past as decisive as those that opened the way for society to address equally corrosive prejudices of race, gender, and nation. Whatever justification exists for exercising influence in matters of conscience lies in serving the well-being of humankind. At this greatest turning point in the history of civilization, the demands of such service could not be more clear. "The well-being of mankind, its peace and security, are unattainable," Bahá'u'lláh urges, "unless and until its unity is firmly established."

New Translations
of Bahá'u'lláh's Writings

Bahá'u'lláh's writings elucidate virtually every aspect of existence, including subjects as varied as science, philosophy, laws for human conduct, the spiritual nature of existence, and pronouncements about the future of humanity. These divinely inspired writings create the foundation of the Bahá'í Faith, but their intended application is universal. Bahá'u'lláh wrote not to a select group of followers, but to the whole of humanity. The texts are the charter for a new world, and no being is outside the rejuvenating influence of Bahá'u'lláh's revelation, which He describes in these terms:

> Say: In this day, the fertilizing winds of the grace of God have passed over all things. Every creature hath been endowed with all the potentialities it can carry.... Every tree hath been endowed with the choicest fruits, every ocean enriched with the most luminous gems. Man, himself, hath been invested with the gifts of understanding and knowledge. The whole creation hath been made the recipient of the revelation of the All-Merciful, and the earth the repository of things inscrutable to all except God, the Truth, the Knower of things unseen.[1]

---

[1] Bahá'u'lláh, *Summons of the Lord of Hosts* (Haifa: World Centre Publications, 2002), p. 25.

In 2002, World Centre Publications issued two new volumes of English translations of Bahá'u'lláh's writings, *The Summons of the Lord of Hosts* and *Gems of Divine Mysteries*. These new publications not only represent a significant contribution to the understanding and history of the Bahá'í Faith, but also demonstrate the breadth of Bahá'u'lláh's ministry, as they address issues of human leadership, the nature of God's appearance on earth, the meaning of past religious symbols, and the ceaseless journey of the soul towards its Lord.

The Summons of the Lord of Hosts

The Summons of the Lord of Hosts is a 272-page compilation that collects English translations of six major works written by Bahá'u'lláh in the latter half of the nineteenth century.

The book contains the Súriy-i-Haykal (Súrih of the Temple), Súriy-i-Ra'ís (Súrih of the Chief), Lawḥ-i-Ra'ís (Tablet of the Chief), Lawḥ-i-Fu'ád (Tablet to Fu'ád Páshá), Lawḥ-i-Sulṭán (Tablet to the Sultan), and Súriy-i-Mulúk (Súrih to the Kings).[2] Parts of each of these Tablets had been previously translated by Shoghi Effendi and published in other forms, but this is the first time each has appeared in its complete form.

Collectively, the works clearly enunciate Bahá'u'lláh's claim to prophethood and offer a prescription for peaceful and just leadership in the modern world.

The primary work in the volume, the Súriy-i-Haykal, was described by Shoghi Effendi as one of Bahá'u'lláh's "most challenging works" and sets the tone for the volume by establishing the divine source of Bahá'u'lláh's mission.

"Never since the beginning of the world," declares Bahá'u'lláh, "hath the message been so openly proclaimed." That proclamation of His message and its divine source comes in passages such as the following, where Bahá'u'lláh describes receiving the intimations of His mission and station:

---

[2] The Lawḥ-i-Sulṭán is addressed to Náṣiri'd-Dín Sháh, the Shah of Persia, and the Lawḥ-i-Ra'ís and Súriy-i-Ra'ís are addressed to 'Alí Páshá, Grand Vizier of the Ottoman Empire.

While engulfed in tribulations I heard a most wondrous, a most sweet voice, calling above My head. Turning My face, I beheld a Maiden—the embodiment of the remembrance of the name of My Lord—suspended in the air before Me.... Pointing with her finger unto My head, she addressed all who are in heaven and all who are on earth, saying: By God! This is the Best-Beloved of the worlds.[3]

Throughout the Súriy-i-Haykal, Bahá'u'lláh explores the inseparable relationship between the Manifestation and God, in passages such as this:

Say: Naught is seen in My temple but the Temple of God, and in My beauty but His Beauty, and in My being but His Being, and in My self but His Self, and in My movement but His Movement, and in My acquiescence but His Acquiescence, and in My pen but His Pen, the Mighty, the All-Praised. There hath not been in My soul but the Truth, and in Myself naught could be seen but God.

Beware lest ye speak of duality in regard to My Self, for all the atoms of the earth proclaim that there is none other God but Him, the One, the Single, the Mighty, the Loving.[4]

The text of the Súriy-i-Haykal also includes letters addressed to some of the most powerful individual monarchs of the time: Napoleon III, Czar Alexander II, Queen Victoria, Náṣiri'd-Dín Sháh, and Pope Pius IX. In each, Bahá'u'lláh describes His station as a Manifestation of God and challenges the rulers to acknowledge that station.

Bahá'u'lláh's address to Náṣiri'd-Dín Sháh is the longest of these letters. Known as the Lawḥ-i-Sulṭán, it is directed to the Shah of Persia, an enemy of the Bahá'ís who ordered the martyrdom of the Báb and the imprisonment of Bahá'u'lláh in the Síyáh-Chál, among other abuses to the community. In the address to one whom Bahá'u'lláh called the "Prince of Oppressors," He outlines the abuses that He has suffered at the Shah's command and challenges the sovereign to

---

[3] Bahá'u'lláh, *Summons*, pp. 5–6.
[4] Ibid., pp. 23–24.

accept His revelation. He also offers to meet with the Muslim clergy, and to provide whatever definitive proofs of the new revelation they would require to test Bahá'u'lláh's claim.

After the completion of the Súriy-i-Haykal, Bahá'u'lláh instructed that the work be written in the form of a pentacle, symbolic of the human temple. He added a concluding paragraph that Shoghi Effendi described as "words which reveal the importance He attached to those Messages, and indicate their direct association with the prophecy of the Old Testament":[5]

> Thus have We built the Temple with the hands of power and might, could ye but know it. This is the Temple promised unto you in the Book. Draw ye nigh unto it. This is that which profiteth you, could ye but comprehend it. Be fair, O peoples of the earth! Which is preferable, this, or a temple which is built of clay? Set your faces towards it. Thus have ye been commanded by God, the Help in Peril, the Self-Subsisting.[6]

Another major work included in *The Summons of the Lord of Hosts* is the Súriy-i-Mulúk, described by Shoghi Effendi as "the most momentous Tablet revealed by Bahá'u'lláh in which He, for the first time, directs His words collectively to the entire company of the monarchs of East and West."[7] In it, Bahá'u'lláh outlines requirements for rulers, including reduction of armaments, the resolution of international conflicts, and reduction of expenditures that place unnecessary strain on their subjects.

"Lay not aside the fear of God, O kings of the earth, and beware that ye transgress not the bounds which the Almighty hath fixed. … Be vigilant, that ye may not do injustice to anyone, be it to the extent of a grain of mustard seed. Tread ye the path of justice, for this, verily, is the straight path," Bahá'u'lláh asserts in a statement outlining the requirements of just leadership.[8]

---

[5] Shoghi Effendi, *The Promised Day Is Come* (Wilmette, IL: Bahá'í Publishing Trust, 1996), p. 47.

[6] Bahá'u'lláh, *Summons*, p. 137.

[7] Shoghi Effendi, *God Passes By* (Wilmette, IL: Bahá'í Publishing Trust, 1995), p. 171.

[8] Bahá'u'lláh, *Summons*, p. 188.

The Súriy-i-Ra'ís, which addresses the Ottoman Prime Minister 'Alí Páshá, exposes the ways in which the Minister misused his power and betrayed the trust of the people. The Lawḥ-i-Ra'ís contains passages addressed to the same Minister and includes a vehement portrayal of the depth of his depravity, saying, "[T]he fury of God's wrath hath so encompassed you that ye shall never take heed."[9]

The Lawḥ-i-Fu'ád, which refers to the Ottoman Minister Fu'ád Páshá, "describes the spiritual consequences of the abuse of power, and foretells the imminent downfall of his colleague, 'Alí Páshá, and the overthrow of the Sultan himself—prophecies that were widely circulated and whose dramatic fulfillment added greatly to the prestige of their Author."[10]

Gems of Divine Mysteries

Gems of Divine Mysteries (a translation of the Arabic title Javáhiru'l-Asrár) was written in Arabic during Bahá'u'lláh's banishment to Iraq, where He was exiled from 1853 until 1863. Though a relatively small volume, it is an important early epistle that explores the human quest for spiritual enlightenment and the symbols used throughout the history of religious revelation.

Gems is in the form of a letter written in reply to questions asked of Bahá'u'lláh about the Promised One of Islam. Bahá'u'lláh used the questions as an opportunity to elaborate a number of related subjects.

The book relates closely to another of the major works of Bahá'u'lláh, the Kitáb-i-Íqán, which gives an exploration of the progression of divine revelation and the tribulations sustained by the Manifestations of God. Specifically, it addresses the cause of the rejection of the Prophets of the past, the danger of a literal reading of scripture, the meaning of the signs and portents in the Bible concerning the advent of the new Manifestation, and the continuity of divine revelation.

---

[9] Ibid., p. 164.
[10] Universal House of Justice, introduction to *The Summons of the Lord of Hosts*, p. vi.

Bahá'u'lláh explains many of the symbolic terms used in past revelations, such as "resurrection" and "Day of Judgment," symbolic terms that have been misunderstood and have created a barrier between mankind and God's divinely appointed Messengers. In His description of the true meaning of resurrection, Bahá'u'lláh says,

> [H]e who had believed in God and in the Manifestation of His beauty was raised from the grave of heedlessness, gathered together in the sacred ground of the heart, quickened to the life of faith and certitude, and admitted into the paradise of the divine presence. What paradise can be loftier than this, what ingathering mightier, and what resurrection greater? Indeed, should a soul be acquainted with these mysteries, he would grasp that which none other hath fathomed.[11]

Gems further describes the quest for unity with God. In this, it bears similarity to *The Seven Valleys*, a primarily mystical work of Bahá'u'lláh that describes seven stages, described as a series of valleys, through which a seeker's soul progresses as it grows closer to God.

Gems explains these seven stages using an extended metaphor of a progression of cities called "the Garden of Search," "the City of Love and Rapture," "the City of Divine Unity," "the Garden of Wonderment," "the City of Absolute Nothingness," "the City of Immortality," and "the City that hath no name or description."

In this final city, where the seeker achieves the apex of re-union,

> flow the oceans of eternity, whilst this city itself revolveth round the seat of eternity. Therein the sun of the Unseen shineth resplendent above the horizon of the Unseen, a sun that hath its own heavens and its own moons, which partake of its light and which rise from and set upon the ocean of the Unseen. Nor can I ever hope to impart even a dewdrop of that which hath been decreed therein, as none is acquainted with its mysteries save God, its Creator and Fashioner, and His Manifestations.[12]

---

[11] Bahá'u'lláh, *Gems of Divine Mysteries* (Haifa: World Centre Publications, 2002), p. 42.

[12] Ibid., p. 77.

Rendering the Translations

These newly issued volumes are the first full translations published since the release of the the first authorized English translation of the Kitáb-i-Aqdas, Bahá'u'lláh's book of laws, in 1992. The preparation of translations from the original Persian or Arabic was undertaken by the Research Department of the Universal House of Justice. The English renderings are a result of combined efforts of a number of translators, all of whom strive to follow the pattern established by Shoghi Effendi.

In some cases, Bahá'u'lláh would Himself write the Tablets, but it was typical for Him to reveal verses aloud to an amanuensis. The dictation was sometimes recorded in what has been called "revelation writing"—a shorthand script written with extreme quickness owing to the speed with which the words were uttered. These original "revelation writing" drafts were later revised and approved by Bahá'u'lláh.

These "revelation drafts," as well as the many other transcriptions of Bahá'u'lláh's writings, are held in the International Bahá'í Archives in Haifa. The collection encompasses approximately 17,000 items, some of which are in Bahá'u'lláh's own handwriting, while others are transcriptions made either by Bahá'u'lláh's amanuenses or by other known scribes, under Bahá'u'lláh's direction.

The thousands of epistles revealed by Bahá'u'lláh, when taken together, constitute a volume more than 70 times the size of the Qur'an and more than 15 times the size of the Old and New Testaments of the Bible. Though less than 10 percent of Bahá'u'lláh's writings have been translated, those completed represent works of major significance.

The work of the Research Department to study and translate the remaining bulk of the writings of the Faith is ongoing, with new volumes planned for future release that will continue to contribute to understanding of the Faith both for those among its followers as well as the historians and scholars who study it.

World Summit on Sustainable Development

Held from 26 August to 4 September 2002 in Johannesburg, South Africa, the World Summit on Sustainable Development was dedicated to evaluating progress since 1992's Earth Summit and defining new strategies for achieving sustainability.

In Rio de Janeiro, Brazil, there stands a five-meter-high, hourglass-shaped sculpture that contains soil from some 150 nations. Called the Peace Monument, the sculpture is a symbol of people's connection both to their environment and to each other. That connection is eloquently summarized in the monument's inscription, from the writings of Bahá'u'lláh: "the earth is but one country, and mankind its citizens."

The Peace Monument was inaugurated in 1992, when representatives from governments and nongovernmental organizations (NGOs) gathered in Rio de Janeiro for the Earth Summit,[1] a landmark conference to assess global issues surrounding the environment and sustainable development. That summit drew the international community one step closer to the realization of the goal of the interconnectedness and ultimate unity of the planet. The Bahá'í International Community was deeply engaged in both preparation beforehand and meetings at the summit.

Ten years later, the World Summit on Sustainable Development (WSSD) in Johannesburg, South Africa, was held to judge progress

---

[1] Formally known as the United Nations Conference on Environment and Development.

since the Rio Summit. Bringing together 104 heads of state and government and thousands of NGOs, it was the largest UN conference ever. Once again, Bahá'ís contributed to many aspects of the conference and continued to stress not only the importance of unity but also the need for highlighting spiritual and religious issues in discussions on sustainable development.

A Recognition of Unity

A total of 191 countries participated in the summit, and 21,340 accreditation passes were issued. Organized by the United Nations, the summit had the goal of inspiring action towards the creation of an environmentally sound world while addressing humanity's needs for food, water, shelter, sanitation, energy, health services, and economic security.

The summit itself, which focused on government negotiations, was held at the Sandton Convention Center just outside Johannesburg. A parallel Civil Society Forum of NGOs, which attracted some 22,000 delegates, was held separately at Nasrec. The Ubuntu Village, an exhibition space that was open to government leaders, NGOs, major groups such as businesses, and the public, was created for exhibits, cultural performances, and other events designed to help facilitate new partnerships for sustainable development.

A notable factor was the increased involvement of business leaders, scientists, farmers, and other groups not traditionally part of UN conferences on the environment. This increased diversity of participants was accompanied by an affirmation of a growing sense of interconnectedness and interdependence.

"[R]ecognition has grown that, indeed, the world has grown into a global village," said Thabo Mbeki, President of South Africa, who served as the summit's chairman. "The survival of everybody in this village demands that we develop a universal consensus to act together to ensure that there is no longer any river that divides our common habitat into poor and wealthy parts. This indicates that the noble concept of human solidarity has, once again, regained currency as a driving force in the reconstruction and development of our common world."

The summit's declaration also reinforced the need for unity within the spheres that constitute sustainable development, stating that it must be built on three "interdependent and mutually reinforcing pillars"—economic development, social development, and environmental protection—and established "at local, national, regional, and global levels."

For the Bahá'í representatives, the summit's recognition of the need for unity is an important step in the right direction. Some 30 representatives of six Bahá'í and Bahá'í-inspired organizations took part in activities at all of the summit's three venues. Delegations from the Bahá'í International Community included representatives from Bahá'í communities in Brazil, Canada, and South Africa. In addition, two Bahá'í-inspired organizations, the International Environment Forum (IEF) and the European Bahá'í Business Forum (EBBF), which operate on Bahá'í principles but have no formal connection to Bahá'í institutions, sent delegations. The IEF and EBBF shared an exhibit at the NGO Forum and presented several workshops on topics related to sustainable development.

The Bahá'í International Community and the Bahá'í community of South Africa created two exhibits, one for the Ubuntu Village and the other for the NGO Forum, highlighting the Bahá'í approach to development. They showcased Bahá'í projects that reflect values and principles at "the heart of development," such as trustworthiness, the equality of women and men, and justice.

Other contributions included those in the arts. Two Bahá'í youth performing-arts troupes, Beyond Words and Ablaze, offered performances, and a display of "Children's Art for the Environment" featured art from an annual competition run by the Bahá'ís in the Cape Town area.

Outcomes

Much was expected from Johannesburg, especially in terms of concrete commitments from governments. For the most part, these consisted of reaffirmations or reiterations of commitments made at the Millennium Summit in 2000 and other recent UN conferences.

On another level, however, the Johannesburg Declaration and the summit's Plan of Implementation demonstrate both growth and development in the global understanding of sustainable development since the Earth Summit—particularly in terms of recognizing links between poverty, environmental protection, and the use of natural resources.

"The deep fault line that divides human society between the rich and the poor and the ever-increasing gap between the developed and developing worlds pose a major threat to global prosperity, security and stability," states the summit's declaration.

Additionally, the decision to hold the summit in Africa demonstrated an awareness of the needs of that continent, which stands as the least developed in the world and in dire need of attention from the international community.

Another key outcome of the Johannesburg Summit was a clear acknowledgment that sustainable development cannot be achieved without widespread collaboration among all sectors of global society. This is most clearly seen in the creation of new "Type II" partnerships between governments, businesses, and civil society, in contrast to traditional "Type I" government-to-government agreements. The Rio Declaration on Environment and Development and *Agenda 21* are considered to be Type I agreements, as are the Johannesburg Declaration and its final Plan of Implementation.

Designed to stress practical collaboration on the front lines of environmental action and development, some 280 Type II partnerships were launched at the summit. They include actions like those embodied in an initiative to collect bicycles in Europe to refurbish and sell in Africa, so as to reduce CO_2 and alleviate poverty; a plan involving Asian governments and wildlife groups aimed at recognizing and protecting landing sites for migratory birds; and the creation of a public/private network in the South Pacific to help protect coral reefs and associated fisheries.

The Role of Religion

For their part, the Bahá'í participants expressed the need for expanding the vocabulary of development to include spirituality and the role of religion in the dialogue.

In 2001, the Bahá'í International Community issued the state-ment entitled "Sustainable Development: The Spiritual Dimension."[2] For this conference the delegation presented a follow-up statement, "Religion and Development at the Crossroads: Convergence or Divergence?", that outlines the need for a reassessment of the role of religion in development.[3]

"The statement [to the WSSD] raises a bold and challenging call to the UN and to the leaders of the world's religions," said Peter Adri-ance, the lead representative of the Bahá'í International Community to the summit. "It asks the UN to more fully recognize the key role religion must play in the quest for sustainable development and it calls on religious leaders to reject all forms of religious fanaticism as impediments to development and peace."

The Bahá'í International Community's statement makes a clear call for a further exploration of the role of spirituality and religion:

> Despite … significant achievements, the United Nations has yet to grasp fully both the constructive role that religion can play in creating a peaceful and prosperous global order, and the destruc-tive impact that religious fanaticism can have on the stability and progress of the world…. For its part, the United Nations might begin the process of substantively involving religion in delibera-tions on humankind's future by hosting an initial gathering of religious leaders.[4]

Even though the WSSD acknowledged the need for greater unity, unity without its spiritual underpinnings is nothing more than an ar-rangement of convenience. When based on spiritual understanding, however, it is a reality whose reflection needs to be seen in all efforts for the advancement of human society. As 'Abdu'l-Bahá said,

> No matter how far the material world advances, it cannot establish the happiness of mankind. Only when material and spiritual civilization are linked and coordinated will happiness be

---

[2] This statement can be found in *The Bahá'í World 2001–2002*, pp. 279–85.

[3] For the text of this statement, see pp. 231–39.

[4] Ibid., pp. 231–38.

assured. Then material civilization will not contribute its energies to the forces of evil in destroying the oneness of humanity, for in material civilization good and evil advance together and maintain the same pace.[5]

The idea is not completely foreign to the development community. The 500-page document *Agenda 21*, which emerged from the Earth Summit and outlines an extensive plan of action for the world's governments, businesses, and NGOs in pursuit of sustainable development, has served as a blueprint for action in the 10 years since that conference.

Agenda 21, in sections dealing with subjects as diverse as human health and deforestation, includes several mentions of the need for spirituality as well as social, economic, and other factors. Despite this, however, a true consensus on what spirituality means and how to include it in the discussions about development remains to be reached.

The motivation that drives Bahá'ís to participate in these gatherings is an an acknowledgement of the need for the integration of spiritual concerns into development issues, which arises from the essential reality of humankind. As the Bahá'í International Community writes in "Sustainable Development: The Spiritual Dimension":

> For the vast majority of the world's people the idea that human nature is fundamentally spiritual is an incontrovertible truth. Indeed, this perception of reality is the defining cultural experience for most of the world's people and is inseparable from how they perceive themselves and the world around them. It is, therefore, only by bringing a focus on the spiritual dimension of human reality that development policies and programs can truly reflect the experiences, conditions, and aspirations of the planet's inhabitants and elicit their heartfelt support and active participation.[6]

---

[5] 'Abdu'l-Bahá, *The Promulgation of Universal Peace: Talks Delivered by 'Abdu'l-Bahá during His Visit to the United States and Canada in 1912*, rev. ed. (Wilmette, IL: Bahá'í Publishing Trust, 1995), p. 109.

[6] See *The Bahá'í World, 2001–2002*, p. 280.

Race Unity
and Social Cohesion

During the summer of 2001, England was marred by riots rooted mainly in racial strife. More than a thousand people ultimately participated in the unrest, which left hundreds injured and caused nearly US$20 million in damages. The events forced an examination of the society that spawned them, with government and citizens seeking answers to the questions of why the riots had happened and how to prevent them from erupting again.

Racism may not be the sole cause, but in a country where more than half of the people feel they live in a racist society,[1] it is certainly a pervasive and insidious disease that erodes the underpinnings of society. In the words of the National Spiritual Assembly of the Bahá'ís of the United Kingdom, its effects are "undoubtedly a major cause of division, and a force for harm in society." The National Assembly continues,

> At the root of this and all forms of discrimination is the erroneous idea that humankind is somehow composed of separate and distinct races, peoples, or castes, and that those subgroups

---

[1] According to a May 2002 poll conducted by ICM Research, available at http://www.icmresearch.co.uk/reviews/2002/bbc-race-poll.may-2002.htm.

innately possess varying intellectual, moral, and/or other capacities, which in turn justify different forms of treatment. The reality is that there is only the one human race, a single people inhabiting the planet Earth, one human family bound together in a common destiny.[2]

The government launched inquiries into "community cohesion" that identified not only racial strife but other elements, such as public service failures and inequitable access to social services, as factors in the social unrest. But even these other factors can be ultimately seen to be caused by separation, segregation, and underrepresentation in politics—the symptoms of creating a system with an undoubted hierarchy of value associated with ethnic and cultural heritage.

But addressing these symptoms by creating laws to encourage integration and increasing public works is not the key to uniting a society that is divided along racial lines. Even such measures as increasing interaction between races and ensuring equal representation address only part of the problem.

Racism does not exist in a vacuum. These attitudes and prejudices penetrate to all levels of society, including its political, economic, and cultural frameworks, and such deep social divisions cannot be undone by legislation alone. As the National Spiritual Assembly of the United Kingdom pointed out in its May 2002 address to the people of the UK, "while anti-racist initiatives are clearly essential, and regulating behavior by legislation has a place, they are uncertain modifiers of basic attitudes and beliefs. Unless these latter are changed, it is doubtful if a truly cohesive society can ever be more than an unachievable ideal."[3]

Evidence of the inadequacy of law unto itself can be seen in the experiences of countries like the United States and South Africa. Racist laws in the United States were largely repealed in the 1960s, during the American Civil Rights Movement, and apartheid in South Africa ended in the 1990s, but in spite of freedom from legal

---

[2] National Spiritual Assembly of the Bahá'ís of the United Kingdom, "Social Cohesion: Dwelling in the Same Land," May 2002. For the full text, see pp. 257–63.

[3] Ibid., p. 259.

restrictions, neither of these countries is free from racism's blight. Its healing is a complex process, and one that must finally rest not in civil authority, but within the hearts of people.

Clearly, there exists a need to bridge the gap between the laws and the hearts. It was in this regard that the British Bahá'í community sought to bring the Bahá'í perspective into discussions on causes of and solutions to disconnection in society through its Institute for Social Cohesion, a forum for research and discussion.

The institute's first national colloquium in May 2002 hinged on the question, "What makes a society cohesive?" Nearly 130 people attended, including British government representatives from the Home Office, the Race Equality Unit, and the Community Cohesion Unit; MP John Battle, the Prime Minister's informal interfaith adviser; and high-ranking members of the British Police Department. Significant nongovernmental organizations (NGOs) represented included the Council of Ethnic Minority Voluntary Sector Organizations (CEMVO), the Citizenship Foundation, and BUILD, an ethnic minority mentoring and networking organization.

Related to the work of the institute, the British Bahá'í community has issued four statements on the subject of community cohesion. The first, "Community Cohesion: A Bahá'í Perspective," was issued in May 2001, and the most recent, "Social Cohesion: Prospect and Promise," was issed in January 2003.

"This is a turbulent time in the history of mankind," said Barney Leith, Secretary of the National Spiritual Assembly of the United Kingdom, at the colloquium, "and all around us the cohesion of our society is being disintegrated. Religion has the capacity to bring this cohesion back. The Bahá'í community feels it can make its contribution by providing this forum for dialogue."

The National Spiritual Assembly hopes through the colloquium to influence processes towards world peace and to contribute to healing rifts in British society. Mr. Leith also pointed out that the Bahá'í community is pleased that its initiatives are being found increasingly useful by government officials, parliamentarians, and organizations of civil society.

He stressed the "increasing need expressed by policy makers for coherent ideas and policies based on principle" and the fact that Bahá'ís are being offered opportunities to show that the principles that govern their Faith can be used to contribute actively and positively to British society.

The institute sponsors conferences and symposia on the processes and issues that shape and sustain cohesive, unified societies, and the role of spiritual values in underpinning sustainable, cohesive societies will also be explored. Four special interest groups have been formed to work as informal information-sharing networks, for which the institute offers administrative support. The eventual goal of the institute is to establish an academic resource that will research questions related to social cohesion, to be attached to universities in Britain.

"The institute will provide a long-term, nonpartisan environment where academics, activists, parliamentarians, and members of society can contribute to repairing social breakdown of all kinds," said Dan Wheatley, external affairs spokesman for the UK Bahá'í community.

Government representatives publicly thanked the Bahá'í community for running the colloquium, and some also emphasized that no one else had tried or been able to bring together such a diverse group of people to discuss these important issues. The diversity of opinions and the intense need for change expressed in the dialogue have formed the basis of a search for common ground and a sense not only of shared community but of a common future.

Origins of Racism

The problems facing Britain are far from unique. Similar problems are found elsewhere in Europe, with its rising immigration; in Africa, where the scars of colonialism are slow to heal; in America, where damage done by the policies of slavery is still evident; and in virtually every other country in the world.

It would be easy to dismiss racism as nothing more than a by-product of modern societies, where the world has been compressed into a "global village" and immigration is creating increasingly diverse societies. In fact, many are tempted to see the stress in race relations as an inevitable result of the confrontation between irreconcilable cultural and ethnic differences.

In stark contrast are examples found in the work of author Frank Snowden. He gives compelling evidence not only for the possibility of racial amity but also that certain racist attitudes are a relatively modern invention. In his examinations of the ancient Mediterranean world, he shows that Greek, Roman, Egyptian, and Ethiopian societies intermingled for centuries in a spirit of cooperation and mutual respect. He notes that most scholars who have examined the evidence

> have come to conclusions such as these: the ancients did not fall into the error of biological racism; black skin color was not a sign of inferiority; Greeks and Romans did not establish color as an obstacle to integration in society; and ancient society was one that for all its faults and failures never made color the basis for judging a man.[4]

Much has changed in the thousands of years since those ancient civilizations commingled without regard for skin color. Snowden's conclusions come amidst an ongoing debate among scientists and sociologists over the origins of both race and racism. Though the current tide tends towards acceptance that the old concepts of "race" are inventions of ignorance, the effects of slavery, xenophobia, and other social factors have all funneled into the problems of the modern world, where people are often judged based on their race or ethnicity. The world in which we now live is replete with nations and peoples struggling to find solutions to these problems.

Bahá'í Approach to Racial Unity

The Bahá'í writings affirmed the reality of racial unity more than 150 years ago, when Bahá'u'lláh wrote that all people were "one same substance" and "created … from the same dust."[5]

'Abdu'l-Bahá acknowledged that differences exist, while stressing that they are not insurmountable obstacles to unity. In lectures in the United States in the early twentieth century, he spoke on the value of racial unity, notwithstanding that the country was barely

---

[4] Quoted in Richard Thomas, *Race Unity: An Imperative for Social Progress*, rev. ed. (Ottawa, ON: Association for Bahá'í Studies, 1993), p. 8.

[5] Bahá'u'lláh, *The Hidden Words* (Wilmette, IL: Bahá'í Publishing Trust, 1994), Arabic no. 68, p. 20.

50 years removed from its system of slavery and the idea of equality was an unpopular one in some quarters. While many people at the time sought to establish the scientific basis of the inferiority of certain races, 'Abdu'l-Bahá asserted, "The differences existing between nations and peoples will soon be annulled."[6]

He further explained,

> In the human kingdom itself there are points of contact, properties common to all mankind; likewise, there are points of distinction which separate race from race, individual from individual. If the points of contact, which are the common properties of humanity, overcome the peculiar points of distinction, unity is assured. On the other hand, if the points of differentiation overcome the points of agreement, disunion and weakness result. … In fact numerous points of partnership and agreement exist between the two races; whereas the one point of distinction is that of color. Shall this, the least of all distinctions, be allowed to separate you as races and individuals?[7]

Bahá'u'lláh called upon people not to accept the separations between them but to actively strive to eliminate them, writing, "O contending peoples and kindreds of the earth! Set your faces towards unity, and let the radiance of its light shine upon you. Gather ye together, and for the sake of God resolve to root out whatever is the source of contention amongst you."[8] There must be true amity, and indeed even a celebration of differences, where the variety of colors are valued even as the differing flowers in a garden. As 'Abdu'l-Bahá wrote,

> How unpleasing to the eye if all the flowers and plants, the leaves and blossoms, the fruits, the branches, and the trees of that garden were all of the same shape and color! Diversity of hues, form, and shape, enricheth and adorneth the garden, and heighteneth the

---

[6] 'Abdu'l-Bahá, *The Promulgation of Universal Peace: Talks Delivered by 'Abdu'l-Bahá during His Visit to the United States and Canada in 1912*, rev. ed. (Wilmette, IL: Bahá'í Publishing Trust, 1995), p. 66.

[7] Ibid., p. 67–68.

[8] Bahá'u'lláh, *Gleanings from the Writings of Bahá'u'lláh* (Wilmette, IL: Bahá'í Publishing Trust, 1994), p. 216.

effect thereof. In like manner, when divers shades of thought, temperament and character, are brought together under the power and influence of one central agency, the beauty and glory of human perfection will be revealed and made manifest.[9]

Bahá'í activities are guided not only by the reality of spiritual equality, but also by the idea that human power alone cannot eliminate racism. 'Abdu'l-Bahá stated clearly: "[T]here is need of a superior power to overcome human prejudices, a power which nothing in the world of mankind can withstand and which will overshadow the effect of all other forces at work in human conditions. That irresistible power is the love of God."[10]

The presence of a "superior power" does not exempt humanity from its responsibilities or its difficult struggles, however. Shoghi Effendi delineated the requirements for true unity. While discussing racial division in the United States, he explained that the responsibility rests on both sides:

> Let neither think that the solution of so vast a problem is a matter that exclusively concerns the other. Let neither think that such a problem can either easily or immediately be resolved. Let neither think that they can wait confidently for the solution of this problem until the initiative has been taken, and the favorable circumstances created.… Let neither think that anything short of genuine love, extreme patience, true humility, consummate tact, sound initiative, mature wisdom, and deliberate, persistent, and prayerful effort, can succeed in blotting out the stain which this patent evil has left on the fair name of their common country.[11]

It is within this spectrum of spiritual virtues such as patience, humility, and wisdom that solutions must be constructed. While Bahá'ís do not dictate solutions, nor claim to possess easy or exhaustive remedies, they do seek honest dialogue. They are motivated by a desire for unity and not by the blame and finger-pointing that so

9 'Abdu'l-Bahá, *Selections from the Writings of 'Abdu'l-Bahá* (Wilmette, IL: Bahá'í Publishing Trust, 1997), pp. 291–92.
10 'Abdu'l-Bahá, *Promulgation of Universal Peace*, p. 68.
11 Shoghi Effendi, *The Advent of Divine Justice* (Wilmette, IL: Bahá'í Publishing Trust, 1990), pp. 40–41.

often overshadow the question of race and racism. In Bahá'í communities throughout the world, individual and collective efforts to aid in the process of healing are proving that the goal of unity is not out of reach.[12]

Patterns of Integration

Though the writings of the Faith are a firm foundation for the unification of the world, the Bahá'í communities are still learning how to implement them. In each country and in each community, the needs and the challenges are different. Bahá'ís have no precise formula for addressing these problems, but no matter how different the situation or divisive the elements, they have built a record of achievement whose successes are worthy of attention from all sectors of society.

AUSTRALIA

In Australia, the intersection of communities comes not only from the relationship between the indigenous population and the descendants of the British colonists, but also from the influx of refugees from Asian countries who seek a haven from the chaos in their own states. The Bahá'í community is committed to creating an environment that not only appreciates the history of the land and its ancient peoples, but also welcomes newcomers.

Australian Bahá'ís, interested in making a contribution to national reconciliation efforts, submitted a report in 2002 to the Senate Legal and Constitutional References Committee's Inquiry into the Progress towards National Reconciliation. The submission describes racism as the most "fundamental barrier" to reconciliation and describes progress towards reconciliation as "slow and marked with setbacks" despite notable progress in some areas.

"The recent resurgence of divisive racial attitudes in Australia, the increased number of racial incidents, and the unrelieved deprivation faced by many Aboriginal and Torres Strait Islander Australians make the need for solutions ever more pressing," it says. "Healing

---

[12] For more information about Bahá'í activities towards racial unity, see pp. 51–55 of this volume.

the wounds and building a society in which people of diverse backgrounds live as members of one family are the most urgent issues confronting Australia today. Our nation's peace and prosperity and our standing in the international community depend to a great extent on their resolution."

In 1999, the Bahá'í community appointed an Indigenous Advisory Group, consisting of Aboriginal and Torres Strait Islander members of the Bahá'í community, to advise the National Spiritual Assembly of the Bahá'ís of Australia on matters including indigenous community development and indigenous protocols. Other initiatives include the development of relationships with the traditional custodians of the land on which the Bahá'í House of Worship and national Bahá'í center are located, participation in the Advisory Group on Faith Communities to the Council for Aboriginal Reconciliation, and support for its Week of Prayer for Reconciliation.

Within the community, too, much has been done to maintain diversity and assist in reinforcing the importance of traditional cultures. Indigenous Australians have been part of the Australian Bahá'í community since the 1950s, have participated in its development and national administration, and have represented the Faith at national and international events. The Bahá'í community encourages historical research into early contacts between the Australian Bahá'í community and indigenous Australians, and renders Bahá'í scriptures into indigenous languages as a means of fostering mutual understanding and supporting the spiritual development of Aboriginal and Torres Strait Islander Bahá'ís. Institute courses focused particularly on youth have also been developed to educate members of the Bahá'í community in basic issues of indigenous cultural practices and protocol, and to encourage personal commitments to the reconciliation process.

In response to the increasing stress regarding immigration, the Australian Bahá'ís contributed a report to the Department of Immigration and Multicultural Affairs in relation to the 1999–2000 Migration and Humanitarian Programs. The submission contended that immigration to Australia can be increased without creating a negative impact on the economy or the environment. It acknowledged a need for migrants with viable skills in order for the migration program to receive public support, and argued that a larger humanitarian intake is a moral imperative. "Given the global scale of refugee and humanitarian flows, a setting of 12,000 for Australia's humanitarian program is lower than we should contemplate," the submission says. "Australia faces the challenge of continuing to respond ... to the legitimate aspirations of our fellow human beings for a better life."

The Bahá'í community has also participated in and sponsored events during the annual National Refugee Week, ranging from the holding of seminars on the problems facing refugees to the hosting of simple receptions and prayer gatherings. The issue of sheltering refugees is of particular poignancy to a community in which many members were forced to flee their native Iran because of religious persecution.

UNITED STATES

Racism is regarded by the Bahá'í community in the United States of America as its "most challenging issue," but it is one in which notable strides have been made. Bahá'í groups in the country were among the first religious communities to hold fully integrated meetings, in the early 1900s. In the 1920s and 1930s, the Bahá'ís in the United States also began holding public "race amity" meetings. One such event in 1921, sponsored by the Bahá'í community in Springfield, Massachusetts, drew some 1,200 people. Race Amity Day eventually became Race Unity Day, an event that is now commemorated annually in localities all over the world. In many countries, the Bahá'ís have worked with the government to have the day nationally recognized.

In 1991, the National Spiritual Assembly issued the statement "The Vision of Race Unity," which was widely distributed throughout the country and offers a hopeful vision of the future for both the country and the whole of mankind. It states,

> Bahá'ís see unity as the law of life; consequently, all prejudices are perceived as diseases that threaten life.... Bahá'ís believe that both spiritual and material development are dependent upon love and unity. Therefore, the Bahá'ís offer the teachings of their Faith and the example of their community for examination, convinced that these can make a contribution toward the eradication of racism endemic in American society. We do so with firm faith in the

assistance of our Creator, Who, out of His infinite love, brought forth all humanity from the same stock and intended that all belong to the same household. We believe, moreover, that the day of the unification of the entire human race has come.[13]

In pursuit of that goal, Bahá'ís in the United States have also lent support to other prominent initiatives. Bahá'ís organize or are substantial contributors to countless Martin Luther King Jr. Day observances throughout the country. Representatives of the National Spiritual Assembly served on the MLK Jr. Federal Holiday Commission. Bahá'ís have also supported the activities of the King Center in Atlanta and played a major role in King Week festivities each year.

The Bahá'í community also collaborated closely with President Clinton's year-long Initiative on Race, launched in July 1997 to stimulate a dialogue on race relations throughout the country, which engendered a series of local town meetings and regional religious forums. Local Bahá'í communities throughout the country participated in those forums and, as a result, Bahá'ís were asked to serve on the planning committee for a summit in October 1998 of 40 national faith leaders to discuss how religious communities can contribute to improving race relations. The Bahá'ís were later asked to participate on the planning committee for a second conference with the President and some 150 faith leaders in March 2000.

In another campaign to promote race unity, the US Bahá'ís produced and broadcast of a series of videos designed to reach households in every part of the country with messages about spiritual solutions to social problems. The first video, "The Power of Race Unity," is about four individuals who actively work for racial reconciliation in their communities. It continues to be broadcast on cable television channels along with public service commercials on the themes "Children Without Prejudice," "World Citizen," and "One Race."

SOUTH AFRICA

The campaign of apartheid in South Africa provided the world with one of its most striking and shameful examples of institutionalized

---

[13] National Spiritual Assembly of the Bahá'ís of the United States, "The Vision of Race Unity" (1991), available at http://us.bahai.org/ourvision/vision.htm.

racism. Apartheid was the rule of the land from 1948 until 1992. Despite this program, the Bahá'í community, established in South Africa since 1911, remained completely integrated throughout those trying years.

Under the watchful eye of the South African government's special police, who were charged with maintaining racial separation, Bahá'ís held administrative and worship meetings in private homes, since integrated meetings in public were forbidden.

In such meetings, whites usually entered through the front door, while blacks came in through the kitchen. Yet, despite such restrictions, the first national Bahá'í governing council of South Africa, elected in 1956, had four white and five black members—a degree of integration that was extremely rare, if not unique, for any sort of national organization in South Africa at the time.

In 1997, while many other religious communities throughout South Africa offered apologies to the Truth and Reconciliation Commission for their practices under apartheid, the National Spiritual Assembly of the Bahá'ís of South Africa issued a statement titled "A Pathway to Peace and Justice" that summarized the important place of racial integration in Bahá'í belief.[14] It gave a summary of the endurance of the Bahá'í community during the apartheid years and explained that, despite difficulty and harsh legislation, the Bahá'ís clung to the ideals of their Faith.

Of the 10,000 people in the South African Bahá'í community today, more than 90 percent would have been classified as "non-white" under apartheid laws. Members come from nearly all the tribal and ethnic groups in the country. And although many of those groups, such as the Zulu and Xhosa tribes, are in conflict with one another, tribal members are united in their beliefs as Bahá'ís.

RWANDA

In Rwanda, violence by the Hutu majority against the Tutsi minority resulted in the deaths of some 800,000 people in 1994. As the country struggled to create unity and rebuild trust between the ethnic groups, the National Spiritual Assembly of the Bahá'í community

---

[14] The text of this statement can be found in *The Bahá'í World 1997–98*, pp. 229–32.

issued a statement in March 2000 to the National Commission for Unity and Reconciliation urging consideration of the principle of human oneness as a basis for reconciliation in the country.

"Bahá'ís believe that humankind has always constituted one species, but that prejudice, ignorance, power seeking, and egotism have prevented many people from recognizing and accepting this oneness," stated the Rwandan National Assembly, urging the adoption of a program for moral education that would seek both to abolish prejudices and to foster social and economic development.

BRAZIL

The national Bahá'í community in Brazil has had to contend with deep divisions of race and class since its beginnings, in a country where the vast chasm between rich and poor also separates black from white.

In just over 80 years since the inception of the community, though, the Bahá'ís have established a reputation for their work to unite the varying elements of Brazilian society. As a result, Brazilian Bahá'ís were invited by the government to assist in national preparations for the 2001 World Conference against Racism, held in Durban, South Africa.[15] In the fall of 2000, the national Bahá'í community sent a delegation to preparatory conferences in Brazil and participated in a Seminar of Experts.

In 2002, the Brazilian School of Nations was featured at the International Meeting of the Global Network of Education for Peace. The school seeks to raise up a new generation of leaders instilled with the ideal of world citizenship. Established in Brasilia, where there are some 85 foreign embassies, the school has more than 550 students from at least 25 national backgrounds. With courses from kindergarten through grade eight, the school offers a distinctive curriculum that blends an emphasis on cross-cultural experiences with moral and religious education in a bilingual setting.

In an effort to promote and appreciate diversity within their own community, Bahá'ís in Salvador, in the state of Bahia, organized a Bahá'í gathering of Afro-Descendants in 1996. The event gave special

---

[15] For a report of this conference, see *The Bahá'í World 2001–2002*, pp. 125–32.

attention to Afro-Brazilian cultural elements that are present in the arts, cooking, dress, and history. The gathering also aimed to help participants recover lost social and family cultural traditions, seeking to raise the self-esteem of Afro-Descendants. The gatherings now occur annually; more than 170 people attended the meeting in March 2003.

BAHÁ'Í INTERNATIONAL COMMUNITY

Beyond their efforts to build a model of racial integration within their own communities, Bahá'ís have also actively sought to promote the ideal of unity at an international level, using a wide range of nonviolent and peaceful means. These activities include work with the United Nations and its agencies; collaboration with governments, like-minded NGOs, and religious groups; educational initiatives; media-based outreach campaigns; grassroots initiatives; youth workshops; and individual initiatives that encompass a variety of innovative and creative approaches to local problems and concerns.

In 1997, for example, the Bahá'í International Community (BIC) launched a global campaign to promote human rights education, in support of the UN Decade for Human Rights Education (1995–2004). The campaign encourages national Bahá'í communities to become involved with their governments and with other NGOs in promoting human rights education, outlining a broad program of action that includes as a key element efforts to promote tolerance and an end to racial discrimination.

More than 100 of the BIC's national affiliates participated in training sessions at the start of the campaign, and 50 have already undertaken some form of human rights education activities. In addition, 39 have held in-country training for those who, in support of the Decade, will be interacting with government officials and NGOs, either nationally or locally.

Conclusion

As noble as these efforts are, they cannot be seen as ends unto themselves. Racial unity is a goal for humanity, but ultimately it is only a stepping stone to the unity of humanity in all spheres, one in which all prejudices are erased and mankind can finally be regarded as having reached both its destiny and its natural equilibrium.

As with all efforts where sincere change is sought, the issues must be approached with understanding, tolerance, and a commitment to persevere until solutions are found. These efforts cannot survive if they exist only as a reaction to antisocial forces. Rather, they must, if they are to be lasting in influence and scope, be a propellant towards ever greater unity among all people.

For real progress to be made, the problem of racism must be addressed through practical efforts and the sincere belief, free of cynicism and utopian idealism, that the unity of people can be established. This, the Bahá'í community is resolved to do. Shoghi Effendi succinctly summed up this resolve in the following words:

> Let there be no mistake. The principle of the Oneness of Mankind—the pivot round which all the teachings of Bahá'u'lláh revolve—is no mere outburst of ignorant emotionalism or an expression of vague and pious hope. Its appeal is not to be merely identified with a reawakening of the spirit of brotherhood and good-will among men, nor does it aim solely at the fostering of harmonious cooperation among individual peoples and nations. Its implications are deeper.... Its message is applicable not only to the individual, but concerns itself primarily with the nature of those essential relationships that must bind all the states and nations as members of one human family.[16]

---

[16] Shoghi Effendi, *The World Order of Bahá'u'lláh: Selected Letters*, 2nd rev. ed. (Wilmette, IL: Bahá'í Publishing Trust, 1993), pp. 42–43.

Bahá'í International Community
ACTIVITIES

The Bahá'í International Community (BIC) represents, at the United Nations and at international gatherings, the more than five million Bahá'ís living in some 237 countries and dependent territories around the world. Its 182 national and regional administrative bodies are engaged in a wide range of activities aimed at creating a just and peaceful society. In recent years, Bahá'í International Community activities at the local, national, and international levels have centered on four major themes—human rights, the advancement of women, global prosperity, and moral development.

The Bahá'í International Community's United Nations Office and its Office of Public Information play complementary roles in this work. The United Nations Office offers Bahá'í perspectives on global issues, supports UN programs, and assists its national affiliates to work with governments and other organizations in their own countries to shape policies and programs that will foster peace and prosperity. The Office of Public Information coordinates and stimulates the public information efforts of national Bahá'í communities, disseminates information about the Bahá'í Faith around the world, oversees production of the award-winning newsletter *One Country*, and maintains the official Web sites of the Bahá'í International Community.

United Nations

The BIC has United Nations Offices in New York and Geneva and maintains representations to United Nations (UN) regional commissions in Addis Ababa, Bangkok, and Santiago, and to UN offices in Nairobi, Rome, and Vienna.[1] A feature of this year's activities has been the growing role of national Bahá'í communities and regional representatives in the external affairs work, both in their own countries and in the global arena. They have received training and encouragement from the Bahá'í International Community's United Nations Office to expand their cooperation with their own governments and with the United Nations in their countries and regions.

Bani Dugal, Director of the BIC's Office for the Advancement of Women, was this year named the Bahá'í International Community's Principal Representative to the United Nations.

ADVANCEMENT OF WOMEN

The Office for the Advancement of Women was fully involved in the UN General Assembly's Special Session on Children, which was convened in New York in May 2002 to assess progress towards goals set at the 1990 World Summit for Children. The Special Session, originally scheduled for 19–21 September 2001, was postponed for eight months because of security considerations after the events of 11 September. During the three-day Special Session, the Bahá'í offices served as the venue for 16 workshops, panel discussions, and

---

[1] Since the founding of the United Nations in 1945, the Bahá'í International Community has consistently supported the principles set forth in the UN Charter and has helped to achieve the UN's social and educational objectives. Formally affiliated with the UN since 1947, the Bahá'í International Community was granted special consultative status with the United Nations Economic and Social Council (ECOSOC) in 1970 as an international nongovernmental organization (NGO). Consultative status with the United Nations International Children's Fund (UNICEF) was accorded in 1976, and then with the United Nations Development Fund for Women (UNIFEM) in 1989. That same year, the BIC established a working relationship with the World Health Organization (WHO). Its Office of the Environment, established in 1989, and its Office for the Advancement of Women, established in 1992, function as adjuncts of the United Nations Office.

caucus meetings. The BIC circulated *A Bahá'í Vision for Children,* a compilation of its past statements on children addressing such topics as the rights of children, the importance of educating girls, the need to protect children from sexual abuse, and the role of youth in protecting human rights. Bahá'ís were also represented on a panel entitled "Religions for Children: Challenges and Best Practices," sponsored by the Committee of Religious NGOs.

As chair of the NGO Committee on UNICEF, the BIC helped organize a number of activities at the Special Session, among them an interactive workshop entitled "Girls as Their Own Advocates," sponsored jointly by the NGO Committees on UNICEF and Women. Among the 15 young people who addressed the audience of over 200 at the workshop was Anjali Mody, a Bahá'í youth delegate from India. While acknowledging India for its progressive constitution, Anjali drew attention to the widespread traditional discrimination that leaves a majority of girls in India uneducated and malnourished. She cited as a hopeful example the work of the Barli Development Institute for Rural Women in central India,[2] which offers a program of empowerment—including literacy, income-generating skills, and character development—for young women living in an area where only four percent of women and girls are literate. At a follow-up senior-level NGO consultation sponsored by UNICEF in July, Bani Dugal explored the topic "Maintaining a Political Momentum for the Children's Agenda."

National Bahá'í communities have continued to establish Offices for the Advancement of Women to assist in promoting the full participation of women both in the life of the Bahá'í community and in the world at large. At last count 69 National Spiritual Assemblies had established such offices, committees, and task forces to carry out this work. The Bahá'í International Community supports these offices with materials, advice, and guidance. It also draws on those who have gained experience at the national level to help represent the BIC at such UN events as the Special Session on Children and

---

[2] The Barli Institute, which is now an independent NGO, had its beginnings in 1983 as a project for the advancement of women undertaken by the National Spiritual Assembly of the Bahá'ís of India. A profile of the institute can be found in *The Bahá'í World 2000–2001,* pp. 219–27.

the Commission on the Status of Women. At the October 2002 Global Peace Initiative of Women Religious and Spiritual Leaders in Geneva, an outcome of the 2000 Millennium World Peace Summit, a member of the Swiss Bahá'í community, Silvia Fröhlich, represented the Bahá'í International Community and presented the community's statement.[3]

The Bahá'í communities of Canada, Hawaii, the United Kingdom, and the United States were represented on the BIC delegation at this year's 47th session of the UN Commission on the Status of Women. Convened in March 2003, the Commission focused on two themes: ending violence against women, and ensuring that women have access to media and information and communication technologies (ICT) and that these technologies are used to empower women. With the UN Office of the High Commissioner for Human Rights, the BIC cosponsored a panel on "Ending Violence Against Women." Approximately 89 people, including 16 from government missions and delegations, attended the panel featuring UN and government experts, an expert on gender-based persecution from the Tahirih Justice Center in Washington, DC, and a Bahá'í expert, Dr. Michael Penn, coauthor of a recent book, *Overcoming Violence against Women and Girls*. Dr. Penn was also invited to address a monthly meeting of the UN Values Caucus on the value of recognizing one's own worth. National NGOs made valuable contributions to the Commission. With other UK NGOs, the Association of Bahá'í Women of the UK cosponsored a panel entitled "You Can't Beat a Woman: High and Low-Tech Ways to Prevent Violence against Women." This panel focused on grassroots efforts to empower and protect survivors of domestic violence in Europe, South America, Africa, and the Middle East, including efforts undertaken by faith groups.

The BIC's concern about the impact of HIV/AIDS, especially on women and children, was reflected in a variety of activities this year. At the Commission on the Status of Women, Bahá'ís were represented on a panel on "Women, Religion, and HIV/AIDS," organized by the World Conference of Religions for Peace (WCRP). At the August 2002 exceptional session of the UN Committee on the Convention on the Elimination of Discrimination against Women

---

[3] For the text of this statement, see pp. 241–42.

(CEDAW), the BIC cohosted a luncheon panel on "HIV/AIDS and the Human Rights of Women: Health, Law and UN Priorities" with two other human rights NGOs. And, as it has in years past, the BIC hosted a celebration of Human Rights Day on the theme "No One is Alone" with African Action on AIDS, an NGO that supports schools for AIDS orphans in Africa.

REGIONAL AND NATIONAL PARTICIPATION IN UN ACTIVITIES

For the first time, Bahá'í representatives to four regional UN offices and commissions were invited to New York City in September 2002 for formal training in UN diplomatic work. The training was timed to coincide with the 55th annual UN Department of Public Information (DPI) Conference "Rebuilding Societies Emerging from Conflict: A Shared Responsibility" so that the regional representatives could take advantage of the meeting at the UN.

The training has stimulated activity in the regions and created a closer connection between the regional representatives and the BIC United Nations Office. At the Economic and Social Commission for Asia and the Pacific (ESCAP), Bahá'í activity has increased, with involvement in planning and executing World Peace Day and International Women's Day celebrations and participation in the regional UN Girls' Education Initiative (UNGEI) organized by UNICEF. At two separate UNGEI regional partnership meetings the Bahá'í representative was invited to make presentations on "Bahá'í Consultation" and the "Bahá'í-inspired Montessori School in Lucknow, India." He also moderated a session on "Freedom of Religion and Belief" for the Asian Civil Society Forum 2002.

HUMAN RIGHTS

The Bahá'í International Community's long-standing dedication to human rights is firmly grounded in the conviction that human rights are indispensable to the creation of a peaceful, prosperous, and sustainable world order. Throughout the year, the Geneva Office, in particular, participates in UN and NGO activities focused largely on human rights and religious freedom. Twice this year, BIC statements focused attention on the rights of minorities. At the 54th session of the Sub-Commission on the Promotion and Protection of Human

Rights in July and August 2002, the BIC submitted a statement offering support for the Sub-Committee's Working Group on Minorities.[4] In May 2002, at the eighth session of that working group, the BIC statement raised questions about the practice followed by some governments of "recognizing" certain minorities in order to disenfranchise others. The Bahá'í International Community has also continued its efforts to secure relief from persecution for the Bahá'ís in Iran and in Egypt, where several Bahá'ís remain imprisoned for their beliefs.[5]

The Bahá'í International Community is active in the defense of its own community and protecting the rights of Bahá'ís throughout the world to practice their faith, working through the United Nations' human rights machinery and meeting personally with diplomats on behalf of Bahá'ís experiencing difficulties in their countries. The role of National Spiritual Assemblies, which liaise with their governments on behalf of the Bahá'ís in Iran, is particularly important now that some governments are considering dialogue with Iran as a way to encourage that country to improve its human rights record. At annual training seminars organized by the BIC United Nations Office, representatives of National Spiritual Assemblies come together for consultations aimed at coordinating their efforts to defend the Faith and for workshops designed to sharpen their diplomatic skills. The seventh such training session was held in Acuto, Italy, in September 2002. A similar training session for National Spiritual Assemblies in Latin America and the Caribbean was held for the first time in Orlando, Florida, in October 2002.

MEETINGS

The Bahá'í International Community held offices on six NGO consultative bodies, cochairing the NGO Committee on UNICEF in New York and the Subgroup on Education, Literacy, and Mass Media for the NGO Group for the Rights of the Child in Geneva; and serving as Vice-Chair of the NGO Committees on the Status of Women and

---

[4] For the text of this statement, see pp. 243–45.

[5] For information about the situation of the Bahá'í communities in Iran and Egypt, see the article on pp. 139–44 and the statements on pp. 247–53 and pp. 255–56.

Freedom of Religion or Belief in New York, and Racism in Geneva. BIC also cochaired, for the NGO Committee on the Status of Women, the Planning Group for NGO Consultation Day at the Commission on the Status of Women. In New York the BIC cohosted with the NGO Committee on UNIFEM two receptions honoring CEDAW Committee members and a workshop entitled "Update on CEDAW: Looking Ahead." At the August session of CEDAW, the BIC hosted with another NGO a panel luncheon on "HIV/AIDS and the Human Rights of Women: Health, Law, and UN Priorities."

Other meetings and UN sessions monitored by the Bahá'í International Community this year included the 57th session of the UN General Assembly (GA); the 2nd UN GA Ad Hoc Committee for the Negotiation of a Convention against Corruption; the 10th session of the Commission on Sustainable Development; the 41st session of the Commission for Social Development; the Substantive Session of ECOSOC; the 55th session of the Economic and Social Council for Asia and the Pacific (ESCAP); the Committees on the Rights of the Child, Social, Economic, and Cultural Rights, and the Elimination of Racial Discrimination; the 27th and 28th sessions of the UN Committee on CEDAW; and meetings of the Human Rights Committee, the UNICEF/ WHO Joint Committee on Health Policy, the UNICEF Executive Board, the 90th session of the International Labour Organization (ILO), and the 53rd session of the Executive Committee of the UN High Commissioner for Refugees' Program.

Public Information

Based at the Bahá'í World Centre in Haifa, Israel, with an Office in Paris, the Bahá'í International Community's Office of Public Information oversees and organizes public information work throughout the worldwide Bahá'í community and liaises with a network of National Public Information Officers (NPIO) who carry out the external affairs and public information work of National Spiritual Assemblies. The Office of the Bahá'í International Community's Special Representative in London plays a vital role in organizing diplomatic and other social functions that serve the interests of the Faith at the international level.

The Haifa Office also receives dignitaries and other important visitors to the Bahá'í World Centre. From 21 April 2002 to 21 April 2003, the Office arranged more than 253 visits of nearly 2500 dignitaries, leaders of thought, and prominent people from 62 countries. Visitors from Israel included judges, representatives of the Haifa Police Department, members of the Knesset and representatives of other government ministries, including the Ministry of Religious Affairs, the Ministry of Finance, the Ministry of Tourism, and the Ministry of Foreign Affairs. The Office also hosted film crews, journalists, and photographers from local and national TV channels.

The Office received 16 Ambassadors from 14 countries, and government ministers and officials from Australia, Brazil, Canada, China, the Czech Republic, Finland, France, Germany, Ghana, Greece, Guatemala, India, Ireland, Italy, Kazakhstan, Lithuania, the Netherlands, Paraguay, the Philippines, the Republic of the Congo, Russia, Singapore, Slovakia, South Africa, South Korea, Sri Lanka, Switzerland, Turkey, the United Kingdom, the United States, Uzbekistan, Venezuela, and Yugoslavia.

In addition to these visits, the Office also manages a Guided Tours Operations Office that oversees a reservation system for public tours of the terraced gardens. Weekly, an average of nearly 3,000 people take the guided group tours. In total, more than 1.4 million people have visited the gardens since their public opening in June 2001.

The Paris Office contributes to the work of the BIC by assisting in public information efforts in Europe and the francophone world and through continued involvement with the EU, UNESCO (the United Nations Educational, Scientific, and Cultural Organization), and Eastern Europe's Stability Pact (formerly the Royaumont Process).[6] OPI-Paris supports the Stability Pact through its continuing involvement with the project "Promoting Positive Messages in the Media." This year, activities included follow-up of the project in Romanian Schools in Bucharest and in Cluj-Napoca, Giurgiu, and Braila. The Office also participated in follow-up projects in Bosnia

[6] For more on the BIC's involvement in this initiative, see *The Bahá'í World 1998–99*, pp. 145–50.

and Herzegovina, including a seminar on "Positive Messages through Theatrical Expressions in Schools," organized by the Pedagogical Institute of Tuzla.

The Office's ongoing efforts to support national Bahá'í communities in their public information efforts included planning the 10th annual European Public Information Management Seminar, in Budapest, Hungary, in June 2003. The Office also carried out regional seminars in several countries, including the Czech Republic, Malaysia, Morocco, and Tunisia, and continued in the production of its European Public Information Bulletin, which published its 106th issue in April 2003.

As part of its partnership with UNESCO for the International Decade for a Culture of Peace and Nonviolence against the Children of the World, the Paris Office continued assisting European National Spiritual Assemblies and Bahá'í-inspired associations with their registration as partners. All 37 European national communities are now registered, as are 9 local communities and 26 European Bahá'í-inspired organizations.

The Office of Public Information's publications, both print and Web-based, are intended to provide information about the news and activities of the Bahá'í International Community. The official Web site of the Bahá'í International Community, located at http://www.bahai.org/, is the flagship site of the Bahá'í presence on the Web and receives an average of 50,000 visitors monthly. The site contains excerpts from the Bahá'í writings, information about the history and teachings of the Bahá'í Faith, and perspectives of the community on issues facing mankind. Links to Web sites for 76 national Bahá'í communities are also available on the site.

The Bahá'í World News Service continued its third year of publication via its Web site at http://www.bahaiworldnews.org/, also receiving more than 50,000 visits per month.

One Country, the official newsletter of the Bahá'í International Community, entered its 14th year of publication. Published quarterly in English, French, German, Chinese, Spanish, and Russian, it reaches some 53,000 readers in some 180 countries while maintaining a presence on the World Wide Web at http://www.onecountry.org/.

During the year, many of *One Country*'s stories focused on sustainable development, with an emphasis on innovative approaches to protecting and preserving the environment. The October–December 2002 issue carried a profile of Dr. Austin Bowden-Kerby and his ground-breaking efforts to protect coral reefs in Fiji, along with a report on the efforts of the Barli Development Institute for Rural Women to encourage the use of solar cookers among indigenous women in India. The previous issue, July–September 2002, focused on the World Summit on Sustainable Development in Johannesburg and Bahá'í efforts to emphasize the ethical and spiritual dimensions of sustainable development there. Other stories during the year focused on grassroots education projects, such as efforts by the Bahá'í community of Puka Puka, Bolivia, and the Ngabe-Bugle community in Panama to establish better local educational opportunities. Editorials discussed Bahá'í approaches to global concerns such as terrorism, the intersection of religion and development, and "materialism" as the "modern malady."

One Country won four awards during 2002–03. In April 2002, the Religion Communicators Council gave *One Country* an Award of Excellence for the story "In London, a ground-breaking exploration into the science of morality," which appeared in the January–March 2002 issue. The council also gave *One Country* a Certificate of Merit for "In Bolivia, a distinctive training program in moral leadership shines brightly" about Nur University, which appeared in the same issue. In July, Communications Concepts awarded *One Country* two Apex Awards for Publication Excellence. The edition as a whole won in the category of printed newsletters, and the cover story for the July–September 2002 issue, "In Johannesburg, a shift in emphasis on sustainable development," won in the news writing category.

Update on the Situation of the Bahá'ís in Iran and Egypt

eresy. Conspiracy. Unprotected infidels. These are the terms used by the government of Iran to describe the Bahá'í Faith and its adherents in the land of the Faith's birth. Although, with 300,000 members, the Bahá'ís constitute the largest religious minority in the country they are not a *recognized* minority under the Iranian Constitution and thus have no civil, political, social, economic, or cultural rights.

A series of brief examples will illustrate this point:

- When the Iranian government instituted a law granting equal compensation in "blood money" to members of recognized minorities, the Bahá'ís were excluded.

- While the Islamic Human Rights Commission claims to have succeeded in resolving cases submitted to it by Bahá'ís, no action has actually been taken to defend Bahá'ís' rights; rather, the situations of some Bahá'ís who submitted cases have worsened.

- When a Bahá'í appealed to the Islamic Revolutionary Court for the return of property confiscated from his home, the court rejected his case because the owner had held Bahá'í classes there and because he owned a large number of Bahá'í books. In fact, the courts in Iran routinely uphold confiscations of Bahá'í property.

■ While a public statement has been released urging tolerance towards non-Muslim minorities—even those not recognized in the constitution—it is possible that the Bahá'ís may be excluded. A leading ayatollah has stated that rights such as life, shelter, employment, education, and marriage will not pertain to minority groups that conspire against or weaken the foundation of the Islamic government, or that alter people's opinion of it or spy on it for foreigners. Since the government has repeatedly accused the Bahá'í community of these crimes and has labeled it as "illegal," it is possible that one could interpret the Bahá'ís as being excluded.

■ In the spring of 2002, as students at the Bahá'í Institute of Higher Education—established by the Bahá'í community to provide post-secondary education for students who are denied access to universities in Iran—were preparing to sit for their exams, officials took away their exam papers, computers, and other materials in what appeared to be a coordinated series of raids.

As a non-Bahá'í Iranian scholar has noted:

while the Islamic Republic's policies towards the spiritual leaders of Bahá'ís have endangered their identity and existence as a religious community, government officials' treatment of ordinary Bahá'í individuals has, in a day-by-day increasing fashion, made continuation of their loyalty to this religion and their religious unity and solidarity difficult. Furthermore, cases of deprivation, violation of rights, and discrimination are blatantly reflected in the mass media as if they should be counted as normal and acceptable events of life in Iran.[1]

---

[1] Dr. Reza Afshari, "Violation of the Human Rights of the Bahá'ís in the Islamic Republic" (provisional translation), *Iran Nameh* 19.1–2 [Winter 1379–Spring 1380 (2001)].

In April 2002, the 58th session of the United Nations Commission on Human Rights rejected the resolution on the Islamic Republic of Iran, marking the first time in 18 years that the United Nations had not passed a resolution condemning the human rights situation in that country, with particular mention of the continuing plight of the Bahá'ís. The Universal House of Justice termed this failure "regrettable" and noted, "Given the continuing discrimination and oppression of the beleaguered Bahá'í community in Iran, as certified in the Commission's reports to it from its own Rapporteur and Special Representative, it is unfortunate that the Commission has chosen to ignore these facts and its own findings."[2]

As a consequence, during the past year the United Nations Commission on Human Rights suspended international monitoring of human rights in Iran, and the Bahá'ís have seen increases in the numbers of arbitrary arrests and short-term detentions of members of their community; teachers and students have been subjected to harassment for attempting to pursue education that has been systematically denied to them by the state; property confiscations continue; and individuals who have attempted to obtain redress have invariably met with denial.

In an oral statement to the Commission on Human Rights in Geneva on 3 April 2003, the Bahá'í International Community noted that UN monitoring has been "of great use," and without it "the Bahá'í community in Iran would have been subjected to even more widespread and grievous forms of persecution." While the Iranian government's dialogue on human rights with the European Union and its invitations to human rights monitors are "positive," they "should not be considered as achievements in and of themselves." Rather, the process should be analyzed and progress should be assessed on a regular basis.

The Bahá'í International Community has proposed as benchmarks a series of recommendations set out in 1996 by Professor Abdelfattah Amor, the United Nations Special Rapporteur on religious intolerance. These call for the reinstitution of the following rights for the Bahá'í community:

---

[2] Universal House of Justice, letter to selected National Spiritual Assemblies, 23 April 2002.

- to bury their dead
- to enjoy freedom of movement
- to have unimpeded access to education and employment
- to have security of the person and physical integrity
- to have the freedom to manifest their belief
- to receive equal treatment by the judiciary
- to have equal rights with other citizens
- the review and setting aside of all death sentences pronounced against Bahá'ís on the basis of their belief
- the return of community properties and compensation for the destruction of places of worship
- the reestablishment of Bahá'í institutions

Taking up the theme of assessment of progress, the NGO Human Rights Watch (HRW) in December 2002 called on the European Union to set "clear and measurable benchmarks" for monitoring the progress of its human rights dialogue with Iran. Among the 10 specific points mentioned by HRW as "critical tests of good faith by the government of Iran and substantive progress in any human rights dialogue" is one that calls for the initiation of "a program of action to identify and address discrimination against minority groups, for instance by providing education and employment entitlements to people of the Baha'i faith." Human Rights Watch proposed that the benchmarks "be made public and used to evaluate progress after an initial period of 12 months."

Other international agencies have also been vocal in their assertion of the Bahá'í community's rights. For example, in June 2002 the 90th Session of the International Labour Organization (ILO) referred to the ongoing discrimination against the Bahá'ís in Iran, and its Committee of Experts on the Application of Conventions and Recommendations (CEACR) also mentioned the subject. The CEACR made two significant observations and recommendations. First, in connection to the newly established National Committee for the Promotion of the Rights of Religious Minorities, "which is to review the problems that religious minorities face and recommend corrective policies," the CEACR expressed its hope that the committee "will review the problems of the nonrecognized religious minorities and will include members of the nonrecognized minorities in its work." This would include the Bahá'ís. Second, the report discusses "the treatment in education and employment of members of unrecognized religions, in particular the members of the Bahá'í faith," noting that "the situation of the Bahá'ís goes beyond formal restrictions and exclusions, which may exist, and extends to the societal attitude towards the members of this group." The CEACR also mentions the Special Representative's interim report, which states that the "Bahá'í community continues to experience discrimination in education and employment and other areas."

In Egypt, too, the Bahá'ís are not free to profess their Faith. As the Bahá'í International Community mentioned on 9 April 2003 in an oral statement to the UN's Commission on Human Rights in Geneva, "All members of the community are under strict surveillance. They have no access to any form of legal marriage, cannot obtain custody of children, child allowances or alimony, and are often denied access to pensions and inheritance. Not being legally married, they cannot even obtain a family record—a document required by law in Egypt for many official purposes."

The roots of this injustice lie in Presidential Decree No. 263, issued by President Nasser in 1960, which dissolved Bahá'í institutions, banned the Faith's activities, and suppressed its community life. For example, Bahá'ís have been arrested for speaking about their beliefs to friends in their own homes, and for participating in small, private gatherings to say prayers and to read their sacred writings. As the Bahá'ís stated to the Human Rights Commission, "The Decree is still used today to instigate police investigations, arrests, domicile searches, and the destruction of Bahá'í religious literature, and it is restrictively interpreted by the courts in ways that reduce the status of the Bahá'ís to that of second-class citizens."

The media and the courts regularly denounce the Bahá'ís as apostates, and government appointees have given "an air of official approval" to incitement to hatred and violence against the Bahá'í community, refusing to take action against calls for its members to be killed.

The Bahá'í International Community brought these violations of freedom of religion or belief to the attention of a subcommission of the UN's Human Rights Committee during its 2002 session. While the Committee deplored the ban on worship imposed on the community, official "obstructions and restrictions" that specifically target them have not been removed.

In summary, the conditions under which the Bahá'ís in countries such as Iran and Egypt suffer can best be described as sustained harassment and slow strangulation, which are harder to monitor than executions and imprisonments. Nevertheless, such systematic action is extremely damaging, and the attention of the international community is one of the few means by which Bahá'ís in those countries may dare to hope for redress.

ESSAYS, STATEMENTS, AND PROFILES

Obligation and Responsibility in Constructing a World Civilization

Dr. Hoda Mahmoudi examines the nature
of a spiritualized society founded on
altruism and reciprocity and based on the
principles described in the Bahá'í writings.

Constructing a world commonwealth grounded in obligation and responsibility is not an easy task. The twentieth century has shown the capacity of human beings to inflict unimaginable pain, suffering, and destruction upon one another. In terms of civil violence, mass murder, and genocide, no other century rivals that of the twentieth, and it remains to be seen what the twenty-first century has to offer in this regard. The collapse of communism and the end of the Cold War, rather than bringing an end to a long-standing ideological battle, seem to have fuelled the flames of nationalism, ethnic rivalries, and religious hatred, thus bringing to the surface, in an extreme form, the terror and ugliness of ethnic cleansing. At any given time around the globe, countless atrocities are inflicted by one group of human beings upon another. In fact, an assessment of the current global community cannot help but conclude that at the early stages of the twenty-first century, humanity, rather than acting on the reality of its interdependence and its need for collaboration, is instead pursuing a course that hinders the possibility of building bonds of cooperation and peaceful existence, and appears to stand on the brink of total disorder and chaos.

As the forces of globalization continue to unfold, the world community finds itself in a quagmire of growing political instability, intensifying economic inequality, and the weakening of family, educational, and religious authority. Never before in history have the widely dispersed, diverse peoples and cultures of the planet lived in such close proximity to one another. And yet within this emerging global community deep attitudes of suspicion, distrust, and hatred persist among its diverse populations. Those engaged in the study of cultures have, on the one hand, pointed to multiculturalism as a means for democratic society to recognize and promote equal representation of all, including equal access to economic means.[1] But multiculturalism is challenged by deep-rooted prejudices and attitudes of superiority and control amongst certain groups or cultures that actively impede possibilities of removing barriers, resolving differences, and promoting advancement towards coexistence.

Others, like Samuel Huntington, view the emerging global community as one wherein "the clash of civilizations" or conflict between cultures is inevitable.[2] In particular, Huntington views the post-Cold War era as one in which "cultural identities" are "shaping the patterns of cohesion, disintegration, and conflict."[3] He describes this "new world" thus:

> In the post-Cold War world flags count and so do other symbols of cultural identity, including crosses, crescents, and even head coverings, because culture counts, and cultural identity is what is most meaningful to most people. People are discovering new but often old identities and marching under new but often old flags which lead to wars with new but often old enemies.[4]

For many, modernity and its initial optimism and promise for a better, more advanced economic system and rationalization in organization is viewed as a failed experiment. Many critics believe that

---

[1] Amy Gutmann, ed., *Multiculturalism: Examining the Politics of Recognition* (Princeton, NJ: Princeton University Press, 1994), p. 3.

[2] Samuel P. Huntington, *The Clash of Civilizations and the Remaking of World Order* (New York: Simon and Schuster, 1998).

[3] Ibid., p. 20.

[4] Ibid.

modern society is incapable of resolving its basic social ills, much less the more complex global uncertainties that challenge humankind to search for new paradigms of international life and civil organization and governance. Sociologist Robert Bellah and others describe this seeming impotence of the modern age:

> There is a widespread feeling that the promise of the modern era is slipping away from us. A movement of enlightenment and liberation that was to have freed us from superstition and tyranny has led in the twentieth century to a world in which ideological fanaticism and political oppression have reached extremes unknown in previous history.[5]

In *Seedbeds of Virtue*, Mary Ann Glendon points out how in postmodern academy, words like "virtue" and "character have nearly disappeared from the lexicon of the modern human sciences."[6] Others have observed a decline in public morality as democratic societies have spread, as growth in prosperity has occurred, and as personal freedom has expanded.[7]

Jonathan Sacks, in his book *The Dignity of Difference: How to Avoid the Clash of Civilizations*, suggests that the current conflict-ridden global community is in need of common values that promote coexistence if we are to avoid the clash of civilizations. He writes,

> [N]ation-states seem increasingly unable to control global phenomena from multinational corporations to ecological devastation, and we have not yet evolved a form of global governance. Market capitalism has increased wealth beyond the imagination of previous generations, but cannot, in and of itself, distribute it equally or even equitably. There are problems that cannot be solved within the terms set by modernity, for the simple reason that they are not procedural, but rather valuational or, to use

---

[5] Robert N. Bellah et al., *Habits of the Heart: Individualism and Commitment in American Life* (Berkeley: University of California Press, 1985), p. 277.

[6] Mary Ann Glendon and David Blankenhorn, eds., *Seedbeds of Virtue: Sources of Competence, Character, and Citizenship in American Society* (Lanham, MD: Madison Books, 1995), p. 5.

[7] James Q. Wilson, "Liberalism, Modernism, and the Good Life," in *Seedbeds of Virtue*, pp. 17–34.

the simple word, moral. There is no way of bypassing difficult moral choices by way of a scientific decision—a procedure that states: "Maximize X." We first have to decide which X we wish to maximize, and how to weigh X against Y when the pursuit of one damages the fulfilment of the other. The human project is inescapably a moral project. That is one reason why the great faiths, with their history of reflection on moral issues, must be part of the conversation.[8]

Sociologist Philip Selznick defines modernity as referring to "the special features of the technologically advanced industrial, commercial, urban society that has taken shape in the West since the eighteenth century, anticipated, of course, by earlier trends and ideas."[9] He presents a constructive perspective of modern life by suggesting that

> Modern life offers a welcome if risky challenge to the moral order. As self-determination is enlarged, as awareness is sharpened, the complexity of moral choice increases. The responsibility of individuals and groups becomes in many ways more self-conscious and more demanding. More is asked of us and we ask more of ourselves.[10]

In the late twentieth century, postmodernism emerged as a reaction to modernity, rejecting scientific objectivity, challenging the notion of coherence, and refuting the existence of any authoritative principles. Postmodernism rejects any form of truth, whether philosophical, scientific, or religious. Zygmunt Bauman, writing about the characteristics of postmodern literature, but making an observation relevant to society at large, states,

> What the inherently polysemous and controversial idea of *postmodernity* most often refers to ... is first and foremost an acceptance of the ineradicable plurality of the world—not a temporary state

---

[8] Jonathan Sacks, *The Dignity of Difference: How to Avoid the Clash of Civilizations* (London: Continuum, 2002), p. 195.

[9] Philip Selznick, *The Moral Commonwealth: Social Theory and the Promise of Community* (Berkeley: University of California Press, 1992), p. 7.

[10] Ibid., p. 4.

on the road to the not-yet-attained perfection, sooner or later to be left behind, but the constructive quality of existence. By the same token, postmodernity means a resolute emancipation from the characteristically modern urge to overcome difference and promote sameness.... In the plural and pluralistic world of postmodernity, every form of life is *permitted on principle*; or, rather, no agreed principles are evident which may render any form of life impermissible.[11]

In his discussion of the challenge of postmodernism, Philip Selznick points to its validity in relation to the "many insidious aspects of modern life, including hidden forms of power and manipulation."[12] He refers to postmodernism as the "wayward child of modernism" and suggests that "its central message carries 'the logic of modernism to its farthest reaches.'" He then elaborates on this point:

It does so ... without retaining the intellectual, moral, and aesthetic strengths of modernism; without the belief that there is genuine truth to be discerned; without confidence in the possibility of creating new and better ways of manifesting the human spirit; without tacit commitment to continuity as well as change. What there was of exuberant optimism has been displaced by cynicism and despair. With some fidelity postmodern theorists reflect—and dramatize—the weakening of selfhood in late modernity.[13]

New ideologies continue to emerge, some with the goal of providing, on the one hand, solutions to the social ills presently at work throughout the world, and on the other, with grim explanations for the failure of any form of intervention that might be the source of remedy for the many global disorders. The unparalleled levels of violence, the proliferation of political corruption, the increased

---

[11] Zygmunt Bauman, "Strangers: The Social Construction of Universality and Particularity," in *Telos* 28, no. 23 (1988–89), quoted in Robert Kagan, *In Over Our Heads: The Mental Demands of Modern Life* (Cambridge, MA: Harvard University Press, 1994), p. 326.

[12] Selznick, *Moral Commonwealth*, p. 13.

[13] Ibid.

lawlessness, the breakdown in the code of ethics, the lax attitude toward ecological disintegration, the overall disregard for human rights, all such disorders seem to have brought humanity to its darkest hour. It is no wonder that the individual's response to such dreadful developments is one of a paralysis of will, a sense of deep pessimism, and profound disaffection. At the heart of the current predicament in which a beleaguered global community finds itself, are complex questions about the future direction of humankind. Is there the potential for a way out of the present dark condition in which humanity finds itself? Is it possible for humans to find a common vision in advancing reasonable solutions to the present course of disintegration? Who can or should take responsibility for reversing the present bleak conditions faced by humankind?

The aim of this paper is to examine the challenging pronouncement advanced by Bahá'u'lláh, of the need for humankind in the present age to recognize and bring about a world community that is founded on the unification of the human race and the establishment of a new world order that is responsive to the needs of a single human race. The paper discusses the teachings of the Bahá'í Faith that address the establishment of the "constructive social forces which, because they are consistent with human nature, will encourage harmony and cooperation instead of war and conflict."[14]

Cognizant of the capacity of human beings to do both good and evil, the paper examines, from the spiritual framework set forth in the Bahá'í writings, what it means to be human. It discusses the potential of the development, through moral education, of spiritual qualities leading to individual and institutional actions that aim to promote the welfare of others as more important than one's own. It develops the Bahá'í concepts of reciprocity and altruism as providing a foundation for the formation of a society centered on "constructiveness and accomplishment in all the planes of human activity."[15]

---

[14] Universal House of Justice, *The Promise of World Peace* (Haifa: Bahá'í World Centre, 1985), p. 3.

[15] 'Abdu'l-Bahá, *The Promulgation of Universal Peace: Talks Delivered by 'Abdu'l-Bahá during His Visit to the United States and Canada in 1912*, rev. ed. (Wilmette, IL: Bahá'í Publishing Trust, 1995), p. 338.

The Claim of Bahá'u'lláh

In the middle of the nineteenth century, Bahá'u'lláh imparted His vision of the oneness of humankind and the earth as a common homeland. In the 1860s, while an exile of the Ottoman Empire, Bahá'u'lláh wrote about the need for the creation of a "New World Order," stating,

> The winds of despair are, alas, blowing from every direction, and the strife that divides and afflicts the human race is daily increasing. The signs of impending convulsions and chaos can now be discerned, inasmuch as the prevailing order appears to be lamentably defective....
>
> Soon will the present day Order be rolled up and a new one spread out in its stead.[16]

Some 70 years later, Shoghi Effendi wrote that the "dark forces ... of hate, rebellion, anarchy, and reaction are threatening the very stability of human society."[17] He expounded on the need for a new system (world order) as set forth by Bahá'u'lláh and set into motion a plan for its development towards the organization of an emerging global community. In 1936, he wrote the following about the disorder facing humanity and the need for its unification:

> Beset on every side by the cumulative evidences of disintegration, of turmoil and of bankruptcy, serious-minded men and women, in almost every walk of life, are beginning to doubt whether society, as it is now organized, can, through its unaided efforts, extricate itself from the slough into which it is steadily sinking. Every system, short of the unification of the human race, has been tried, repeatedly tried, and been found wanting.[18]

---

[16] Bahá'u'lláh, cited in Shoghi Effendi, *The World Order of Bahá'u'lláh: Selected Letters,* 2nd rev. ed. (Wilmette, IL: Bahá'í Publishing Trust, 1993), pp. 32, 161.

[17] Shoghi Effendi, *Bahá'í Administration: Selected Messages 1922–1932* (Wilmette, IL: Bahá'í Publishing Trust, 1995), p. 52.

[18] Shoghi Effendi, *World Order of Bahá'u'lláh,* p. 190.

Unification of the Human Race

A large part of Bahá'u'lláh's writings is dedicated to the progressive nature of God's revelation and man's relationship to it. There is only one God, described in Bahá'u'lláh's writings as an "unknowable Essence ... exalted beyond every human attribute, such as corporeal existence, ascent and descent, egress and regress."[19] "Know thou," Bahá'u'lláh asserts, "that every created thing is a sign of the revelation of God."[20] Consequently, it is through the Will of God that successive revelations, or religions, are made known to humanity. The Bahá'í teachings view divine revelation not as a static, unique event, but as a continuing process that is the central feature of human history. There is only one religion. That there have been and will continue to be Prophets who introduce humankind to God's progressive revelation does not imply that religion is in competition with itself. Rather, as explained by Bahá'u'lláh, "if thou callest them [Manifestations of God] all by one name, and dost ascribe to them the same attributes, thou hast not erred from the truth.... For they are all but one person, one soul, one spirit, one being, one revelation."[21] The spirit that inspired all the Founders of the great religions of the past, and will inspire Those to come in the future, is recognized as one and the same. Their original teachings contain the same basic ethical and moral precepts, prominent among which are the teachings that promote reciprocity and altruism. The tenets that change from one religious dispensation to another are the social laws and practices. Thus, religious truth is understood to be relative, progressive, and developmental.

Manifestations of God appear because humanity is in need of spiritual renewal. With every new revelation, a new Prophet, or Manifestation of God, appears with a twofold purpose. The first, according to Bahá'u'lláh, is "to liberate the children of men from the darkness of ignorance, and guide them to the light of true understanding.

---

[19] Bahá'u'lláh, *Gleanings from the Writings of Bahá'u'lláh* (Wilmette, IL: Bahá'í Publishing Trust, 1994), p. 46.

[20] Ibid., p. 184.

[21] Ibid., pp. 51 and 54.

The second is to ensure the peace and tranquillity of mankind, and provide all the means by which they can be established."[22]

According to Bahá'u'lláh, the first step towards the establishment of peace begins with the acceptance of the principle of the oneness of the human race. He states, "The well-being of mankind, its peace and security are unattainable unless and until its unity is firmly established."[23] He proclaims the principle of unity as the central purpose of His Faith. "So powerful is the light of unity," declares Bahá'u'lláh, "that it can illuminate the whole earth."[24] The image that comes into view regarding the unification of the human race is that of a global community in which all inhabitants recognize and accept their membership in one human family. In Bahá'u'lláh's own words, "The world is but one country, and mankind its citizens."[25] Shoghi Effendi explains that the "coming of age of the human race," as proclaimed by Bahá'u'lláh, is associated with the unification of the human race, which will evolve into "the stage at which the oneness of the whole body of nations will be made the ruling principle of international life."[26]

Bahá'u'lláh's vision of the emerging international community calls for the widening of the existing foundations of society. It demands the reshaping of institutions in order that they be in harmony with "the needs of an ever-changing world."[27] In the following passage Shoghi Effendi summarizes what Bahá'u'lláh foreshadowed for the evolving global society:

> Unification of the whole of mankind is the hall-mark of the stage which human society is now approaching. Unity of family, of tribe, of city-state, and nation have been successively attempted and fully established. World unity is the goal towards which a harassed humanity is striving. Nation-building has come to an end. The anarchy inherent in state sovereignty is moving towards

---

[22] Ibid., pp. 79–80.
[23] Bahá'u'lláh, cited in Shoghi Effendi, *World Order of Bahá'u'lláh*, p. 203.
[24] Bahá'u'lláh, *Epistle to the Son of the Wolf* (Wilmette, IL: Bahá'í Publishing Trust, 1995), p. 14.
[25] Bahá'u'lláh, *Gleanings*, p. 250.
[26] Shoghi Effendi, *World Order of Bahá'u'lláh*, p. 193.
[27] Ibid., p. 41.

a climax. A world, growing to maturity, must abandon this fetish, recognize the oneness and wholeness of human relationships, and establish once and for all the machinery that can best incarnate this fundamental principle of its life.[28]

Given this vision of the oneness of humankind and the need for a new global world order, the question arises as to how the Bahá'í Faith envisages the development of such a system. In particular, what are the roles of the individual and of Bahá'í institutions in constructing a social life based on the unification of humankind living in a truly interdependent world commonwealth? How is such a system possible given the present moribund condition of the world community? Is it possible—or even realistic—to assume that human beings can bring about cooperation and constructiveness in social relationships?

The Bahá'í teachings address the development of social patterns that are necessary for the well-being of humankind. For the individual Bahá'í, personal commitment to the laws and principles of Bahá'u'lláh is the key to transforming oneself, which leads, in turn, to the transformation of civilization. One's inner life and attitudes cannot be separated from one's public life. The ethics and values that guide the individual are not separate from those of society.

In the following passage, Shoghi Effendi expounds on the importance of the interconnectedness of the individual and society:

> We cannot segregate the human heart from the environment outside us and say that once one of these is reformed everything will be improved. Man is organic with the world. His inner life molds the environment and is itself also deeply affected by it. The one acts upon the other and every abiding change in the life of man is the result of these mutual reactions.[29]

The Bahá'í teachings shift the focus of religious practice from individual salvation or enlightenment to the collective responsibility

---

[28] Ibid., p. 202.

[29] Letter written on behalf of Shoghi Effendi to an individual believer, 17 February 1933, in *Conservation of the Earth's Resources*, prepared by the Research Department of the Universal House of Justice (October 1989), in *The Compilation of Compilations*, vol. 1 (Ingleside, NSW: Bahá'í Publications Australia, 1991), p. 84.

for the progress of humanity as a whole. The Bahá'í conception of social life is essentially based on the subordination of the individual will to that of society. The Bahá'í teachings address social conditions and global problems as directly related to the individual's spiritual life and sense of responsibility; Bahá'í principles such as world peace, the equality of women and men, harmony between science and religion, the equitable distribution of wealth and resources, and the elimination of all forms of prejudice are, for Bahá'ís, inseparable from religious belief and practice.

This emphasis on collective progress has important implications for the relationship of individual entities—whether individual persons, institutions, nations, or other groups—to the larger society of which they form a part. As Shoghi Effendi describes, the relationship between these entities is based on the principle of the subordination of "every particularistic interest, be it personal, regional, or national, to the paramount interests of humanity." This, in turn, is based on the idea that "in a world of inter-dependent peoples and nations the advantage of the part is best to be reached by the advantage of the whole."[30]

Yet the "interests of humanity as a whole" are not conceived in terms of a vague abstraction that could be appropriated by a particular dominant group and interpreted as identical with its own interests but, rather, as a complex dynamic relationship between the parts and the whole, in which the viability of the whole is served by ensuring the well-being of all its individual parts, an enterprise for which all share responsibility.

This conception is demonstrated at its most basic level in the relationship of the individual person and society, in which a complex balance is sought between individual freedom and responsibility. Cooperation between society and the individual is stressed in the Bahá'í writings, as is the fostering of "a climate in which the untold potentialities of the individual members of society can develop." Such a relationship, as it is envisioned, "must allow 'free scope' for 'individuality to assert itself' through modes of spontaneity, initiative, and diversity that ensure the viability of society." Even while the will of

---

[30] Shoghi Effendi, *World Order of Bahá'u'lláh*, p. 198.

the individual is subordinate to that of society, "the individual is not lost in the mass but becomes the focus of primary development."[31]

Thus, a fundamental principle of social relations and structures for Bahá'ís lies in the realization of belief through practice. The fulfilment of individual potential is to be sought not in pursuing self-centered desires but in contributing to the benefit and well-being of others, and in the belief that "the honor and distinction of the individual consist in this, that he among all the world's multitudes should be a source of social good."[32] This challenging assertion as put forth in Bahá'í teachings cannot be fully understood without an examination of the Bahá'í perspective of what it means to be a human being and what is the purpose of life for humans.

The Dual Nature of the Human Being

The paleontologist Ian Tattersall, in his book *Becoming Human*, describes what he believes sets humans apart from animals: "[I]f we have to identify any single characteristic that sets us apart, one of the things that is truly extraordinary about human beings is their finely honed perception of the world beyond their social milieu."[33]

Differences between human beings and animals are explained with great care in the Bahá'í writings. Animals are "captive of the senses" and do not have "the powers of ideation and conscious reflection"; "they are without education and training" and "have no touch with the spiritual world and are without conception of God."[34] And yet, animals are described as being keener than humans when it comes to bodily senses. Animals manifest superiority to humans in their "powers such as hearing, sight, smell, taste, and touch,"[35]

---

[31] Universal House of Justice, *Individual Rights and Freedoms in the World Order of Bahá'u'lláh: A Statement by the Universal House of Justice* (Wilmette, IL: Bahá'í Publishing Trust, 1989), pp. 20–21.

[32] 'Abdu'l-Bahá, *The Secret of Divine Civilization* (Wilmette, IL: Bahá'í Publishing Trust, 1994), p. 2.

[33] Ian Tattersall, *Becoming Human: Evolution and Human Uniqueness* (New York: Harcourt Brace & Co., 1998), p. 195.

[34] 'Abdu'l-Bahá, *Promulgation of Universal Peace*, pp. 255, 172–73, 311.

[35] 'Abdu'l-Bahá, *Some Answered Questions* (Wilmette, IL: Bahá'í Publishing Trust, 1994), p. 187.

but they are unable to "perceive intellectual realities." 'Abdu'l-Bahá
writes,

> For example, that which is within the range of its vision the
> animal sees, but that which is beyond the range of sight it is
> not possible for it to perceive, and it cannot imagine it. So it is
> not possible for the animal to understand that the earth has the
> form of a globe. But man from known things proves unknown
> things and discovers unknown truths.[36]

The Bahá'í writings describe the "human spirit" as the "rational
soul," unique to humans and absent in the world of nature, explain-
ing that the "rational soul is the substance through which the body
exists."[37] Regarding the nature of the human spirit, 'Abdu'l-Bahá
says,

> When you wish to reflect upon or consider a matter, you consult
> something within you. You say, shall I do it, or shall I not do it?
> Is it better to make this journey or abandon it? Whom do you
> consult? Who is within you deciding this question? Surely there
> is a distinct power, an intelligent ego. Were it not distinct from
> your ego, you would not be consulting it. It is greater than the
> faculty of thought. It is your spirit which teaches you, which
> advises and decides upon matters.[38]

Although humans are different from animals in significant ways,
as described above, they nevertheless, have a dual nature. 'Abdu'l-
Bahá describes this duality in the human being, stating,

> [A]s an animal he is subject to nature, but in his spiritual or
> conscious being he transcends the world of material existence.
> His spiritual powers, being nobler and higher, possess virtues
> of which nature intrinsically has no evidence; therefore, they
> triumph over natural conditions.[39]

---

[36] Ibid., p. 187.
[37] Ibid., p. 240.
[38] 'Abdu'l-Bahá, *Promulgation of Universal Peace*, p. 242.
[39] Ibid., p. 81.

In another place 'Abdu'l-Bahá states the following about the duality of human beings:

> But the spirit of man has two aspects: one divine, one satanic— that is to say, it is capable of the utmost perfection, or it is capable of the utmost imperfection. If it acquires virtues, it is the most noble of the existing beings; and if it acquires vices, it becomes the most degraded.[40]

Humans, then, have the capacity for both good and evil acts. However, the force of darkness must be overcome through deliberate attention and great effort in the development of the force of light or goodness. Shoghi Effendi, in a letter written on his behalf, explained the Bahá'í perspective that "evil exists … and we cannot close our eyes to it, even though it is a negative existence. We must seek to supplant it by good."[41] It is through spiritual education that the individual learns to demonstrate the constructive force through deeds. 'Abdu'l-Bahá explains that it is the role of religion to provide spiritual education, which, in turn, is a means for the alleviation of the destructive forces. He states, "Close investigation will show that the primary cause of oppression and injustice, of unrighteousness, irregularity, and disorder, is the people's lack of religious faith and the fact that they are uneducated."[42]

Being Human

The Bahá'í viewpoint on human nature is not based on a specific philosophical, anthropological, political, or sociological theory. The station and purpose of human beings is explicitly defined by Bahá'u'lláh in the following passage:

> Having created the world and all that liveth and moveth therein, He [God], through the direct operation of His unconstrained and

---

[40] 'Abdu'l-Bahá, *Some Answered Questions*, p. 144.

[41] Shoghi Effendi, *Unfolding Destiny: The Messages from the Guardian of the Bahá'í Faith to the Bahá'í Community of the British Isles* (London: Bahá'í Publishing Trust, 1981), pp. 457–58.

[42] 'Abdu'l-Bahá, *Secret of Divine Civilization*, p. 18.

sovereign Will, chose to confer upon man the unique distinction and capacity to know Him and to love Him—a capacity that must needs be regarded as the generating impulse and the primary purpose underlying the whole of creation.[43]

This unique distinction bestowed upon man confers responsibility and capacity for the cultivation of spiritual virtues in the service of the collective advancement of society.

In addition to describing God's purpose in creating man and his unique station, Bahá'u'lláh addresses the lofty purpose inherent in every individual to become the "source of all goodness … and an example of uprightness to mankind."[44] He states, "Noble have I created thee, yet thou hast abased thyself. Rise then unto that for which thou wast created."[45] Furthermore, He declares, "We love to see you at all times consorting in amity and concord … and to inhale from your acts the fragrance of friendliness and unity, of loving-kindness and fellowship."[46] The Bahá'í teachings insist that the individual leave behind outdated traditions, prejudices, superstitions, narrow-mindedness, and provincial tendencies that keep humanity apart. They invite the individual to acquire a "world embracing" vision that accepts the equality, well-being, and oneness of all people.

The Universal House of Justice explains the purpose for spiritual laws by comparing them to the laws that govern the physical lives of humans. It states,

Just as there are laws governing our physical lives, requiring that we must supply our bodies with certain foods, maintain them within a certain range of temperatures, and so forth, if we wish to avoid physical disabilities, so also there are laws governing our spiritual lives. These laws are revealed to mankind in each age by the Manifestation of God, and obedience to them is of vital importance if each human being, and mankind in general, is to develop properly and harmoniously. Moreover, these various

---

[43] Bahá'u'lláh, *Gleanings*, p. 65.

[44] Ibid., p. 315.

[45] Bahá'u'lláh, *The Hidden Words* (Wilmette, IL: Bahá'í Publishing Trust, 1994), Arabic no. 22, p. 9.

[46] Bahá'u'lláh, *Gleanings*, p. 315.

aspects are interdependent. If an individual violates the spiritual laws for his own development he will cause injury not only to himself but to the society in which he lives. Similarly, the condition of society has a direct effect on the individuals who must live within it.[47]

The station of man is thus one of refinement and righteousness through the application of spiritual principles and laws. In this process, individuals are responsible for their actions toward others and thus strive to become a source of positive influence on others as well as on the environment or the society in which they are actively involved.

What Bahá'u'lláh asks is that individuals embrace a vision far beyond the narrow confines of their traditional norms, wherein one's family, clan, culture, or nation is considered as superior and separate. A vastly expanded circle of social interaction is called for. A higher level of consciousness and moral commitment is required in an international community that has developed highly complex levels of social interaction. Shoghi Effendi elucidates this point in the following passage:

> Let there be no misgivings as to the animating purpose of the world-wide Law of Bahá'u'lláh. Far from aiming at the subversion of the existing foundations of society, it seeks to broaden its basis, to remold its institutions in a manner consonant with the needs of an ever-changing world. It can conflict with no legitimate allegiances, nor can it undermine essential loyalties. Its purpose is neither to stifle the flame of a sane and intelligent patriotism in men's hearts, nor to abolish the system of national autonomy so essential if the evils of excessive centralization are to be avoided. It does not ignore, nor does it attempt to suppress, the diversity of ethical origins, of climate, of history, of language and tradition, of thought and habit, that differentiate the peoples and nations of the world. It calls for a wider loyalty, for a larger aspiration than any that has animated the human

---

[47] Universal House of Justice, letter to all National Spiritual Assemblies, 6 February 1973, in *Messages from the Universal House of Justice, 1963–1986* (Wilmette, IL: Bahá'í Publishing Trust, 1996), p. 231.

race. It insists upon the subordination of national impulses and interests to the imperative claims of a unified world. It repudiates excessive centralization on one hand, and disclaims all attempts at uniformity on the other. Its watchword is unity in diversity.[48]

Thus, the Bahá'í teachings affirm the capacity of individuals and humanity as a whole to develop behavior aimed at establishing constructiveness, cooperation, and agreement in social interactions. Such beneficial forces require that great attention and energy be devoted to the socialization of the individual though a strong spiritual or moral education.

Moral Education

Human beings, according to the Bahá'í perspective, are fundamentally spiritual. But developing spiritual capacity requires moral education. Developing the spiritual side of humans is a comprehensive, life-long process. The Bahá'í writings are realistic in their assessment of the capacity of humans to pursue selfish motives or to inflict great harm on others. In the following passage, 'Abdu'l-Bahá explains the deep roots of man's self-centered tendency and prescribes spiritual education as a requisite for overcoming it:

> [I]t is impossible for a human being to turn aside from his own selfish advantages and sacrifice his own good for the good of the community except through true religious faith. For self-love is kneaded into the very clay of man, and it is not possible that, without any hope of a substantial reward, he should neglect his own present material good. That individual, however, who puts his faith in God and believes in the words of God—because he is promised and certain of a plentiful reward in the next life, and because worldly benefits as compared to the abiding joy and glory of future planes of existence are nothing to him—will for the sake of God abandon his own peace and profit and will freely consecrate his heart and soul to the common good.[49]

---

[48] Shoghi Effendi, *World Order of Bahá'u'lláh*, pp. 41–42.
[49] 'Abdu'l-Bahá, *Secret of Divine Civilization*, pp. 96–97.

The Bahá'í teachings on spiritual education focus on training children from a young age in "goodly character and good morals," and on guiding them to "all the virtues of humankind."[50] Spiritual education is centered on the development of that distinctive quality, the spiritual nature, which the Bahá'í teachings explain as being unique to human beings. 'Abdu'l-Bahá, in the following passage, explains the significance of raising children to have a strong spiritual constitution:

> A child is as a young plant: it will grow in whatever way you train it. If you rear it to be truthful, and kind, and righteous, it will grow straight, it will be fresh and tender, and will flourish. But if not, then from the faulty training it will grow bent, and stay awry, and there will be no hope of changing it.[51]

This training is so important that the Bahá'í teachings assert, "Training in morals and good conduct is far more important than book learning."[52] This principle is further elucidated in the following passage:

> A child that is cleanly, agreeable, of good character, well-behaved—even though he be ignorant—is preferable to a child that is rude, unwashed, ill-natured, and yet becoming deeply versed in all the sciences and arts. The reason for this is that the child who conducts himself well, even though he be ignorant, is of benefit to others, while an ill-natured, ill-behaved child is corrupted and harmful to others, even though he be learned. If, however, the child be trained to be both learned and good, the result is light upon light.[53]

Bahá'í child socialization aims to develop a prosocial orientation in children, who are encouraged to recognize themselves as members of a community that begins with the family and extends to include

---

[50] 'Abdu'l-Bahá, *Selections from the Writings of 'Abdu'l-Bahá* (Wilmette, IL: Bahá'í Publishing Trust, 1997), p. 133.

[51] 'Abdu'l-Bahá, in "Bahá'í Education," in *Compilation of Compilations,* vol. I, p. 287.

[52] 'Abdu'l-Bahá, *Selections*, p. 143.

[53] Ibid.

all of humanity. Prosocial behavior is defined as the psychological mechanism of social action which includes helping, sharing, and caring for others. Bahá'í children are taught appreciation for the principle of unity in diversity and a respect for others regardless of race, class, or nationality; they are encouraged to develop a sense of personal spiritual responsibility to act toward others with compassion as well as justice and equity, and to sacrifice their own material self-interests for others in need. As adults, Bahá'ís are expected to make a commitment to continue internalizing such patterns until they become the foundation of the personality itself. Spiritual development is seen as an infinite process of self-transformation—that is, a continual, conscious refining of one's behavior in the crucible of social interaction. The cultivation of spiritual, altruistic qualities remains the aim and central focus of life for the adult Bahá'í.

Spiritual life is not separated from the realm of social relations but integrated with it. In this way, it becomes the means for authentic change that is positive and aimed at advancing society. The Universal House of Justice explains the distinctive significance of the spiritual nature of humans and its positive influence in history thus:

> The endowments which distinguish the human race from all other forms of life are summed up in what is known as the human spirit; the mind is its essential quality. These endowments have enabled humanity to build civilizations and to prosper materially. But such accomplishments alone have never satisfied the human spirit, whose mysterious nature inclines it towards transcendence, a reaching towards an invisible realm, towards the ultimate reality, that unknowable essence of essences called God.[54]

Promoting the Welfare of Others

Shoghi Effendi explains that the breakdown in the present social conditions of the world is an outcome of the decline of true religion as a social force. He writes,

---

[54] Universal House of Justice, *Promise of World Peace*, p. 5.

The perversion of human nature, the degradation of human conduct, the corruption and dissolution of human institutions, reveal themselves, under such circumstances, in their worst and most revolting aspects. Human character is debased, confidence is shaken, the nerves of discipline are relaxed, the voice of human conscience is stilled, the sense of decency and shame is obscured, conceptions of duty, of solidarity, of reciprocity and loyalty are distorted, and the very feeling of peacefulness, of joy, and of hope is gradually extinguished.[55]

If human beings are responsible for the current degenerative condition facing society, they are, likewise, in a position to do something about it. Bahá'u'lláh describes the role of religion as a social force with the capacity to promote the good of society but also warns about its capacity to harm. He states,

Religion is the greatest of all means for the establishment of order in the world and for the peaceful contentment of all that dwell therein.... The weakening of the pillars of religion hath strengthened the hands of the ignorant and made them bold and arrogant.... Religion is a radiant light and an impregnable stronghold for the protection and welfare of the peoples of the world, for the fear of God impelleth man to hold fast to that which is good, and shun all evil. Should the lamp of religion be obscured, chaos and confusion will ensue, and the lights of fairness, of justice, of tranquility and peace cease to shine. Know thou, that they who are truly wise have likened the world unto the human temple. As the body of man needeth a garment to clothe it, so the body of mankind must needs be adorned with the mantle of justice and wisdom. Its robe is the Revelation vouchsafed unto it by God.[56]

Religion, then, not only has the potential for, but also has a direct role in, the advancement of the moral order. Religious teachings can become the source for cohesion and solidarity in social relationships among all the cultures and peoples of the world. The individual can

---

[55] Shoghi Effendi, *World Order of Bahá'u'lláh*, p. 187.
[56] Bahá'u'lláh, ibid., p. 186.

become a positive force whose actions become the cause of the well-being of others. Shoghi Effendi explains,

> Indeed, the chief reason for the evils now rampant in society is a lack of spirituality. The materialistic civilization of our age has so much absorbed the energy and interest of mankind, that people in general no longer feel the necessity of raising themselves above the forces and conditions of their daily material existence. There is not sufficient demand for things that we should call spiritual to differentiate them from the needs and requirements of our physical existence. The universal crisis affecting mankind is, therefore, essentially spiritual in its causes.[57]

The more fundamental moral or spiritual attributes that are at the heart of influencing society and advancing it from one that is purely materialistic to one that strikes a balance between the material and spiritual, are outlined by the Universal House of Justice as follows: "the virtues that befit human dignity are trustworthiness, forbearance, mercy, compassion, and loving-kindness towards all peoples."[58] It is through the application of these virtues in one's daily life and through the work of Bahá'í institutions that real change can come about in human interactions. Such virtues belong to every person, since all are capable of internalizing them. It is through deeds that individuals take responsibility for a moral order.

Reciprocity and Altruism

Social relationships involve "requirements that must be met if groups are to survive and flourish."[59] Philip Selznick believes that these requirements include "leadership, communication, specialization, and symbolic affirmation of group identity."[60] But then there are other requirements that "generate moral obligations," such as "maintaining

---

[57] From a letter written on behalf of Shoghi Effendi to an individual believer, 8 December 1935, in "Youth," in *Compilation of Compilations*, vol. 2, p. 425.

[58] Universal House of Justice, *Promise of World Peace*, p. 25.

[59] Selznick, *Moral Commonwealth*, p. 97.

[60] Ibid.

order, protecting property, and facilitating cooperation."[61] As an example of such obligations, Selznick writes,

> [A] norm of reciprocity ("people should help those who have helped them; people should not injure those who have helped them") is, in one form or another, universally recognized. Such principles are not accidental developments. They are solutions to problems, rediscovered innumerable times as ways of dealing with ever-present demands of organization and solidarity.[62]

Although the norm of reciprocity appears to be universally recognized, its actual practice and implementation are impossible without a system that promotes the fundamentals of individual moral development. Reciprocity can be guaranteed only as a result of individual consciousness, internalization of spiritual values, and a social system that actively promotes and supports such values within its institutions. Only then can a moral order based on reciprocity evolve.

The Bahá'í writings describe the evolution of a moral order in language that places significant responsibility upon the individual in learning to distinguish between what is right and what is wrong. Bahá'u'lláh states, "We have counselled all people, in the most clear and eloquent language, to adorn their characters with trustworthiness and godliness, and with such qualities as are conducive to the elevation of man's station in the world of being."[63]

He asserts, "The betterment of the world can be accomplished through pure and goodly deeds, through commendable and seemly conduct."[64] A moral order, as envisaged in the Bahá'í writings, is possible provided that the means for mutual responsibility and a genuine concern and consideration for others in all social interactions are successfully developed among the members of society.

Reciprocity is a concept that is highly valued in the Bahá'í teachings. It is the one principle that aims to bring about true altruistic

---

[61] Ibid.

[62] Ibid.

[63] Bahá'u'lláh, in "Trustworthiness," in *Compilation of Compilations*, vol. 2, p. 332.

[64] Bahá'u'lláh, cited in Shoghi Effendi, *The Advent of Divine Justice* (Wilmette, IL: Bahá'í Publishing Trust, 1990), pp. 24–25.

intentions in social interactions. It is an integral part of a system of social exchange based on return or giving back. It strives to bring about solidarity, a sense of duty to others. Altruism, the Latin root of which means "other," is defined as unselfish regard for or devotion to the welfare of others.[65] In the social sciences, it is considered to be a highly multifaceted concept.[66] Sociologists such as Auguste Comte, Emile Durkheim, and others have acknowledged the presence of altruism in society. In their book, *The Altruistic Personality: Rescuers of Jews in Nazi Europe*, Samuel and Pearl Oliner point out that "the act [of altruism] needs to be performed entirely for its own sake apart from any considerations of self-satisfaction, pleasure, or utility."[67] Thus, self-interest as an inherent trait of human beings is challenged and the notion "that human behavior can be motivated by self-transcendence" is upheld.[68] Sociologist Helen Fein has developed a theory of "collective altruism," suggesting that altruistic people "help persons outside their borders to whom they owe no conventional obligation" and whom they view as members within their own "universe of obligation."[69] Fein explains that for the altruistic person there is no "Other."[70]

Two types of altruistic behavior are mentioned in the literature: universalistic or inclusive, and specialized or bounded. Lawrence A. Blum concludes, "The more inclusive the altruism, the more worth it has."[71] Selznick defines particularism as *bounded* altruism or "an ethic of commitment to individuals who matter because of the special connections they have, not because of their general characteristics.…

---

[65] *Webster's New Collegiate Dictionary*, 9th ed.

[66] For a more in-depth discussion of the roots of altruism see, Samuel P. Oliner and Pearl M. Oliner, *The Altruistic Personality: Rescuers of Jews in Nazi Germany* (New York: The Free Press, 1988).

[67] Ibid., p. 5.

[68] Ibid., p. 358 n. 5.

[69] Helen Fein, *Genocide: A Sociological Perspective* (London: Sage Publications, 1993), pp. 65–66.

[70] Ibid., p. 65.

[71] Lawrence A. Blum, "Altruism and the Moral Value of Rescue: Resisting Persecution, Racism, and Genocide," in *Embracing the Other: Philosophical, Psychological, and Historical Perspectives on Altruism*, ed. Pearl M. Oliner et al. (New York: New York University Press, 1992), p. 35.

The 'other' to be regarded, for whom self-sacrifice is appropriate, be-
longs to one's own family or community."[72] Universalism, or *inclusive
altruism*, according to Selznick, is found when, "[i]n defining objects
of moral concern, the special interests of persons and groups are set
aside."[73] Selznick explains that with inclusive altruism, "people are
classified according to such objective criteria as age, need, talent, or
achievement, in the light of general policies or purposes, without
considering the special claims of kinship or group affiliation. This is
the morality of fairness, the familiar logic of the 'rule of law.'"[74] He
describes the importance of inclusive altruism, stating,

> [U]niversalism is a natural accompaniment to the formation
> of communities. As opportunities for cooperation are enlarged
> and their benefits perceived, the application of altruism is no
> longer limited to a small band of close relatives. Particularism
> is diluted as the community expands. More and more people
> are recognized, first as fellow-creatures and then as colleagues or
> members of the same in-group. In the modern nation-state the
> particularistic connotations of "citizen," though far from lost,
> are greatly attenuated.[75]

The Bahá'í perspective is clearly more aligned with the inclusive
or universal form of altruism. It correlates with the Bahá'í claim of
the need for acceptance of the unification of all people, the consciousness that humanity has now reached the point where it must
live as one human family because of the challenges and requirements
of the age in which we live. 'Abdu'l-Bahá elaborates on this theme:

> The supreme need of humanity is cooperation and reciprocity.
> The stronger the ties of fellowship and solidarity amongst men,
> the greater will be the power of constructiveness and accomplish-
> ment in all the planes of human activity. Without cooperation
> and reciprocal attitude the individual member of human society
> remains self-centered, uninspired by altruistic purposes, limited

---

[72] Selznick, *Moral Commonwealth*, p. 194.
[73] Ibid.
[74] Ibid.
[75] Ibid., p. 195.

and solitary in development like the animal and plant organisms of the lower kingdoms.[76]

Elsewhere, the Bahá'í writings explicitly delineate altruistic norms, holding in high regard those who "nurture altruistic aims and plans for the well-being of their fellow men."[77] Other teachings reflect the values and attitudes conducive to an altruistic orientation,[78] including a sense of unity with and responsibility towards others beyond one's own social group; a strong family orientation; emphasis on relationship rather than status; generosity; trustworthiness; appreciation of diversity; as well as ethical values of justice and caring.

It is noteworthy that both the ethical principles of justice and of caring—important motivators of altruistic behavior—are emphasized in the Bahá'í writings, where they are not viewed as contradictory or exclusive but as inseparably connected. Even when the ethic of justice is enjoined, it is usually as a practice to be performed out of concern for others. Justice is presented as the practice of equity, often linked with "safeguard[ing] the rights of the downtrodden."[79] The Bahá'í conception of justice means that all have a right to receive care.

Well over half a century before Carol Gilligan called attention to the complementarity of the "masculine" ethic of justice and the "feminine" ethic of caring,[80] 'Abdu'l-Bahá had written, "The Kingdom of God is founded upon equity and justice, and also upon mercy, compassion, and kindness to every living soul. Strive ye then with all your heart to treat compassionately all humankind."[81] Yet, He then qualified this statement, asserting that oppression must be opposed: "Kindness cannot be shown the tyrant, the deceiver, or the thief, because … it maketh them to continue in their perversity as before."[82] Individuals are encouraged to develop their capacities

---

[76] 'Abdu'l-Bahá, *Promulgation of Universal Peace*, p. 338.
[77] 'Abdu'l-Bahá, *Selections*, p. 72.
[78] See Oliner and Oliner, *Altruistic Personality*, n. 66.
[79] Bahá'u'lláh, *Gleanings*, p. 247.
[80] Carol Gilligan, *In a Different Voice: Psychological Theory and Women's Development* (Cambridge, MA: Harvard University Press, 1982).
[81] 'Abdu'l-Bahá, *Selections*, p. 158.
[82] Ibid.

in identifying those who are oppressors, whether they manifest this trait through physical force, dominance, terrorism, dishonesty, seduction, villainy, or evil. 'Abdu'l-Bahá's statement is clear in insisting that we are to withhold goodwill and kindness when faced with the demoralizing behavior of tyrants, deceivers, or thieves, since such foul behavior brings harm upon others and becomes the cause of distrust, oppression, and injustice. These violations of individual rights may not be tolerated under any circumstances within the context of a moral order.

Bahá'í Institutions and the Promotion of Altruism

The Bahá'í teachings recognize that the transformation of individuals into altruistic persons cannot take place outside the social context, which must provide a matrix for that transformation. Research has drawn attention to the importance of group norms in motivating moral behavior, whether directly, as a response to social expectations, or indirectly, as internalized personal norms.[83] The findings of Oliner and Oliner further underscore what they refer to as the normocentric orientation in motivating the altruism of rescuers of Jews during World War II.[84] Oliner and Oliner write: "[A] normocentric reaction is not rooted in direct connection with the victim, but rather in a feeling of obligation to a social reference group with whom the actor identifies and whose explicit and implicit rules he feels obliged to obey."[85]

Such findings imply that not only must altruistic qualities be fostered in individuals, but a social framework must also be provided within which extensivity and altruism are highly valued and represent the norms of the group itself. The creation of such a society is inseparable from the development of individual altruistic personalities, for so long as groups value egocentrism, unfettered individualism, ethnocentrism, status seeking, dominance, and a materialistic

---

[83] See J. Reykowski, "Motivation of Prosocial Behavior," in *Cooperation and Helping Behavior: Theories and Research*, ed. V. J. Derlaga and J. Grizelak (New York: Academic Press, 1982), pp. 355–75.

[84] Oliner and Oliner, *Altruistic Personality*, pp. 199–209.

[85] Ibid., p. 199.

orientation, altruism will remain an exception to the rule, and the altruistic personality will appear as deviant in comparison to the rest of the group. In Bahá'í society this situation is reversed: altruism is not an aberrant behavior contrary to convention, because the normative expectations (which individuals are ultimately expected to internalize) are altruistic.

Where Bahá'í socialization and moral education are aimed at developing the spiritual side of the person, the Bahá'í administrative order (or Bahá'í institutions) seeks to advance spiritual values, principles and laws through formal means. Bahá'í institutions are viewed as an instrument through which the spirit of the teachings of Bahá'u'lláh is realized collectively. In sociological terms, these institutions constitute a rational system of moral agency. That is, as institutions they embody values beyond mere efficiency or technical excellence. Their aim is the creation of a new world civilization grounded in spiritual principles relevant to the needs of this age.

Bahá'u'lláh conceived the formation of Bahá'í institutions, and their functions and responsibilities are expounded upon in the writings of 'Abdu'l-Bahá and Shoghi Effendi. These governing bodies promote the progress and development of the community through the application of spiritual principles and laws. Among their responsibilities are educational programs for children and adults, community devotional meetings, application and observance of Bahá'í laws and principles relevant to the rank and file of members, and the overall spiritual protection and well-being of the community as it advances towards the implementation of the goals of the Bahá'í religion. The goals are arrived at and outlined through a consultative (inclusive) system where the Universal House of Justice, being at the highest level of Bahá'í institutions, communicates its vision and plan to each national institution, referred to as the National Spiritual Assembly, and in turn, to the regional and local institutions, thus coordinating the work of the Bahá'í community at the global level.

Thus, in the Bahá'í view, it is through the individual practice as well as the institutionalization of the principle of unity in diversity that human society can evolve to an unprecedented level of cohesion and cooperation, and transcend the limitations implicit in the current state of separation and competitiveness. While the Bahá'í conception of unity in diversity should not be viewed as merely a version of liberal pluralism, the safeguarding and encouraging of diverse elements within the Bahá'í community is a major institutional principle. It is embedded within Bahá'í institutions through practices that, because they apply at all levels of administrative and community functioning—local, national, and international—require the participation and support of the entire Bahá'í community. Under liberal pluralism diverse groups lobby the power structure in order to ensure that their interests are represented, while in the Bahá'í community every individual, regardless of class, culture, gender, race, or nationality, is responsible for upholding and applying the spiritual principles and laws laid down by Bahá'u'lláh, which form the structure of a social order. In the Bahá'í context, there is only one community, which is united around the general teachings of Bahá'u'lláh. Through the application of these principles and laws the betterment of all members is realized and not simply a particular group or segment of society which aims to promote its own particularistic agenda.

Most prominent of these practices is consultation, a group decision-making process whose goal is to reach solutions to problems by consensus. Bahá'í consultation encourages the open and frank expression of diverse views on the topic under discussion, in an atmosphere of love and respect that also allows the "clash of differing opinions" that can strike the "shining spark of truth."[86] Each member of the consultative group has an equal right of expression, and no blocs or factions—or any subdivisions of the group—are permitted. Inseparable from the Bahá'í consultative process is the development of sensitivity and respect for the different voices whose expression of opinion may not fit into conventional or dominant cultural modes of communication. Since the group attempts to work towards consensus on an issue, voting only as a last resort, the process does not necessarily require reduction to duality: alternatives need not be narrowed down to the two poles "for" and "against." Instead, the consultative process itself, drawing on the interactive contributions of all its diverse members, is looked to as the creative source of new solutions.

---

[86] 'Abdu'l-Bahá, quoted in Shoghi Effendi, *Bahá'í Administration*, p. 21.

Consultation is regarded both as a method for generative decision making and conflict resolution and as an instrument for reinforcing the unity of a diverse group. It is the method by which the Bahá'í administrative institutions conduct the affairs of the Bahá'í community, but Bahá'ís are also encouraged to use consultation in all aspects of their lives, whether in the family, neighborhood, or workplace.

Another way in which Bahá'í administrative institutions are structured to implement unity in diversity involves practices intended to ensure the participation of minority ethnic populations. (The definition of what constitutes a "minority" is left to the discretion of the National Spiritual Assembly of each country.) "To discriminate against any race, on the ground of its being socially backward, politically immature, and numerically in a minority" is considered to be "a flagrant violation of the spirit" of the Bahá'í teachings.[87] In principle, protecting the "just interests of any minority element within the Bahá'í community" and ensuring that all have the opportunity to contribute their perspectives to the collaborative efforts of the group are considered so important that representatives of minority populations "are not only enabled to enjoy equal rights and privileges, but they are even favored and accorded priority."[88] Bahá'í communities are instructed that it is their duty to ensure that "Bahá'í representative institutions, be they Assemblies, conventions, conferences, or committees, may have represented on them as many of these divers elements, racial or otherwise, as possible."[89]

One way in which this principle is practiced is the minority tie rule of Bahá'í elections. In the course of elections for Bahá'í administrative institutional membership—elections that are conducted without nominations or campaigning and are decided by plurality vote—if voting results in a tie between persons, one of whom represents a minority, "priority should unhesitatingly be accorded the party representing the minority, and this for no other reason except to stimulate and encourage it, and afford it an opportunity to further the interests of the community."[90] In addition to its direct effect in

---

[87] Shoghi Effendi, *Advent of Divine Justice*, p. 29.

[88] Universal House of Justice, *Messages from the Universal House of Justice, 1968–1973* (Wilmette, IL: Bahá'í Publishing Trust, 1976), p. 49.

[89] Shoghi Effendi, *Advent of Divine Justice*, p. 36.

[90] Ibid.

increasing minority representation in Bahá'í administrative institutions, the practice of this rule heightens the sensitivity of the group to its minority membership and reaffirms the group commitment to valuing and encouraging minority participation. For the individual Bahá'í, conceding a tie vote to the minority representative becomes a concrete opportunity to practice sacrifice of self-interest for the other, within a context of social approval.

Whether applied in community administration, in the family, in education, or in the economy, the Bahá'í principles and practices are viewed as catalysts whose application will ultimately bring about social transformation leading to the development of an altruistic global society. Such a society, in the Bahá'í context, begins with the individual striving daily toward personal transformation—the deliberate internalization of spiritual teachings incorporating altruistic, extensive values as personal norms. The Bahá'í teachings strive to imbue individuals with an inclusive orientation transcending—though not suppressing—other group loyalties and valuing the well-being of the entire planet and all its inhabitants. Throughout the Bahá'í writings, the vision imparted to the individual is that of a peaceful, just, and caring civilization whose foundation rests on the cornerstone of the unity of all human beings, a unity that is to be consolidated and protected by institutions that reflect and promote the principles of unity, equality, and altruistic service as normative expectations.

Conclusion

As a community whose membership includes individuals from virtually every race, class, religion, ethnicity, and nationality, Bahá'ís are laboring hard to bring about a global community based on constructive, altruistic social relationships. They believe that it is their duty to strive towards the establishment of a moral order in which the pernicious aspects of human nature are overcome by the positive, spiritual tendencies inherent in every individual. From the Bahá'í perspective, real change towards a cooperative, progressive global community requires that the spiritual framework of society become strengthened. Nothing, Bahá'ís believe, short of a legitimate commitment to the fortification of the spiritual nature of humans can hope to bring true and lasting happiness to human existence. Janet and Peter Khan, in their book, *Advancement of Women: A Bahá'í Perspective*, explain,

> To a Bahá'í, the ideal spiritual life does not conform to the traditional model of an individual engaged in solitary spiritual discipline, remote from interaction with other people and removed from the transactions of social life. Rather the Bahá'í teachings direct attention to the interactive relationship between individual and social development, calling for a holistic approach in which the actions of the individual and of the social organism mutually reinforce each other and give rise to evolutionary change.[91]

The Bahá'ís envision a world commonwealth in which, as described by Shoghi Effendi, "the consciousness of world citizenship, the founding of a world civilization and culture … continue indefinitely to progress and develop."[92] In that civilization, as a result of the "practical consequence of the spiritualization of the world and the fusion of all its races, creeds, classes and nations,"[93] peace will be established.

---

[91] Janet A. Khan and Peter J. Khan, *Advancement of Women: A Bahá'í Perspective* (Wilmette, IL: Bahá'í Publishing Trust, 1998), p. 7.

[92] Shoghi Effendi, *World Order of Bahá'u'lláh*, p. 163.

[93] Ibid., p. 162.

Facing the Global HIV/AIDS Epidemic
A BAHÁ'Í PERSPECTIVE

*Dawn K. Smith, MD, MS, MPH, examines
a faith-based approach to the social and
public health consequences of HIV/AIDS.*

Although written decades before the recognition of HIV and AIDS, the words of Shoghi Effendi can aptly be used to describe the effects of this epidemic on the world we live in at the beginning of the twenty-first century:

> A yawning gulf threatens to involve in one common disaster both the satisfied and dissatisfied nations, democracies and dictatorships, capitalists and wage-earners, Europeans and Asiatics, Jew and Gentile, white and colored.… Sore-tried and disillusioned, humanity has no doubt lost its orientation and would seem to have lost as well its faith and hope. It is hovering, unshepherded and visionless, on the brink of disaster.[1]

It is unusual to discuss what perspective religion has on a specific disease. We do not ask for the Buddhist perspective on measles, the Catholic view on malaria, or the Islamic view on tuberculosis. All of these are major causes of illness and premature death in the world. The still-expanding HIV/AIDS epidemic is different from these other infectious diseases in that it is driven by, and magnifies the negative

---

[1] Shoghi Effendi. *The World Order of Bahá'u'lláh: Selected Letters*, 2nd rev. ed. (Wilmette, IL: Bahá'í Publishing Trust, 1993), p. 190.

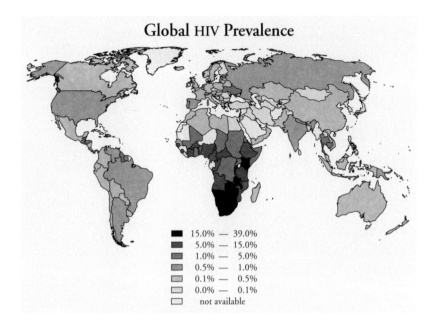

effects of, the social and institutional problems of civilization to an extent never before seen. It is this catalytic nature that gives impetus to the frequent call for the world's religions to define their "position" on HIV/AIDS.

The Global HIV Epidemic

Religion has always been concerned with humanitarian support for the ill, and the intensity of this global pandemic demands an unprecedented level of action in response to this traditional concern. In the 22 years since the first reports were published about a new and fatal illness named acquired immunodeficiency syndrome (AIDS), then with cause unknown, and the 20 years since its cause—the human immunodeficiency virus (HIV)—was discovered, this epidemic has spread steadily and tragically throughout the world. [2] At the end of 2002, the Joint United Nations Program on HIV/AIDS (UNAIDS)

---

[2] For more information about the initial discovery of AIDS, see Centers for Disease Control, "Pneumocystis pneumonia—Los Angeles," *Morbidity and Mortality Weekly Reports* 30 (1981): 250–52. For more on the initial reports of HIV, see F. Barre-Sinoussi, J.C. Chermann, F. Rey et al., "Isolation (cont'd)

Lifetime risk of AIDS death for 15-year-old boys, assuming unchanged or halved risk of becoming infected with HIV in selected countries

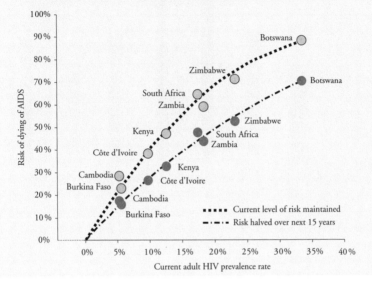

and the World Health Organization (WHO) reported that 42 million people were living with HIV infection, 5 million having been newly infected; 3.1 million died in 2002 alone.[3]

Sub-Saharan Africa—especially southern Africa—has suffered the heaviest impact of any region of the world, accounting for 70 percent of all new infections and 77 percent of deaths worldwide. But rapid growth of the epidemic is now also occurring in the two most populous countries of the world. In India there were estimated to be 4 million people infected at the end of 2002, more than in any other country besides South Africa. In China, home to one-fifth of the world's people, at least one million are living with HIV infection, and the number of infections is increasing 30 percent per year.

---

of a T-lymphotropic retrovirus from a patient at risk for acquired immune deficiency syndrome (AIDS)," *Science* 220, no. 4599 (1983): 868–71.

[3] UNAIDS, WHO, *AIDS Epidemic Update: December 2002*, available at http://www.unaids.org/html/pub/publications/irc-pub06/epi03_00_en_html.htm.

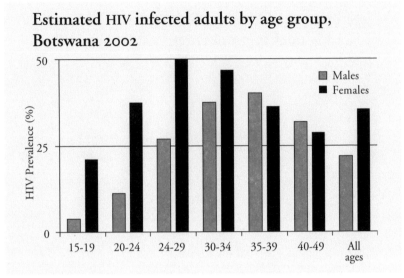

Estimated HIV infected adults by age group, Botswana 2002

Botswana is the most heavily infected population in the world and exemplifies the human devastation that this epidemic is capable of causing. In 2002, more than one-third (35.4 percent) of the population 15–49 years of age was already infected with HIV, with the highest prevalence among older adolescents and young adults.[4]

This high rate of infection in its young population and the resulting premature deaths have resulted in negative population growth (i.e., more deaths than births) in a country with more than 40 years of uninterrupted peace and a stable, representative government that has used the nation's mineral and agricultural resources to achieve exemplary gains in social and economic development for its people. Life expectancy at birth (the age to which an average person born in a year could expect to survive), which had risen steadily over the last 50 years and would have been 70 without the HIV epidemic, has now fallen to 39 and is expected to reach 27 by the end of this decade.[5]

---

[4] Botswana National AIDS Coordinating Agency, "*Botswana 2002: Second Generation HIV/AIDS Surveillance: A Technical Report,*" November 2002.

[5] USAID, "Life Expectancy Will Drop Worldwide Due to AIDS," July 2002, available at http://www.usaid.gov/press/releases/2002/pr020708.html.

Although the burden of illness and death being caused by this epidemic is deeply disturbing, its consequences are not limited to these health outcomes. Economic productivity declines as the impact on human resources increases. For example, fewer school teachers, nurses, and administrators are available to provide public services; social infrastructure is both increasingly strained and shrinking; poverty increases; food generation decreases; and families are disrupted as young adults sicken and die, leaving behind dependent children and elders. We are truly hovering on the brink of an unprecedented disaster.

Components of a Response by Bahá'ís

Bahá'ís are instructed not to live in monastic isolation from the rest of the world and its problems.[6] The Bahá'í community has been swept into this global problem and, like the rest of the world, is searching to find ways to contribute more aggressively and effectively to the struggle against this evolving holocaust. As a letter written on behalf of Shoghi Effendi in 1932 expressed it, "When such a crisis sweeps over the world no person should hope to remain intact. We belong to an organic unit and when one part of the organism suffers all the rest of the body will feel its consequence."[7]

ACQUIRING KNOWLEDGE

The ability to "know" is one of the most important blessings given to mankind. Ignorance is one of the key elements fueling the HIV epidemic and the too-often cruel or inappropriate responses to it. The Bahá'í writings state,

> God has conferred upon and added to man a distinctive power—the faculty of intellectual investigation into the secrets of creation, the acquisition of higher knowledge—the greatest virtue

---

[6] Shoghi Effendi, *God Passes By* (Wilmette, IL: Bahá'í Publishing Trust, 1995), p. 214.

[7] From a letter written on behalf of Shoghi Effendi to a Bahá'í family, 14 April 1932, in *Lights of Guidance: A Bahá'í Reference File,* compiled by Helen Hornby, 3rd rev. ed. (New Delhi: Bahá'í Publishing Trust, 1994), no. 446, p. 133.

of which is scientific enlightenment. This endowment is the most praiseworthy power of man, for through its employment and exercise, the betterment of the human race is accomplished.[8]

Scientific investigation has been at the core of the global response to the HIV epidemic since its recognition. Medical epidemiology was used to define AIDS; social sciences to elucidate the social networks in which the condition occurred and the pathways by which it spread initially in the United States; and laboratory sciences to isolate its cause and develop treatments. However, the fear and stigma that accompanied the first reports of a new, infectious, fatal illness have persisted in many quarters despite all we have learned. Misinformation and ignorance of the facts underlie many of the negative attitudes and behaviors that are contributing to an inadequate response to the epidemic.

For example, fear of casual contagion causes people in many settings to discriminate against those with HIV infection, denying them access to schooling, jobs, housing, or the care and support of family and former friends. But science has demonstrated clearly that HIV is not casually transmitted.

The virus is very fragile and requires very specific conditions to be able to pass from one person to another.

Direct blood-to-blood transfer is highly efficient and resulted in many early infections among hemophiliacs and transfusion recipients who received direct injection of blood products from infected persons. Now that we have good ways to test donated blood for infectious diseases, this form of spreading HIV is increasingly uncommon. However, direct blood transfer still results in infections among injection-drug users and in situations where a shortage of supplies or poor training leads to reuse of medical injection equipment (e.g., needles) for several patients.

Blood exposure is also the cause of HIV transmission from an infected mother to her child during pregnancy and/or birth. We can now also reduce the frequency of this by treating pregnant

---

[8] 'Abdu'l-Bahá, *The Promulgation of Universal Peace: Talks Delivered by 'Abdu'l-Bahá during His Visit to the United States and Canada in 1912*, rev. ed. (Wilmette, IL: Bahá'í Publishing Trust, 1995), p. 31.

women and infants over a few months with anti-HIV (antiretroviral) medications.

Genital tract secretions and breast milk can also contain relatively high levels of HIV and lead to sexual transmission of HIV and infection of infants through breastfeeding.

However, tears, sweat, saliva, and other body fluids to which we may be exposed casually (by touch, coughing, or sneezing, for example) do not carry HIV. HIV cannot penetrate intact skin. So there is no justification for the physical and social isolation of people with HIV infection. Simply learning how HIV is transmitted (passed between people), and how it is not, frees us to assist people who are infected with HIV and those close to them without fears for our own health.

In one community in the US, a believer went to his religious leaders to tell them about his HIV infection and get their advice about how to tell the others in his community. It was decided that a community meeting would be held at a member's home. When people arrived, they found that the hostess, an elderly woman, had placed chairs outside in the driveway so that the HIV-positive person wouldn't have to come into her home. On the one hand, this demonstrated her unrealistic fear of HIV and set a poor tone for the meeting. On the other hand, despite her fear, she was the one willing to host the meeting.

Exercise of our ability to "know" should not be limited, however, to knowledge about transmission. Bahá'ís have an obligation to learn about the broader issues surrounding the HIV epidemic, its causes, its effects, and actions that can retard its spread and mitigate its effects:

> The present condition of the world—its economic instability, social dissensions, political dissatisfaction, and international distrust—should awaken the youth from their slumber and make them enquire what the future is going to bring. It is surely they who will suffer most if some calamity sweep over the world. They should therefore open their eyes to the existing conditions, study the evil forces that are at play, and then with a concerted effort arise and bring about the necessary reforms—reforms that

shall contain within their scope the spiritual as well as social and political phases of human life.[9]

If the Bahá'ís want to be really effective in teaching the Cause they need to be much better informed and able to discuss intelligently, intellectually, the present condition of the world and its problems.[10]

Too often members and representatives of the world's religions have used the HIV/AIDS epidemic to promote discord, insisting that it is solely a problem of the irreligious or that this illness is a punishment from God, meted out to "sinners" or the "unfaithful." This attitude has been used either to ignore the presence of HIV infection in religious communities or to isolate and accuse members who are infected. Along with the fear of casual infection, this abuse of religion leads to stigma and discrimination. In contrast to this negative stance, 'Abdu'l-Bahá emphasized the role of religion in promoting unity and in working in harmony with science. He said,

> [R]eligion must be the cause of unity, harmony, and agreement among mankind. If it is the cause of discord and hostility, if it leads to separation and creates conflict, the absence of religion would be preferable in the world.
>
> Furthermore, He [Bahá'u'lláh] proclaims that religion must be in harmony with science and reason. If it does not conform to science and reconcile with reason, it is superstition.[11]

HIV-related stigma and discrimination are not only unjust and unkind at the individual level, but they are themselves a contributor to new infections. They deter people from seeking or using a variety of services that can reduce the risk of further HIV transmission. For example, particularly in the developing world, many women are

---

[9] From a letter written on behalf of Shoghi Effendi to an individual believer, 13 March 1932, in *Lights of Guidance*, no. 2125, p. 628.

[10] From a letter written on behalf of Shoghi Effendi to an individual believer, 5 July 1949, in "Guidelines for Teaching," in *Compilation of Compilations*, vol. 2 (Ingleside, NSW: Bahá'í Publications Australia, 1991), p. 314.

[11] 'Abdu'l-Bahá, *Promulgation of Universal Peace*, pp. 454–55.

infected through the risk behaviors of their husbands. But because they fear the reaction of their husbands and families even to being tested for HIV, many refuse testing during pregnancy or, if tested and found positive, refuse antiretroviral medicines that would protect their infants from getting infected and would prolong their own lives.

DEALING WITH BEHAVIORS
THAT RISK HIV INFECTION

The HIV epidemic presents a special challenge to the Bahá'í Faith and other major religions because it is most often spread by sexual behaviors proscribed in sacred texts.[12] Bahá'u'lláh counseled His followers: "Ye are forbidden to commit adultery, sodomy, and lechery. Avoid them, O concourse of the faithful."[13]

Worldwide, approximately 75 percent of HIV infections are sexually acquired, another 10 percent by injection-drug use, and 10 percent from infected mothers to their children during pregnancy, birth, and breastfeeding. The remaining 5 percent occur through transfusion or contaminated medical injections.

While a large majority of HIV is transmitted by heterosexual sex, because AIDS was first recognized among homosexual men in the US and Europe, it is still widely perceived as a "gay plague." And because the teachings of many religions about homosexual behavior are controversial, particularly in the HIV/AIDS community, it is worth spending a moment to discuss this aspect of the Bahá'í teachings.

Sex in the Faith is not a sin-laden concept. We are told that sexual feelings are a divine gift that provides a forceful means to deepen and express love, but only when acted on in a proper context. Sexual intercourse is only permitted between a man and woman who are married to each other. Individual believers are responsible for controlling their sexual desires whenever they occur outside of that context. A variety of behaviors is recognized to occur in human societies but is to be resisted and controlled as part of an individual's spiritual,

[12] See Geoffrey Parrinder, *Sexual Morality in the World's Religions* (Oxford: Oneworld Publications, 1980).
[13] Bahá'u'lláh, in "A Chaste and Holy Life," in *Compilation of Compilations*, vol. 1, p. 57.

moral, and social responsibilities. These include premarital sex, homosexual sex, adultery, and sex with children. In the same way that the Bible commands that a man should not "covet" another's wife, the Bahá'í teachings urge mastery not only of behaviors, but also of inappropriate impulses and desires that precede them. As stated in a letter written on behalf of Shoghi Effendi,

> The world today is submerged, amongst other things, in an over-exaggeration of the importance of physical love, and a dearth of spiritual values. In as far as possible the believers should try to realize this…. [T]hey should seek to establish bonds of comradeship and love which are eternal and founded on the spiritual life of man, not on his physical life. This is one of the many fields in which it is incumbent on the Bahá'ís to set the example and lead the way to a true human standard of life, when the soul of man is exalted and his body but the tool for his enlightened spirit.[14]

On the other hand, we are enjoined from asceticism or a "bigoted Puritanism."[15] In this sense, the Bahá'í teachings strike a difficult balance between recognizing that both positive and negative sexual impulses exist, setting clear boundaries for the healthy enjoyment of sex, and reminding us that sexuality is only one of several important opportunities during our lifetime for self-mastery and spiritual development.

Within this framework of understanding sexuality in general, the teachings prohibiting homosexual behaviors both recognize that there may be medical or inborn factors leading to homosexual desire and emphasize the need to struggle against unhealthy desires and resist engaging in prohibited behavior:

> Man's physical existence on this earth is a period during which the moral exercise of his free will is tried and tested in order to prepare his soul for the other worlds of God, and we must welcome affliction and tribulations as opportunities for improvement in our

[14] From a letter written on behalf of Shoghi Effendi to an individual believer, 28 September 1941, in *Messages from the Universal House of Justice, 1963–1986* (Wilmette, IL: Bahá'í Publishing Trust, 1996), p. 233–34.

[15] Shoghi Effendi, *The Advent of Divine Justice* (Wilmette, IL: Bahá'í Publishing Trust, 1990), p. 33.

eternal selves. The House of Justice points out that homosexuals are not the only segment of human society laboring at this daily task—every human being is beset by such inner promptings as pride, greed, selfishness, lustful heterosexual or homosexual desires, to name a few which must be overcome, and overcome them we must if we are to fulfill the purpose of our human existence.[16]

This approach is extremely helpful in considering the full range of sexual behaviors that are resulting in widespread HIV transmission. If sex occurred only between married partners, there would be no epidemic. And to the extent that religion or other factors help people to move towards that goal, the epidemic will slow. Unfortunately, the prevailing thought is that sexual fidelity and exclusivity, even if desirable, is not attainable. Therefore, people argue, we have to rely on condoms and a future vaccine to control the epidemic and not waste time on, for example, abstinence education. Despite 20 years of aggressive condom promotion, we still have a rapidly growing epidemic. And in the several countries where HIV prevalence has gone down (e.g., Uganda) or remained low (e.g., Senegal), rates of premarital sex and the number of sexual partnerships reported by individuals are decreasing or low. Many of the same people now argue that we have to address gender inequity and poverty to control the HIV/AIDS epidemic—problems that are older, more generalized, and more entrenched than those brought by the "sexual liberation" of the past 100 years.

This resistance to believing that people can, with help, meet a high standard of behavior, particularly one that is in their own best interest, is pervasive and extends also to the question of substance abuse and its role in HIV transmission. Rather than push for the provision of treatment on demand for all those addicted to injected drugs or disinhibiting drugs like cocaine and alcohol, the HIV/AIDS prevention field is spending most of its valuable social capital on "safer injection" programs like needle exchange and medically supervised injection programs. While these may reduce the risk of transmitting HIV and hepatitis, they do not address the primary

---

[16] From a letter written on behalf of the Universal House of Justice to an individual believer, 16 July 1980, in *Lights of Guidance*, no. 1228, p. 367.

social, emotional, and economic costs of the addictions, either to individuals or the community. Drug use and drinking alcoholic beverages are prohibited in the Bahá'í Faith, but we are also required to support community members struggling with these problems. The Bahá'í writings state,

> It is the nature of man to find enjoyment in that which is gratifying to his senses; if he pursue this path he subverts his individuality to such a degree that the poison of darkness which was the means of death becomes the means of his existence and his nature becomes so degraded and his individuality so deflected that his one purpose in life will be to obtain the death-dealing drug.[17]

One long-term, preventative approach—based on a belief that people can live up to these personal behavior challenges—is being tried by several Bahá'í nongovernmental organizations. The Varqa Foundation, in collaboration with Health for Humanity,[18] has implemented a values-based youth education program in Guyana, "Youth Can Move the World,"[19] which trains youth facilitators for a national program to address sexuality, HIV/AIDS, and other issues within a holistic, values-based curriculum. Similarly, Bahá'ís in Buryatia, in the Russian Federation, have created a "Youth Center for Social Initiatives" to provide HIV/AIDS prevention education, training in moral leadership, and alcohol/drug-free social activities to teens. In addition, they are working with the Ministry of Education to develop a prevention curriculum for the schools, targeting 12- to 15-year-olds.

CARING FOR ONE ANOTHER

While the Bahá'í standard for personal behavior that might risk HIV transmission is very high, so also is the standard for personal behavior towards one another. We are instructed to call ourselves to

---

[17] 'Abdu'l-Bahá, *'Abdu'l-Bahá on Divine Philosophy* (Boston: The Tudor Press, 1918), p. 133.

[18] http://www.healthforhumanity.org/.

[19] http://www.sdnp.org.gy/ycmw/YCMTW/index.html.

account each day but admonished, as individuals, not to judge the behavior of each other:

> Each of us is responsible for one life only, and that is our own. Each of us is immeasurably far from being "perfect as our heavenly Father is perfect" and the task of perfecting our own life and character is one that requires all our attention, our will power and energy. If we allow our attention and energy to be taken up in efforts to keep others right and remedy their faults, we are wasting precious time.[20]

We are emphatically and repeatedly admonished against faultfinding or backbiting about others.[21] And we are specifically instructed that "to regard homosexuals with prejudice or disdain would be entirely against the spirit of the Bahá'í teachings."[22] We are encouraged to be patient with "our own poor selves" and urged to "persevere and add up [our] accomplishments, rather than to dwell on the dark side of things."[23] And if we are the object of negative attitudes or behaviors, we are to respond as we would have wished to be treated:

> In every instance let the friends be considerate and infinitely kind. Let them never be defeated by the malice of the people, by their aggression and their hate, no matter how intense. If others hurl their darts against you, offer them milk and honey in return; if they poison your lives, sweeten their souls; if they injure you, teach them how to be comforted; if they inflict a wound upon you, be a balm to their sores; if they sting you, hold to their lips a refreshing cup.[24]

---

[20] From a letter written on behalf of the Guardian to an individual believer 12 May 1925, in *Lights of Guidance*, no. 318, p. 92.

[21] Ibid.

[22] From a letter written on behalf of the Universal House of Justice to the National Spiritual Assembly of the United States, 11 September 1995.

[23] Shoghi Effendi, *Unfolding Destiny: The Messages from the Guardian of the Bahá'í Faith to the Bahá'í Community of the British Isles* (London: Bahá'í Publishing Trust, 1981), p. 456.

[24] 'Abdu'l-Bahá, *Selections from the Writings of 'Abdu'l-Bahá* (Wilmette, IL: Bahá'í Publishing Trust, 1997), p. 24.

Together these teachings reinforce the principle that each member of the global family has an important role to play in helping us to grow and develop, being supportive and nonjudgmental of others, and being forgiving of the errors and occasional harshness of others. These attitudes and actions underlie a compassionate response to the HIV/AIDS epidemic as well as to other difficult situations encountered in our lives.

One story about 'Abdu'l-Bahá, who nearly died of tuberculosis (consumption) as a youth, is exemplary of how such teachings can be applied in our everyday lives:

> In the very early days of the knowledge of the Cause of Bahá'u'lláh in America, Mrs. [Lua] Getsinger was in 'Akká, having made the pilgrimage to the prison city to see the Master. She was with Him one day when He said to her that He was too busy today to call upon a friend of His who was very ill and poor and He wished her to go in His place. "Take him food and care for him as I have been doing," He concluded. He told her where this man was to be found and she went gladly, proud that 'Abdu'l-Bahá should trust her with this mission.
>
> She returned quickly. "Master," she exclaimed, "surely you cannot realize to what a terrible place you sent me. I almost fainted from the awful stench, the filthy rooms, the degrading condition of that man and his house. I fled, lest I contract some horrible disease!"
>
> Sadly and sternly 'Abdu'l-Bahá regarded her. "Dost thou desire to serve God," He said, "serve thy fellow man, for in him dost thou see the image and likeness of God." He told her to go back to this man's house. If it is filthy she should clean it; if this brother of yours is dirty, bathe him; if he is hungry, feed him. Do not return until this is done. Many times had He done this for him and cannot she serve him once?[25]

The teachings at the heart of the Bahá'í Faith are not just abstract principles. Each provides us with an opportunity to demonstrate by our actions the firmness of our belief—and our commitment

---

[25] H.M. Balyuzi, *'Abdu'l-Bahá: The Centre of the Covenant* (Oxford: George Ronald, 1987), p. 196.

to develop the knowledge, skill, and fortitude to live our lives accordingly.

Since its establishment in 1992, the Bahá'í Institute on AIDS, Sexuality, and Addictions (IASA)—which in 1997 became the Bahá'í Network on AIDS, Sexuality, Addictions, and Abuse (BNASAA)—has been working to assist individuals and institutions within the Bahá'í Faith in North America to deal with these issues. Through regional and national workshops, a periodic newsletter, and consultation with the administrative bodies of the Faith, BNASAA stimulates reflection and the exchange of information. It provides a confidential, safe environment where people struggling with these issues, together with their families and friends, can receive love and support.

The Bahá'í Health Agency of South Africa, which has recently been recognized as a nongovernmental AIDS organization, focuses on working within the Bahá'í community to provide resources, consultation, and support for local administrative bodies working with HIV-infected community members. In addition, it advocates abstinence-based prevention activities among youth both within the Bahá'í community and in the general community.

Children on the Brink

If not a single new case of HIV infection occurred from now on, there would still be a devastating impact on the basic structures of civilization because of the amount of illness and death facing us. To carry forward an ever-advancing civilization, it is necessary that each new generation be able to build on the knowledge, experience, and resources of the previous one. All too often, this will not be the case for children in areas heavily impacted by HIV/AIDS.

In 2001, there were already 13.4 million children who had lost one or both parents to HIV infection, 11 million of them in Sub-Saharan Africa. That is the equivalent of one-third of all the school-aged children in the US.[26] By the end of this decade, in 2010, the number will have doubled to 25.3 million worldwide, including 20.1 million

[26] Based on 2003 information from the US Census Bureau.

in Sub-Saharan Africa.[27] Stephen Lewis, the UN Special Envoy for HIV/AIDS in Africa, has called these numbers "hallucinatory," but numbers alone do not give the real picture of the lives of these children.

As parents become ill, if they are employed they have to leave work; if they are farmers or otherwise self-employed they do not have the strength to work. Household income falls while costs go up for medicine, for hospital stays, and eventually for funerals. Children are taken out of school, either to care for ill adults and young children in the household, to work and bring in household income, or because school, book, and uniform fees can no longer be paid. In some cases, schools have closed for lack of teachers because so many of them have died of HIV/AIDS. Girls are taken out of school first, and when things become desperate, they are easy prey for informal sex work. When parents die, children may be taken in by grandparents or aunts and uncles, but this often overtaxes the economic and emotional resources of their new caretakers. And in places where prevalence is high, it is not uncommon to find elderly grandparents trying to care for the young families of several of their adult children who have died of HIV/AIDS. If children are not taken in, because of the stigma associated with HIV/AIDS, foster homes will usually not be available and they may be left trying to care for each other. This phenomenon of child-headed households, in which the eldest child is sometimes only 10 or 12, is unstable—least of all because there are no adults to provide financial support. As a result, many of these children sooner or later end up homeless—street children begging for food or resorting to theft and prostitution to meet their basic survival needs. And of course, these factors leave them at high risk for becoming HIV-infected themselves at a young age.

What will the world be like when 20 or 30 percent of a nation's children have grown up in such dire circumstances? Without the civilizing influences of a parent's love and guidance, without an education? Having many people they love and who loved them die?

---

[27] USAID, UNICEF, UNAIDS, *Children on the Brink 2002: A Joint Report on Orphan Estimates and Program Strategies,* available at http://www.unicef.org/publications/index_4378.html.

With a lifetime of lessons leading them to believe that they have to take what they need because no one will provide it for them?

To date, we have not yet brought to bear our creativity, our intellectual, economic, and political resources, our outrage or our determination that this cannot be allowed to happen.

Bahá'ís are told that the question of orphans is of the utmost importance, that the greatest consideration must be shown them and they must be taught, trained, and educated to become "true servants of the world of humanity and as bright candles in the assemblage of mankind":[28]

> [The Local Spiritual Assembly] must promote by every means in their power the material as well as the spiritual enlightenment of youth, the means for the education of children, institute, whenever possible, Bahá'í educational institutions, organize and supervise their work and provide the best means for their progress and development.[29]

Acting on this and other such statements in their scriptures, Bahá'í individuals and institutions have established private schools around the world (e.g., in Bolivia, Canada, India, and Swaziland). But while orphanages are a traditional humanitarian activity of Christian, Jewish, and Muslim communities around the world, to date, there is little experience in Bahá'í communities with orphan care. A small orphanage in rural Honduras, the Hogar Tierra Santa Orphanage,[30] now houses and educates more than 120 boys and girls with financial support from Bahá'í communities in North America and Europe. But the scope of the HIV/AIDS orphan crisis will require a myriad of approaches, including orphanages, subsidized foster care and adoption, day care programs, free schooling, counseling and protective services, children's villages, and others. There can be no issue on which we can more easily establish consensus across perceived religious, political, and national boundaries than the urgent need to find a way to help these millions of children.

---

[28] 'Abdu'l-Bahá, *Selections*, p. 138.
[29] From a letter written by Shoghi Effendi to the Bahá'ís of the West, Japan, and Australasia, 12 March 1923, in *Lights of Guidance*, no. 417, p. 123.
[30] http://www.tierrasantasupport.org/.

A Call to Action

At the turn of the last century, 'Abdu'l-Bahá admonished members of the Bahá'í community,

> Be ye loving fathers to the orphan, and a refuge to the helpless, and a treasury for the poor, and a cure for the ailing. Be ye the helpers of every victim of oppression, the patrons of the disadvantaged. Think ye at all times of rendering some service to every member of the human race. Pay ye no heed to aversion and rejection, to disdain, hostility, injustice: act ye in the opposite way. Be ye sincerely kind, not in appearance only. Let each one of God's loved ones center his attention on this: to be the Lord's mercy to man; to be the Lord's grace. Let him do some good to every person whose path he crosseth, and be of some benefit to him.[31]

In 2002, Stephen Lewis, the UN Special Envoy for HIV/AIDS in Africa, addressed an assembly of African religious leaders with these words:

> When AIDS has run its course—if it ever runs its course—it will be seen as an annihilating scourge that dwarfs everything that has gone before.
>
> What it leaves in its wake, in country after country, in every one of the countries you represent, are thousands or tens of thousands or hundreds of thousands or, eventually, even millions of children whose lives are a torment of loneliness, despair, rage, bewilderment and loss.
>
> [W]hen the history of the AIDS pandemic is written, you want it said that every religious leader stood up to be counted; that when the tide was turned, the religious leaders did the turning; that when the children of Africa were at horrendous risk, the religious leaders led the rescue mission. It's what all of us beg you to do; I submit to you that it's what your God, of whatever name, would want you to do.[32]

---

[31] 'Abdu'l-Bahá, *Selections*, p 3.

[32] Stephen Lewis, address to the African Religious Leaders Assembly on Children and HIV/AIDS, Nairobi, Kenya, 10 June 2002, available at   (cont'd)

While religious leaders can play a significant role in the fight against AIDS, it is ultimately the responsibility of individual believers and faith communities as a whole. In the Bahá'í Faith, which has no clergy, each person has a vital role to play. In every home, believers can eradicate stigmatizing misconceptions and attitudes and replace them with knowledge about HIV and behaviors that risk infection, and with compassionate support for people in their community. Parents and teachers can work together to develop and implement age-appropriate education materials, grounded in the Bahá'í teachings and explicit in their intent to help youth develop positive attitudes towards their developing sexuality and skills necessary to manage their natural impulses until they are married. As the epidemic continues to spread globally, an approach limited to "just say no" will leave youth increasingly exposed to risks of acquiring HIV infection themselves. In every city or town, Bahá'ís can work with existing community-based organizations to support HIV prevention and care activities. And those with the skills, interests, and resources can establish new faith-based organizations, whether local or international in scope, to address, in ways that are consistent with the Bahá'í teachings, the needs of people most impacted by this epidemic.

It is not by words but by action that Bahá'ís are called to speak to the world: to further the progress of humanity not only through "lip-service" but by "patient lives of active service." If we neglect this work, 'Abdu'l-Bahá said, we cannot claim to truly be Bahá'ís.[33]

In the words of the Bahá'í International Community, "Since the body of humankind is one and indivisible, each member of the race is born into the world as a trust of the whole."[34] The magnitude of the HIV/AIDS epidemic and its devastating impact require us all to rise and fulfill our moral obligations as citizens in this interconnected world.

---

http://www.stephenlewisfoundation.org/docs/20020610-African-RLA-Nairobi.html.

[33] 'Abdu'l-Bahá, *Paris Talks: Addresses given by 'Abdu'l-Bahá in Paris in 1911–1912* (London: Bahá'í Publishing Trust, 1995), p. 80.

[34] Bahá'í International Community, *The Prosperity of Humankind* (1995).

World Watch

Dr. Ann Boyles looks at various ways in which individuals seek to effect social change in a crisis-ridden world.

A growing number of people all over the world, believing that powerful global forces have ignored the well-being of average citizens in favor of the interests of big businesses, transnational corporations, governmental elites, war machines, ecological destruction, and other evils, are taking to the streets to protest. They see their governments as failing, their livelihoods and ways of life threatened. They see convincing evidence of social injustice. They see the human suffering that results from conflicts around the world. Enraged by their own sense of powerlessness and by their leaders' lack of will or ability to address these issues, people are voting with their feet. There is no doubt about the sincerity of their desire to speak out against at least some of the countless ills that plague humanity.

The main flashpoint for the widespread protests has been "globalization," a phenomenon with two distinctly opposite effects. On the one hand, it has served to integrate peoples and countries through "the enormous reduction of costs of transportation and communication, and the breaking down of artificial barriers to the flows of goods, services, capital, knowledge, and (to a lesser extent) people across borders,"[1]

---

[1] Joseph E. Stiglitz, *Globalization and its Discontents* (New York: W.W. Norton, 2003), p. 9.

according to former World Bank economist Joseph E. Stiglitz, winner of the Nobel Prize in economics. It has also contributed to the rise in cross-border institutions such as organizations of civil society and intergovernmental institutions. On the other hand, globalization's economic aspects have had devastating consequences in some countries, as market deregulations imposed by international institutions such as the International Monetary Fund, the World Bank, and the World Trade Organization have erased "the rules and regulations in many developing countries that are designed to stabilize the flows of volatile money into and out of the country."[2] The "Mach 3 financial capitalism" or "tornado capitalism" that has resulted from these unregulated markets has wreaked havoc on entire societies and reforms are needed to protect people from its worst effects, writes Susan George of the Transnational Institute.[3]

But reforms do not appear to be on the horizon, and the hardship is real. The gap between the rich and the poor has become a chasm: In 1996 the combined income of the poorest 45 percent of the world's population, a total of 2.3 billion people, was equal to the net worth of the world's 358 richest people;[4] by 2003, 54 countries were poorer than they had been 10 years earlier;[5] and more than half of the world's largest 100 economies are now corporations, rather than nation-states.[6]

To counter such trends, governments need to play a strong role in protecting their citizens against the ravages of market liberalization, writes James Gustave Speth, former head of the United Nations Development Program, warning that the link between growth and human development "must be deliberately forged by governments

---

[2] Ibid., p. 10.

[3] Susan George, "The Fast Castes," in *New Perspectives Quarterly* (Winter 1997), pp. 10–13.

[4] These figures are taken from the 1996 annual Human Development Report of the United Nations Development Program (UNDP), cited by James Gustave Speth, in "Global Equality: 358 Billionaires vs. 2.3 Billion People," in *New Perspectives Quarterly* (Fall 1996), p. 33.

[5] United Nations Development Program, 2003 Human Development Report.

[6] Noreena Hertz, *The Silent Takeover: Global Capitalism and the Death of Democracy* (New York: The Free Press, 2001).

and regularly fortified by skillful and intelligent policies."[7] But to have the desired effect, such a shift in pace and emphasis would have to be orchestrated through international agreement, and significantly, Susan George notes, "[n]o unifying religion or moral principle is on hand to provide a slow-down mechanism, or sanity and support" during such a transformation.[8] It appears, then, that changes through established routes will be painfully slow, if they happen at all.

Naomi Klein, one of the most vocal spokespeople for the anti-globalization movement, sees the failure of governments to take an active role in guarding the welfare of their citizens in this scenario as a "betrayal" of "the fundamental need for democracies that are responsive and participatory."[9] Noreena Hertz of the Center for International Business at Cambridge University echoes the senti-ment, writing, "The role of nation states has become to a large extent simply that of providing the public goods and infrastructure that business needs at the lowest costs while protecting the world's free trade system."[10]

It is no wonder, then, whether they are troubled by the hardship resulting from the actions of multinational corporations, worried about the alarming deterioration of the environment, horrified by the worsening plight of the world's poor, frustrated by the inaction of their governments, or angered by their government's participa-tion or nonparticipation in various military interventions around the world, that a growing number of people are searching for ways to make themselves heard—to protect themselves or others hurt by these global processes, to express their solidarity with people living half a world away, to take action, to make a difference.

There is much debate in the wider community about the best way to move forward, however. While some advocate the slow route of pursuing reforms within existing legal or administrative avenues, others favor direct action as a faster, more efficient way to remedy social ills.

---

[7]   Speth, "Global Equality," p. 33.
[8]   Susan George, "Fast Castes," p. 13.
[9]   Naomi Klein, *Fences and Windows: Dispatches from the Front Lines of the Globalization Debate* (Toronto: Vintage Canada, 2002), p. xiv.
[10] Hertz, *Silent Takeover*, p. 8.

Underlying the various paradigms encompassed by this latter approach is a long-standing conviction that attacks on the "other"—whether governments, corporations, or institutions—are the most effective means for accelerating change in society. Michael Karlberg of Western Washington University describes this approach as follows:

> Cultural common sense leads many to believe that the best way to organize every social institution is in the form of a contest. Paradoxically, it also leads many to believe that the best way to reform those institutions is through protest—and other adversarial strategies of social change. Protests, demonstrations, partisan organizing, litigation, strikes, and other oppositional strategies are standard methods for pursuing social change. In more extreme cases, violence and terrorism are also employed.[11]

The anti-globalization movement adheres to this "contest" paradigm, but it introduces some unconventional features. The movement has no central leadership; rather, the protesters support many different causes, which assemble in shifting constellations at large events, and coalitions form and evaporate on an issue-oriented basis. This structure, or lack of it, seems itself to be a product of our fragmented postmodern world, but it also reflects the movement's objective of "radical decentralization" and the building of "community-based decision-making potential—whether through unions, neighborhoods, farms, villages, anarchist collectives, or aboriginal self-government"—which it regards as "essential to countering the might of multinational corporations."[12] The "cells" of this grassroots movement are connected through cyberspace, via the Internet—a techno-version of organic networking methods such as painting messages on walls or passing them by word of mouth.[13]

The global gatherings are not only marches, although direct action is certainly the main purpose; they are also "week-long marathons of intense education on global politics, late-night strategy

---

[11] Michael Karlberg, "The Paradox of Protest in a Culture of Contest," *Peace and Change*, vol. 28, no. 3 (July 2003), p. 339.

[12] Klein, *Fences and Windows*, p. 16.

[13] Ibid., p. 223.

sessions in six-way simultaneous translation, festivals of music and street theater."[14] As for the changes they are seeking, Klein writes, "When protesters shout about the evils of globalization, most are not calling for a return to narrow nationalism but for the borders of globalization to be expanded, for trade to be linked to labor rights, environmental protection and democracy."[15]

The effectiveness of the protesters' efforts to promote knowledge and raise people's consciousness on these important global issues is evident by the growing numbers of participants in the events. The movement's spokespersons are well-informed and articulate, and they have attracted like-minded citizens of all ages. However, some problems have arisen. While its objectives are desirable, and while most participants do not call for a return to nationalism nor instigate violent acts, this "movement of movements," with no central coherence based on principle, does encompass radical elements that embrace violence as a useful tool in their struggle. As the numbers of protesters grow and the rhetoric heats up, host governments and police forces feel besieged, so the potential for deadly force is real. And as for the movement's future development, there is no widespread agreement on the course it will take. While some protesters claim that violence has moved leaders to consider and act on issues such as debt relief, others think that it weakens their credibility and want to move beyond protests; they are looking for a new strategy.

Naomi Klein argues that the activists, although serious in intent, refuse "to engage in classic power struggles" in that "their goal … is not to take power for themselves but to challenge power centralization on principle."[16] She refers to the protests as "the precise and thrilling moment when the rabble of the real world crashed the experts-only club where our collective fate is determined"[17] and claims that "a new culture of vibrant direct democracy is emerging, one that is fuelled and strengthened by direct participation, not dampened and discouraged by passive spectatorship."[18]

---

[14] Ibid., p. xxv.
[15] Ibid., pp. 4–5.
[16] Ibid., p. xxvi.
[17] Ibid., p. xvii.
[18] Ibid., pp. xxvi-xxvii.

This increasing emphasis on direct democracy reflects both widespread disillusionment with established political systems and the conviction that the "self-actualizing" power of the individual is the strongest means of effecting change and bringing about social justice. According to individualist and anarchist social theories, to which the anti-globalization movement bears some relation, the state and society block the power and "natural energies" of individuals through their perpetual efforts to control them. [19]

Whether direct action based on such paradigms can actually bring about meaningful and enduring social change remains unclear, however. Can a movement based on adversarial strategies sustain unity within its own ranks—or engender a society that can meet the needs of all its members? According to Karlberg, such strategies have become "paradoxical and self-limiting":

> If they were viable in the past, they now appear to have reached a point of diminishing returns. Adversarial strategies legitimate the assumptions regarding human nature and social organization that sustain the tripartite system. When social activists engage in partisan political organizing, they legitimate the contest models of governance that keep them at a perpetual disadvantage. Likewise, when social activists engage in litigation, they legitimate the adversarial systems of jurisprudence that keep them at a perpetual disadvantage. Even street protests, demonstrations, and acts of civil disobedience legitimate the underlying assumption that contest and opposition are necessary forms of social interaction.
>
> Granted, social activists do "win" occasional "battles" in these adversarial arenas, but the root causes of their concerns largely remain unaddressed and the larger "wars" arguably are not going well. [20]

Within this wider context, the Bahá'í community, which is also concerned with addressing the ills that beset society, sees itself as making one contribution to the struggle for social transformation—but

---

[19] For a helpful discussion of social theories including individualism and anarchism, see Nicholas Abercrombie, Stephen Hill, and Bryan S. Turner, *Sovereign Individuals of Capitalism* (London: Allen and Unwin, 1986).

[20] Karlberg, "Paradox of Protest," p. 339.

with a distinctive vision and approach based on its sacred scriptures. A basic tenet of Bahá'í belief is that humanity, standing on the threshold of its collective maturity, must develop appropriate new qualities, attitudes, and skills. 'Abdu'l-Bahá writes,

> That which was applicable to human needs during the early history of the race could neither meet nor satisfy the demands of this day and period of newness and consummation. Humanity has emerged from its former degrees of limitation and preliminary training. Man must now become imbued with new virtues and powers, new moralities, new capacities.[21]

Bahá'ís believe that among the ideas that will not serve humanity well in its age of maturity are the conviction that human beings are aggressive and quarrelsome by nature and the concept of "us" versus "them."

Humanity is gradually awakening to its essential oneness, but as yet there is no common understanding of the obligations or nature of that unity. The anti-globalization protesters, for example, see themselves as a community that welcomes individuals from different cultures, backgrounds, and levels of education who are more or less unified in their struggle against the worst effects of globalization; they see the anti-globalization protest gatherings as occasions where true democracy and freedom flourish—as windows to the possibilities of a new, more just world. The globalization boosters also see humanity as one, but as a single, gigantic economic market inhabited by consumers of many different cultures. However, such visions of unity are almost always limited, and ideas of difference and conflict are deeply ingrained in both our individual consciousness and our social structure. As the Bahá'í International Community writes:

> Deceptively simple in popular discourse, the concept that humanity constitutes a single people presents fundamental challenges to the way that most of the institutions of contemporary society carry out their functions. Whether in the form of the adversarial structure of civil government, the advocacy principle informing

---

[21] 'Abdu'l-Bahá, *Foundations of World Unity* (Wilmette, IL: Bahá'í Publishing Trust, 1945), pp. 9.

most of civil law, a glorification of the struggle between classes and other social groups, or the competitive spirit dominating so much of modern life, conflict is accepted as the mainspring of human interaction. It represents yet another expression in social organization of the materialistic interpretation of life that has progressively consolidated itself over the past two centuries.[22]

As "idealistic materialists"[23] play their part in the vast historical process destined to lead humanity to the next stage of its development, struggling against "the countless wrongs afflicting a desperate age,"[24] so, too, the Bahá'ís are playing their part. Their efforts attempt to address what they see as the spiritual root of these problems by promoting the wholehearted adoption of the concept of the oneness of the human race. Again, the Bahá'í International Community writes, "Only through the dawning consciousness that they constitute a single people will the inhabitants of the planet be enabled to turn away from the patterns of conflict that have dominated social organization in the past and begin to learn the ways of collaboration and conciliation."[25]

But if adversarial relationships are taken for granted as the norm of operation in society, how, then, can we move from the current model of "containment," where institutions are seen as controlling and limiting the freedom of individuals, to a model of empowerment? Can societal institutions actually be transformed into channels through which individuals can effectively serve society and thus contribute to its healthy growth rather than feeling that they must oppose those institutions in order to force them to make meaningful change? The Bahá'í community asserts that, indeed, societal institutions can be so changed, but to establish such an order, the world requires an "educator" whose teachings address material, human,

---

[22] Bahá'í International Community, *The Prosperity of Humankind* (1995).

[23] Universal House of Justice, letter to a National Spiritual Assembly, 19 November 1974, in *Messages from the Universal House of Justice 1963–1986* (Wilmette, IL: Bahá'í Publishing Trust, 1996), p. 283.

[24] Universal House of Justice, letter to the believers gathered for the events marking the completion of the projects on Mount Carmel, 24 May 2001. The text of this letter appears in *The Bahá'í World 2001–2002*, pp. 69–73.

[25] Bahá'í International Community, *Prosperity of Humankind*.

and spiritual concerns, and whose authority is universally respected. Such an educator "must teach men … to form a social order in order to establish cooperation and mutual aid in living so that material affairs may be organized and regulated for any circumstances that may occur."[26]

Bahá'ís believe that Bahá'u'lláh is the "divine educator" for this age and has been sent by an all-loving Creator to move us to the next stage of humanity's development. Such advancement, however, requires that we change our notions of what is appropriate in societal relationships. In *The Lab, the Temple, and the Market*, Farzam Arbab outlines the challenge that faces humanity in regard to governance:

> Conflict between the individual and the institutions of society—the one clamoring for ever greater freedom and the other demanding ever more complete submission—has been a feature of political life throughout the ages. The model of democracy vigorously propagated in the world today takes this state of conflict for granted but tries to fix the parameters so that the individual's rights are not transgressed in the process. Beyond any question, the version of democracy so far achieved is preferable to the despotic systems of governance to which humanity has been subjected time and again. But the historical process of democratization does not have to end here, at its current immature stage; the interaction between institutional authority to decide and individual power to accomplish has only begun to realize its possibilities. Better arrangements will emerge, however, only when institutions cease to be seen as instruments for imposing on society the views of a particular faction, whether democratically elected or not. To the extent that institutions become channels through which the talents and energies of the members of society can be expressed in service to humanity, a sense of reciprocity will grow in which the individual supports and nurtures institutions and these, in turn, pay sincere attention to the voice of the people whose needs they serve.[27]

---

[26] 'Abdu'l-Bahá, *Some Answered Questions* (Wilmette, IL: Bahá'í Publishing Trust, 1994), p. 9.

[27] Farzam Arbab, "Promoting a Discourse on Science, Religion, and (cont'd)

This sense of reciprocity is now noticeably absent from relationships between individuals and institutions. Institutions—particularly governments—are not seen as "channels" through which citizens' "talents and energies ... can be expressed in service to humanity." Often they are (justly) seen as ladders by which the ambitious can rise and then impose their will on others, practice corruption, and sacrifice the common good to protect the interests of themselves and those who supported their advance. In turn, individuals do not support or "nurture" their governing institutions, and so the vicious circle is complete.

Arbab writes of the necessity of "the transformation of the present mode of governance, based on traditional concepts of power and authority, into one shaped by a genuine posture of learning." While acknowledging the difficulty of the process, he goes on to ask, "[I]s not the shift from governing by force to administering by learning one of the distinguishing features of humanity's passage from childhood to maturity?"[28] The new paradigm advanced by the Bahá'í Faith focuses on empowering individuals to become agents of constructive social change in their communities, or, in the words of one writer, on "cultivating the capacity in individuals and their institutions to participate in their own development."[29]

Inherent in this paradigm is a balance between the rights of the individual and those of the collective. One problem with protests and acts of civil disobedience, whether peaceful or violent, is that they necessarily involve rejection of the authority of the government. While the cause of the protest may be widely seen as praiseworthy, the question remains: if it is accepted that one group can deliberately disobey a decree it perceives as unjust, then why not another group disobeying another law that it sees as unjust, and another group another law? The authoritative standards embodied in civil

Development," in *The Lab, the Temple, and the Market: Reflections at the Intersection of Science, Religion, and Development*, ed. Sharon M.P. Harper (Ottawa, ON: International Development Research Centre, 2000), p. 212.
[28] Ibid., p. 216.
[29] Paul Lample, *Creating a New Mind: Reflections on the Individual, the Institutions, and the Community* (Riviera Beach, FL: Palabra Publications, 1999), p. 107.

jurisprudence are thus undermined to a point where they become empty, and the cohesion of the society is threatened.

A challenging but firm foundational principle of the Baháʾí Faith is obedience to government, stemming from the writings of Baháʾuʾlláh Himself, who stated, "To none is given the right to act in any manner that would run counter to the considered views of them who are in authority."[30] ʿAbduʾl-Bahá described Baháʾís as "the well-wishers of the government, obedient to its laws and bearing love towards all peoples,"[31] and Shoghi Effendi further elaborated that Baháʾís "do not exalt their own consciences over the rulings of the authorities, and hold it a religious duty to be loyal and obedient to the State."[32] In a cablegram written in 1938, he called upon the Baháʾís

> [to] resolve, despite [the] pressure [of] fast crystallizing public opinion, [to] abstain individually and collectively, in word [and] action, informally as well as in all official utterances and publications, from assigning blame, taking sides, however indirectly, in recurring political crises now agitating [and] ultimately engulfing human society.[33]

Baháʾís, then, neither sanction nor oppose partisan political viewpoints, nor do they engage in acts of civil disobedience that would undermine government—even in cases where the government is hostile towards them and their objectives. Two examples serve to illustrate this principle. The first is the Baháʾí community of Iran, which is not recognized under the constitution of the Islamic Republic of that country. In 1983, the community was ordered by the government to disband all administrative structures governing

---

[30] Baháʾuʾlláh, *Gleanings from the Writings of Baháʾuʾlláh* (Wilmette, IL: Baháʾí Publishing Trust, 1994), p. 241.

[31] ʿAbduʾl-Bahá, *Selections from the Writings of ʿAbduʾl-Bahá* (Wilmette, IL: Baháʾí Publishing Trust, 1997), p. 293.

[32] Shoghi Effendi, *Principles of Baháʾí Administration: A Compilation* (London: Baháʾí Publishing Trust, 1973), p. 95.

[33] Shoghi Effendi, cablegram written 24 September 1938, in *Messages to America: Selected Letters and Cablegrams Addressed to the Baháʾís of North America 1932–1946* (Wilmette, IL: Baháʾí Publishing Trust, 1947), p. 15.

its affairs. This was done and, in a final act before it disbanded, the National Spiritual Assembly wrote an open letter that was sent to many government officials, announcing "the suspension of the Bahá'í organizations throughout Iran in order to establish its good intentions and in conformity with its basic tenets concerning complete obedience to the instructions of the Government ... until the time when, God willing, the misunderstandings are eliminated and the realities are at last made manifest to the authorities."[34]

To date, the government's prohibition against Bahá'í administrative institutions remains in effect, and they remain disbanded. The situation is admittedly very difficult, but nevertheless, the Bahá'ís have not become passive "victims" of the regime, in that they and their sister communities around the world continue to pursue all legal means—both within Iran itself and through international channels such as the United Nations—to gain recognition under the constitution and to be granted their basic human and civil rights. Bahá'ís are convinced that their efforts through these channels have mitigated the suffering of the Iranian community.

The second example is the Bahá'í community of South Africa during the apartheid era, which was under constant surveillance by the security police because of its racially integrated membership and activities. In its testimony to the Truth and Reconciliation Commission in 1997, the community stated that its obedience to the previous government stemmed from the Bahá'í Faith's explicit prohibition against involvement in partisan politics and opposition to government. It testified,

> During the time when the previous Government prohibited integration within our communities, rather than divide into separate administrative structures for each population group, we opted to limit membership of the Bahá'í administration to the black adherents who were and remain in the majority of our membership and thereby placed the entire Bahá'í community under the stewardship of its black membership. Happily, such

---

[34] National Spiritual Assembly of the Bahá'ís of Iran, open letter, 3 September 1983, in *Messages of the Universal House of Justice 1963 to 1986*, pp. 599–600.

policies were eased and we were able once again to have racially integrated administrative bodies which were and are democratically elected by and from the entire body of adult adherents of the Bahá'í Faith.[35]

The statement concluded, "through strict adherence to the principles of our Prophet-Founder we have forged ahead and made a modest beginning toward realizing our vision of unity for South Africa by creating a model which can be studied and scrutinized and from which we believe valuable lessons can be learned."

Individual Bahá'ís, when drafted for military service, have faced similar ethical dilemmas regarding the law of the land and their religious convictions. While "Bahá'ís recognize the right and duty of governments to use force for the maintenance of law and order and to protect their people" and the Bahá'í Faith "draws a very definite distinction between the duty of an individual to forgive and 'to be killed rather than to kill' and the duty of society to uphold justice," at the same time "Bahá'ís try to keep themselves out of the internecine conflicts that are raging among their fellow men and to avoid shedding blood in such struggles."[36] Therefore, since they must be obedient to their government, "Bahá'ís do not on the grounds of religious conviction seek to abandon their obligations as citizens"; rather, they apply for legal noncombatant service, "regardless of the effect which that may have on their personal safety, convenience, the kind of activity they must discharge, or the rank to which they may be assigned."[37]

While Bahá'ís seek to obtain noncombatant status to avoid shedding blood, they are not absolute pacifists, as "[n]on-cooperation

---

[35] For the full text of the statement by the National Spiritual Assembly of the Bahá'ís of South Africa to the Truth and Reconciliation Commission, see "A Pathway to Peace and Justice," in *The Bahá'í World 1997–98*, pp. 229–32.

[36] Universal House of Justice, letter to a National Spiritual Assembly, 9 February 1967, in *Lights of Guidance: A Bahá'í Reference File*, compiled by Helen Hornby, 3rd rev. ed. (New Delhi: Bahá'í Publishing Trust, 1994), no. 1354, p. 407.

[37] National Spiritual Assembly of the Bahá'ís of the United States of America, *Developing Distinctive Bahá'í Communities* (Evanston, IL: Office of Assembly Development, 1998), section 19.8.

is too passive a philosophy to become an effective way for social reconstruction."[38] The pacifist stance is viewed as "anti-social," and "its exaltation of the individual conscience leads inevitably to disorder and chaos in society":

> Extreme pacifists are thus very close to the anarchists, in the sense that both of these groups lay an undue emphasis on the rights and merits of the individual. The Bahá'í conception of social life is essentially based on the subordination of the individual will to that of society. It neither suppresses the individual nor does it exalt him to the point of making him an anti-social creature, a menace to society. As in everything, it follows the "golden mean." The only way that society can function is for the minority to follow the will of the majority.[39]

Bahá'ís are obedient to their government to the point where such obedience would force them to deny their core spiritual beliefs. Shoghi Effendi has written that while Bahá'ís "should obey the government under which they live, even at the risk of sacrificing all their administrative affairs and interests, they should under no circumstances suffer their inner religious beliefs and convictions to be violated and transgressed by any authority whatever."[40] To return to the examples of the two communities mentioned earlier: In South Africa, although operating within the restrictions imposed by the government, the Bahá'í community would not and did not abandon its convictions regarding the unity of humankind; and in Iran, thousands of Bahá'ís have been imprisoned since the 1979 revolution and more than 200 have been executed for refusing to recant their Faith when demanded to do so by the authorities.

The Bahá'í view of change as organic in nature provides a perspective that allows the community to pursue it through established,

---

[38] Letter written on behalf of Shoghi Effendi, 21 November 1935, cited by the Universal House of Justice in a letter to an National Spiritual Assembly, 9 February 1967, in *Lights of Guidance*, no. 1354, p. 407.

[39] Ibid.

[40] Shoghi Effendi, *The Light of Divine Guidance: The Messages from the Guardian of the Bahá'í Faith to the Bahá'ís of Germany and Austria*, vol. 1 (Hofheim-Langenhain: Bahá'í-Verlag, 1982), p. 54.

lawful channels. Just as a human being must traverse numerous stages from infancy to adulthood, the political world "cannot instantaneously evolve from the nadir of defectiveness to the zenith of rightness and perfection. Rather, qualified individuals must strive by day and by night, using all those means which will conduce to progress, until the government and the people develop along every line from day to day and even from moment to moment."[41]

Outside the adversarial "contest" paradigm, the Bahá'í community is devoting its energies to building communal patterns to encourage the development of "those means that will conduce to progress." While still very young, the community is gaining valuable experience in nurturing "learning organizations" at the grassroots level and in empowering both individuals and institutions to walk their own path of development. The maturation of democratically elected Bahá'í governing bodies at the local level and the progress of a worldwide system for training human resources both offer encouraging evidence of those patterns within the Bahá'í community itself.[42] But Bahá'ís are also seeking ways to offer the insights and skills inspired by their beliefs to the wider community, notably through social and economic development efforts around the world.

The moral leadership training program initiated by the Bahá'í-inspired Nur University in Santa Cruz, Bolivia, provides one such example. Working at the grassroots, Nur has trained schoolteachers in more than 400 rural communities as agents of social change, and the program is now spreading to other countries and continents. Based on the Bahá'í teachings, it focuses on six defining characteristics:

> consistent service-oriented leadership focused on the common good; active engagement in the process of individual and collective transformation; commitment to fulfilling the twin moral responsibilities of searching for the truth and applying truth in all aspects of one's life; transcendence through vision—that entails connecting with eternal values and renewing a commitment

---

[41] 'Abdu'l-Bahá, *The Secret of Divine Civilization* (Wilmette, IL: Bahá'í Publishing Trust, 1983), pp. 107–08.

[42] For more on the systematic training of human resources, see "Creating a Culture of Growth: The Institute Process in the Bahá'í Community," *The Bahá'í World 2000–2001*, pp. 191–99.

to service and the process of transformation; recognition of the essential nobility of each human being—a nobility that endows the individual with the potential to develop and exercise moral leadership in society; and the exercise of personal, interpersonal and societal leadership capabilities.[43]

Once students have analyzed features of prevailing leadership models, whether authoritarian, paternalistic, manipulative, "know-it-all," or democratic, they move on to explore capabilities essential to moral leadership.

The acquisition of such capabilities will enable individuals to serve effectively as members of institutions that promote social well-being and, in the words of Farzam Arbab,

> to develop in decision-making bodies certain abilities required of them by their functions in society.... These include the abilities to maintain a clear perception of social reality and of the forces operating in it; to detect some of the opportunities offered by each historical moment; to properly assess the resources of the community; to consult freely and harmoniously as a body and with one's constituency; to realize that every decision has both a material and a spiritual dimension; to arrive at decisions; to win the confidence, respect, and genuine support of those affected by these decisions; to effectively use the energies and diverse talents of the available human resources; to integrate the diversity of aspirations and of activities of individuals and groups into one forward movement; to build and maintain unity; to uphold standards of justice; and to implement decisions with an openness and flexibility that avoid all trace of dictatorial behavior.[44]

Nur's training is still relatively small in scope, but as more and more people become empowered with such knowledge, insights, and capabilities, they become effective agents of social change that is grounded in moral principle. Schoolteachers in particular exert a

---

[43] Taken from the description of Nur University on the Mona Foundation's Web site, at http://www.monafoundation.org/projects/nur/profile.shtml.
[44] Arbab, "Promoting a Discourse," p. 216.

strong influence on students and parents, and can thus assist in the transformation of their communities.

FUNDAEC, or Fundación para la Aplicación y Enseñanza de las Ciencias (Foundation for the Application and Teaching of the Sciences), in Colombia, is also concerned with issues surrounding moral education and leadership. It has turned its attention to establishing programs in rural areas through which inhabitants—particularly youth—can develop intellectual and spiritual capacities and attitudes in order to become "valuable human resources for social change."[45] In its description of its objectives, FUNDAEC clearly states its views concerning the most effective way of fostering constructive change:

> [R]ather than trying to reform the present social order, or promote violence in the name of justice and the irresistible march of history, the real task is to search for new options that render rural life meaningful in the context of a global human society, a society that would be radically different from what has taken shape during the past decades of material progress and spiritual bankruptcy. This search, however, cannot be carried out from the planning offices of development agencies and ministries; it has to be part of the effort of rural populations themselves and those who choose to share in their destiny.... [I]t is necessary for each people to have the opportunity to examine its past and present, become aware of the strengths and shortcomings of its culture, and through highly participative processes, search for and walk a viable path of organic change.[46]

It is important, FUNDAEC says, not to romanticize the situation of these populations. Certainly negative external forces act upon them, including "agrarian policies of the country, the unjust distribution of land, the shortcomings of the market, the inappropriateness of available technology, the expansion of a harmful system of education and communication the content of which causes the disintegration of positive values and relationships." But it is also important to

---

[45] CELATER (Latin American Center for Rural Technology and Education), "What is FUNDAEC," sec. II A 1, at http://www.bcca.org/services/lists/noble-creation/fundaec1.html.

[46] Ibid., sec. III A.

recognize that these populations also suffer from internal destructive tendencies, whether "the disintegration of basic structures of family, of decision making, and of the socialization of knowledge," "a rapid deterioration of such traditional values as responsibility, rectitude, and solidarity," or "negative characteristics such as oppressive attitudes towards women and certain patterns of leadership." Neither romanticizing nor patronizing these populations, FUNDAEC aims to educate "new generations who rather than simple objects of oppression can become effective actors in an unavoidable process of profound social change."[47]

In contrast to "idealistic materialists" who see "good" only in terms of material progress,[48] FUNDAEC seeks to integrate "material and spiritual elements into a knowledge system that would enable individuals and entire populations to contribute to the creation of a new social order." Analyzing the results of its work over almost 30 years, FUNDAEC has become convinced that "substantial and sustained improvement in the material conditions of the majority of humanity can only be the fruit of a profound spiritual transformation, for it is within the human soul that social and moral disintegration is producing its most devastating effects."[49]

This recognition that spiritual transformation needs to be the foundation of lasting material improvements is central to the Bahá'í approach to social change. As the Universal House of Justice has expressed it, "Humanity's crying need will not be met by a struggle among competing ambitions or by protest against one or another of the countless wrongs afflicting a desperate age. It calls, rather, for a fundamental change of consciousness."[50] Such a change implies acceptance of the teaching at the heart of the Bahá'í Faith "that the time has come when each human being on earth must learn to accept responsibility for the welfare of the entire human family."[51]

---

[47] Ibid.
[48] Universal House of Justice, letter to a National Spiritual Assembly, 19 November 1974, in *Messages of the Universal House of Justice 1963–1986*, p. 283.
[49] CELATER, "What is FUNDAEC," sec. III C.
[50] Universal House of Justice, letter to the believers gathered for the events marking the completion of the projects on Mount Carmel, 24 May 2001.
[51] Ibid.

Awareness of that responsibility is also, fundamentally, the driving force behind protests such as those organized by the anti-globalization movement. But will the movement be able to sustain itself, over a long period and with a unified vision and sense of purpose, to address the challenges it has taken on? In one of her articles in *Fences and Windows,* Naomi Klein expresses her concern about the future of the anti-globalization movement in a rootless world and asks, "How can a movement be accountable when communities are fraying?"[52] She worries that in the mass demonstrations "the spectacle of displaying a movement is getting confused with the less glamorous business of building one"[53] and recognizes that "there are clearly moments to demonstrate, but perhaps more important, there are moments to build the connections that make demonstration something more than theater."[54] This is an important insight, and the kinds of connections that are forged are extremely important. If those connections rely on temporary overlapping of individualistic agendas or ephemeral political alliances, then they will be weak. If, on the other hand, they arise from a conviction that humanity is one, and that both individuals and institutions play reciprocal roles in serving humanity, then they will endure. Farzam Arbab describes the benefits of such reciprocity, writing,

> [A] new understanding of power and authority has profound implications for the nature of community life and hence for culture. On the community rests the challenge of providing that environment where individual wills blend, where powers are multiplied and manifest themselves in collective action, where higher expressions of the human spirit can appear.[55]

Beyond the barricades, the marches, the violence, and the culture of contest, rich new possibilities open before humanity.

---

[52] Klein, *Fences and Windows,* p. 158.

[53] Ibid., p. 159.

[54] Ibid., p. 158.

[55] Arbab, "Promoting a Discourse," p. 213.

PROFILE:
APRODEPIT

Action pour la Promotion des
Ressources des Organisations de
Defensé de l'Environnement et de la
Pisciculture integrée au Tchad

In May 2002, Action pour la Promotion des Ressources des Organisations de Defensé de l'Environnement et de la Pisciculture
integrée au Tchad (Action for the Promotion of Resources for
Organizations Defending the Environment and Integrated Pisciculture in Chad), or APRODEPIT,[1] observed its first decade of existence
and service to people living along the Chari River in southern Chad.
Government representatives, including the Minister of the Environment and Water, the Minister of Planning and Cooperation, and
the Minister for Social Action and Family, attended the festivities,
as did representatives of local and international nongovernmental
organizations, the European Union, the Canada Fund, and the UN's
Food and Agriculture Organization. The occasion was joyous, as
APRODEPIT had made significant contributions to the region it serves
and there was much to celebrate.

The organization's story began in 1985, against a background of
decreasing water levels in rivers and lakes, harmful practices such as

---

[1] The organization was formerly known as l'Association pour la Promotion
et le Developpement de la Pisciculture integrée au Tchad (the Association
for the Promotion and Development of Integrated Pisciculture of Chad),
but changed its name in 2003.

Men harvest fish farmed using APRODEPIT's *environmentally sound methods.*

the use of dynamite to kill fish, the disappearance of various aquatic species, and a lack of protein in the diet of the people living in the region. In response, a group of 12 families, seeking to find solutions to these serious problems, decided to band together and promote fish breeding. The efforts of the initial group were encouraging enough for it to enlarge the circle by creating a structure that would be national in scope, and so APRODEPIT was formed. A few years later, in 1992, it was recognized by Chad's Ministry of the Interior and the Ministry for Planning and Cooperation as a nongovernmental organization.

Like other Bahá'í-inspired social and economic development activities and organizations, APRODEPIT has focused on building skills and capacities in individuals and communities so that they are empowered to contribute to their own processes of development. The "honor and distinction of the individual," according to the Bahá'í writings, is to "become a source of social good," since it is the role of all peoples "to carry forward an ever-advancing civilization" that is based on the principles of justice and unity. To contribute to such a great enterprise, individuals need access to knowledge; they need to acquire skills; and they need to develop attitudes and qualities that will enable them to lead productive lives. The community, in turn, provides an environment that brings individuals together in constructive, principle-based collective action. The task of Bahá'í-inspired development efforts is to assist individuals and communities to find ways to apply principles and teachings to their particular situations.

Recognizing that both participation by the local population and decentralization of the areas of jurisdiction are necessary for the achievement of just and sustainable development, APRODEPIT's approach has been to provide information, training, and encouragement to local populations so that they can organize their own groups and unions to take action for the protection of the natural resources on which they depend. To this end, the organization has established offices for regional supervision, trains field officers, and sponsors general meetings with those involved in the management of the waters.

APRODEPIT's aim in all of this activity is twofold. First, it supports fishermen's and fish breeders' cooperatives in technical aspects of farming and raising fish, including fish-breeding techniques and the sustained management of fishing resources. Second, it seeks to protect resources by raising the awareness of fishermen about ecologically sound fishing practices, by training them in conservational techniques, by providing groups with nonprohibited equipment for conventional fishing, and by promoting adherence to Chad's fishing regulations.

By 2000, APRODEPIT had set up 172 fish farming projects in lakes, creeks, and artificial ponds in villages throughout southern Chad. With its headquarters in Sarh, on the Chari River, the organization's three main branches—the Chari-Baguimi, the Moyen-Chari, and the Mayo-Kebbi—have developed the capacity to support some 250 fishermen's groups, training field officers and promoting the diversification of self-financing activities.

During 2002, APRODEPIT's efforts to organize the fishermen into groups and to assist them with microcredit loans to acquire materials and tools led it to educate 150 leaders of local organizations about national fishing regulations and the code for responsible fishing, to carry out campaigns to promote the sustainable management of fishing resources in 71 riverside villages, and to conduct extensive studies to understand the economies of villages that depend largely on fishing. Another important aspect of the organization's work is to visit heads of the districts and make them aware of the deterioration of the fishing and other natural resources in their areas. To this end, consultations were held with traditional chiefs, and 12 heads of cantons were visited by 2002.

Focusing on the strengthening of women's capacities, APRODEPIT has helped women to build upon the base of the renewed fishing and fish-breeding resources by encouraging them to buy fish from the farmers, to smoke and cure it, and to sell their products for a profit at nearby markets. To assist the women's groups that have undertaken these activities, APRODEPIT has offered training in smoking and curing procedures and has promoted the development of a savings and credit system for the women to finance their own activities. To date, some 150 women's organizations whose members sell fish and fish products have been eligible for microcredit loans.

As part of its ecological program, APRODEPIT has built consensus in the community to set aside 80 designated creeks exclusively for fish breeding. It has supported supervision of fish reproduction areas in the Léré and Tréné lakes. The organization has also had success in conserving the region's wildlife—notably, in fostering the increase in the hippopotamus population in Moussafoyo from 2 to 50 within 10 years. (Hippos are seen as a keystone species, since they transfer nutrients from land to water. Fish, for example, feed on various invertebrates that eat hippo dung.) As a result of APRODEPIT's efforts, the government designated a large tract of land as a National Nature Reserve, and in 2001 collaboration between the government and fishermen's groups resulted in the placement of an additional five square kilometers of ecologically delicate land in Barh-koh under APRODEPIT's care. APRODEPIT has supported participatory management of the reserve at Gnala, as well as the planting of orchards and trees and the establishment of market gardens in the region.

To pursue a wider range of community development goals, APRODEPIT has expanded its activities to focus on the education of children and women, including unmarried mothers and young girls. These efforts, like APRODEPIT's other activities, which are all founded on Bahá'í principles, also have an approach that is strongly based on community participation. One particular aim is to help men view women as capable partners in devising and implementing social and economic projects in the region. The eventual goal is to curb illiteracy, misery, and ignorance among the underprivileged.

APRODEPIT has supported education through a variety of measures, including providing outreach and assistance to other groups and helping establish village schools. One such initiative, undertaken at the request of local elementary school authorities, has been the facilitation of training for more than 400 teachers of children aged 2 to 6 and of adults, as well as refresher courses for teachers and administrators in several kindergartens in the region. At an experimental nursery school, thousands of children, including those enrolled and many others from the surrounding area, have been vaccinated against diseases such as meningitis, poliomyelitis, smallpox, TB, and

Children celebrate at a graduation ceremony in one of the educational projects supported by APRODEPIT.

APRODEPIT supports meetings like the one pictured here, aimed at strengthening women's capacities.

whooping cough. Lectures, discussions, and training sessions on the control of AIDS have been offered to the public.

In addition, literacy training and vocational programs such as sewing and dyeing have been offered. More than 100 women have participated in the microcredit program Fonds de soutien en matière de population, with the aim of supporting revenue-earning microprojects and activities, particularly to equip those who finish their training in sewing.

At its 10th anniversary celebrations, members of the various groups working with APRODEPIT and the field officers who serve them shared the pleasure of their successes with the public of Sarh and with invited guests. Discussions conducted and facilitated by people directly involved in the projects focused on the role of civil society in the decision-making process, particularly in relation to the challenges of managing fishing resources, to fish breeding in natural lakes and creeks, to the management of a community reserve, to the curing of fish, and to the Bahá'í approach to development. Displays of permitted and prohibited fishing equipment and a market offering various food products and crafts made by women's groups in the region were also featured, along with sports activities and dances from various groups throughout the week.

APRODEPIT looks forward to developing its existing projects further and to undertaking more projects in partnership with other agencies—whether studying the condition of lakes and species of fish in the area it serves, managing the preserves under its care, training more people in fishpond development, fish breeding, and resource management, or offering more support for community schools. Given the expansion of the organization's scope over the first 10 years of its existence, possibilities for assisting the people of southern Chad to build on their success look promising indeed.

Religious Intolerance

Written statement of the Bahá'í International
Community to the 59th session of the United
Nations Commission on Human Rights, held from
17 March to 25 April 2003 in Geneva, Switzerland.

From the reports of the UN Special Rapporteur on Freedom of Religion and Belief, it is clear that serious violations of freedom of religion or belief are continuing the world over. Extremism and fundamentalism are growing day by day, fueling intolerance and hatred on the basis of religion or belief. It is, therefore, gratifying to note the special emphasis that the Special Rapporteur has placed on the need to prevent religious intolerance and discrimination. We also appreciate his calling for an International Consultative Conference to engage the international community in discussions about the role of schools in that preventive process.

The International Consultative Conference on School Education in Relation to Freedom of Religion or Belief, Tolerance, and Nondiscrimination, held in Madrid in November 2001, produced a strong statement affirming the right of children to "be brought up in a spirit of peace, tolerance, mutual understanding, and respect for human rights." The final statement from that conference upheld the urgent need to "promote, through education, the protection and the respect for freedom of religion or belief in order to strengthen peace, understanding, and tolerance among individuals, groups, and nations, and with a view to developing a respect for pluralism."[1]

---

[1] Madrid Final Document, November 2001, operative para. 1.

Widespread respect for freedom of religion or belief is an incredibly important goal in a world torn apart by religious extremism. For this goal to be achieved, however, the children of the world must learn that firmly held religious convictions are compatible with respect for the rights of those whose beliefs differ from their own.

The Madrid Final Document emphasizes the years of primary and secondary school[2] as being the critical time for instilling attitudes of tolerance and nondiscrimination. Indeed the Bahá'í writings confirm that "It is extremely difficult to teach the individual and refine his character once puberty is passed.… Therefore it is in early childhood that a firm foundation must be laid. While the branch is green and tender it can easily be made straight."[3]

An integral feature of any educational initiative that would foster respect for the rights of others must be the notion of the oneness and interdependence of the human race. Oneness and diversity are complementary and inseparable. That human consciousness necessarily operates through an infinite diversity of individual minds and motivations detracts in no way from its essential unity. Indeed, it is precisely the respect for diversity that distinguishes unity from uniformity. Hence, acceptance of the concept of unity in diversity implies the development of a global consciousness, a sense of world citizenship, and a love for all of humanity. It fosters in every individual the realization that, since the body of humankind is one and indivisible, each member of the human race is born into the world as a trust of the whole and has a responsibility to the whole. It further suggests that if a peaceful international community is to emerge, then the complex and varied cultural expressions of humanity must be allowed to develop and flourish and to interact with one another in ever-changing patterns of civilization.

We would, therefore, strongly recommend that the curriculum of every school include the principle of the oneness and interdependence of the human family. The children should also be trained in such virtues as kindliness, cooperation, peacefulness, respect, and tolerance. Children who learn to treat others with respect also

---

[2] Ibid., operative para. 8.
[3] 'Abdu'l-Bahá, *Selections from the Writings of 'Abdu'l-Bahá* (Wilmette, IL: Bahá'í Publishing Trust, 1997), p. 137.

learn to respect themselves. Children who grow up caring about the welfare of others are unlikely to be the purveyors of hatred and intolerance as adults.

We would also urge that children learn to view the riches of humanity's religious heritage through the lens of unity. As stated in the Bahá'í writings, "There can be no doubt whatever that the peoples of the world, of whatever race or religion, derive their inspiration from one heavenly Source, and are the subjects of one God."[4] The world's religions can thus be seen to be one in their nature and purpose with each being a wellspring of knowledge, energy, and inspiration. They each have served to unlock a wider range of capacities within human consciousness and society, impelling the human race towards moral and spiritual maturity. Accordingly, curricula exploring the history and teachings of religion may wish to highlight the complementary aims and functions of the world's faith systems as well as the theological and moral threads that link them.

Clearly much soul searching and reflection will be necessary within and between various religious and belief communities before this principle of the unity of religion will be universally embraced. An important contribution can be made by interreligious dialogue, in deeply pondering the reality of, and urgent need for, a penetrating understanding of the essential oneness of religion, despite the obvious diversity of expression and practice. In the Bahá'í perspective, this is the true purpose of religion: "to establish unity and concord amongst the peoples of the world."[5]

There is a unique power inherent in religion that, if channeled appropriately, can serve as the strongest contributor to unity and understanding amongst the peoples of the world. Religion has shaped human civilization profoundly and positively over many centuries, and the Bahá'í International Community has no doubt that it can and will contribute to establishing bonds of genuine respect among the peoples of the world.

---

[4] Bahá'u'lláh, *Gleanings from the Writings of Bahá'u'lláh* (Wilmette, IL: Bahá'í Publishing Trust, 1994), p. 217.

[5] Bahá'u'lláh, *Tablets of Bahá'u'lláh revealed after the Kitáb-i-Aqdas* (Wilmette, IL: Bahá'í Publishing Trust, 1997), p. 129.

Religion and Development at the Crossroads
CONVERGENCE OR DIVERGENCE?

Statement by the Bahá'í International Community
to the World Summit on Sustainable Development,
Johannesburg, South Africa, 26 August 2002.

O ver the course of the twentieth century, ethnic, racial, and national prejudices have increasingly given way to the recognition that humankind is a single family and the earth its common homeland.[1] The United Nations (UN), which was created in response to this dawning recognition, has worked tirelessly to bring about a world where all peoples and nations can live together in peace and harmony. To help bring about this world, the UN has crafted a remarkable framework of international institutions, processes, conventions, and global action plans that have helped to prevent conflict and warfare, to protect human rights, to nurture equality between women and men, and to uplift the material conditions of countless individuals and communities.

Despite these significant achievements, the United Nations has yet to grasp fully both the constructive role that religion can play in creating a peaceful and prosperous global order, and the destructive

---

[1] Along with this recognition has come the awareness that worldwide peace and prosperity will be impossible so long as human rights are routinely violated, women are denied equality, ethnic and racial minorities are discriminated against, the ravages of poverty are ignored, and unfettered national sovereignty is exercised.

impact that religious fanaticism can have on the stability and progress of the world. This lack of attention to religion can be clearly seen in the development realm, where the United Nations has, for the most part, viewed religious communities merely as channels for the delivery of goods and services, and as mechanisms to carry out development policies and programs. Moreover, while the United Nations' human rights machinery has been used to condemn religious intolerance and persecution,[2] UN development policies and programs[3] have hardly begun to address religious bigotry as a major

---

[2] Unfortunately, the UN has been unable to move beyond its Declaration on the Elimination of All Forms of Intolerance and of Discrimination Based on Religion or Belief, to create a convention on freedom of religion and belief. The ability of the United Nations to transform General Assembly declarations on race and on women into conventions only highlights its lack of success in the area of religion and belief—i.e., after producing the Declaration on the Elimination of All Forms of Racial Discrimination and the Declaration on the Elimination of Discrimination against Women, the UN created the International Convention on the Elimination of All Forms of Racial Discrimination and the Convention on the Elimination of All Forms of Discrimination against Women.

[3] Although some of the global action plans from recent United Nations conferences suggest that misuse of religion poses an obstacle to development, the few references that they do contain neither explore the effects of religious bigotry and violence on development and security, nor offer any notable solutions. [See, e.g., The Vienna Declaration and Program of Action, II-22, 38; The Copenhagen Declaration and Program of Action, 69; The Platform for Action of the Fourth World Conference on Women, 24, 80 (f), 131, 224; The Habitat Agenda, 25; We the Peoples: The Role of the United Nations in the Twenty-First Century, 200; and The Declaration of the World Conference against Racism, Racial Discrimination, Xenophobia, and Related Intolerance, 59–60.] *Agenda 21* mentions religion, but with no reference to the impact that its misuse has on development [see *Agenda 21*, 5.53, 6.1, 6.3, 6.4, 6.12, 6.32, 6.34 (a)(i), 36.13 (a)]. Moreover, the Program for the Further Implementation of *Agenda 21*, which was produced at the Earth Summit +5, contains no mention at all of religion, and the Draft Plan of Implementation for the World Summit on Sustainable Development that was negotiated at the Fourth Preparatory Committee session (27 May–7 June 2002) mentions religion but once, and then only in the context of ensuring that the delivery of basic health care services is "consistent with … cultural and religious values" A/CONF199/PC/L.5, no. 45). This omission of the destructive (cont'd)

obstacle to peace and well-being.[4]

Religion as the Basis of Civilization and Progress

It is becoming increasingly clear that passage to the culminating stage in the millennia-long process of the organization of the planet as

---

effects of religious fanaticism on sustainable development from the global action plans emanating from the Earth Summit, the Earth Summit +5, and the World Summit on Sustainable Development is all the more striking, given that some of the conferences of the 1990s did, at least, express concern about religious intolerance.

[4] In its efforts to combat terrorism, the United Nations has been hesitant to address religious fanaticism. Through a series of resolutions, treaties, and actions, the United Nations has sought concerted international cooperation to combat terrorism, branding it "one of the most serious threats to international peace and security in the twenty-first century" and inimical to "global stability and prosperity" [S/RES/1377 (2001)]. Yet, at the same time, the UN has been reticent to identify religious fanaticism as a source of terrorism, referring to it, if at all, mostly indirectly—e.g., "terrorism motivated by intolerance or extremism" [S/RES/1373 (2001)]. In those few instances when it is mentioned directly, it is included in a list of various justifications—e.g., "criminal acts intended to provoke a state of terror … are … unjustifiable, whatever the considerations of a political, philosophical, ideological, racial, ethnic, religious, or other nature that may be invoked to justify them" [A/RES/55/158, para. 2; see also A/57/37, annex III, article 5, Report of the Ad Hoc Committee (charged with drafting a Comprehensive Convention on International Terrorism) established by General Assembly Resolution 51/210 of 17 December 1996; and the International Convention for the Suppression of the Financing of Terrorism, Article 6]. Interestingly, even the various resolutions that were issued by the Security Council, the General Assembly, and the Commission on Human Rights in response to the terrorist acts of 11 September 2001 failed to identify religious fanaticism as the force animating those acts (to find allusion to this fanatical motivation, one has to look to speeches by the UN Secretary-General: "We are in a moral struggle to fight an evil that is anathema to all faiths" SG/SM8013, message of Secretary-General Kofi Annan to the Warsaw Conference on Combating Terrorism, 6 November 2001). This hesitancy to acknowledge and forcefully condemn the religious bigotry motivating terrorist acts weakens the effectiveness of the UN's efforts to bring an end to international terrorism. For, it is only by identifying and understanding the peculiar motivation behind such acts that they can be effectively combated.

one home for the entire human family cannot be accomplished in a spiritual vacuum. Religion, the Bahá'í scriptures aver, "is the source of illumination, the cause of development and the animating impulse of all human advancement" and "has been the basis of all civilization and progress in the history of mankind."[5] It is the source of meaning and hope for the vast majority of the planet's inhabitants, and it has a limitless power to inspire sacrifice, change, and long-term commitment in its followers.[6] It is, therefore, inconceivable that a peaceful and prosperous global society—a society which nourishes a spectacular diversity of cultures and nations—can be established and sustained without directly and substantively involving the world's great religions in its design and support.[7]

---

[5] 'Abdu'l-Bahá, *The Promulgation of Universal Peace: Talks Delivered by 'Abdu'l-Bahá during His Visit to the United States and Canada in 1912*, rev. ed. (Wilmette, IL: Bahá'í Publishing Trust, 1995), p. 361.

[6] Religion has inspired "in whole populations capacities to love, to forgive, to create, to dare greatly, to overcome prejudice, to sacrifice for the common good, and to discipline the impulses of animal instincts.... Against all odds and with little in the way of meaningful encouragement, it continues to sustain the struggle for survival of uncounted millions and to raise up in all lands heroes and saints whose lives are the most persuasive vindication of the principles contained in the scriptures of their respective faiths." Indeed, "its fundamental laws and cardinal principles have, throughout the ages, constituted the warp and woof" of the social fabric, uniting peoples into communities and serving as the "ultimate authority in giving meaning" and direction to individual and collective life. [See Universal House of Justice, letter to the world's religious leaders, April 2002; Shoghi Effendi, *God Passes By* (Wilmette, IL: Bahá'í Publishing Trust, 1995), p. 223.]

[7] It is untenable to maintain that a regime of international human rights can replace religious purpose as the force capable of inspiring the profound sacrifices and driving the extensive changes necessary for the unification and pacification of humankind. While it is true that international human rights norms and standards are based largely on principles that have their foundation in the world's great religions, such a regime, standing on its own—unmoored from religious purpose—cannot elicit the moral vision and commitment required to establish and sustain universal peace and justice. In fact, severed from the virtues taught by all religions—such as kindness, forgiveness, compassion, generosity, love, sacrifice, responsibility, and service to others—human rights and fundamental freedoms are often used (cont'd)

At the same time, it cannot be denied that the power of religion has also been perverted to turn neighbor against neighbor. The Bahá'í scriptures state that "religion must be the source of fellowship, the cause of unity and the nearness of God to man. If it rouses hatred and strife, it is evident that absence of religion is preferable and an irreligious man is better than one who professes it."[8] So long as religious animosities are allowed to destabilize the world, it will be impossible to foster a global pattern of sustainable development: the central goal of this summit.

Religion and the United Nations Working Together for Peace and Justice

Given the record of religious fanaticism, it is understandable that the United Nations has been hesitant to invite religion into its negotiations. However, the UN can no longer afford to ignore the immeasurable good that religions have done and continue to do in the world, or the salubrious, far-reaching contributions that they can make to the establishment of a peaceful, prosperous, and sustainable global order. Indeed, the United Nations will only succeed in establishing such a global order to the extent that it taps into the power and vision of religion. To do so will require accepting religion not merely as a vehicle for the delivery and execution of development initiatives, but as an active partner in the conceptualization, design,

---

to justify selfish individualism, antisocial lifestyles, overconsumption, ethical relativism, cultural aggrandizement, and national chauvinism.

[8] 'Abdu'l-Bahá, *Promulgation of Universal Peace*, p. 181. This principle is repeatedly stressed in the Bahá'í scriptures—e.g., "If religion proves to be the source of hatred, enmity, and contention, if it becomes the cause of warfare and strife and influences men to kill each other, its absence is preferable" (Ibid., p. 298); "If a religion become the cause of hatred and disharmony, it would be better that it should not exist. To be without such a religion is better than to be with it" ['Abdu'l-Bahá, *'Abdu'l-Bahá in London* (London: Bahá'í Publishing Trust, 1982), p. 28]; "If religion becomes a cause of dislike, hatred, and division, it were better to be without it, and to withdraw from such a religion would be a truly religious act" ['Abdu'l-Bahá, *Paris Talks*, 11th ed. (London: Bahá'í Publishing Trust, 1969), p. 130].

implementation, and evaluation of global policies and programs.[9] The historically justified wall separating the United Nations and religions[10] must fall to the imperatives of a world struggling toward unity and justice.[11]

The real onus, however, is on the religions themselves. Religious followers and, more important, religious leaders must show that they are worthy partners in the great mission of building a sustainable world civilization. To do so will require that religious leaders work conscientiously and untiringly to exorcise religious bigotry and superstition[12] from within their faith traditions. It will necessitate that they embrace freedom of conscience for all people, including

---

[9]   While religious principles have had a palpable influence on the UN, most notably in the human rights realm, the UN has yet to accept the world's religions as genuine partners in its work. The involvement of religious nongovernmental organizations (NGOS) in certain activities at the United Nations, the religious sentiments that UN and governmental officials occasionally express during negotiations, the Permanent Observer status held by the Holy See (representing the state of Vatican City), and other such means through which voices of religion are sometimes raised in the UN can hardly be said to constitute substantive religious involvement in the deliberations and conceptual work of the UN. This lack of involvement is perplexing, given that the world's religious scriptures promise an age of universal peace and world-wide harmony—an age whose establishment is the central purpose of the United Nations.

[10] For an interesting view of the influence of religious NGOS at the UN, see Religion Counts, "Religion and Public Policy at the UN," 2002.

[11] Such initiatives as the World Faiths Development Dialogue (a collaborative initiative between the World Bank and several world religions), and the Millennium World Peace Summit of Religious and Spiritual Leaders (a global gathering of religious leaders that was held, in part, in the UN General Assembly Hall and that involved UN officials, but which was not officially endorsed by the UN) might be seen as initial steps towards directly involving religion in the work of the United Nations. The UN should build on such rudimentary steps to establish mechanisms and processes that will bring, in a meaningful manner, religious values, aspirations, and vision into the heart of the world-embracing enterprise that is the UN.

[12] Religious leaders will need to accept science and religion as the two indispensable knowledge systems that must work together if humankind is to progress. At the same time, those who deny the relevance of religion to the resolution of the seemingly intractable problems confronting (cont'd)

their own followers,[13] and renounce claims to religious exclusivity and finality.[14]

It should not be imagined that the acceptance of religion as a partner within the United Nations will be anything but gradual or that religious hostilities will be eliminated any time soon. But the desperate needs of the human family make further delay in addressing the role of religion unacceptable.

---

humanity must look, with unbiased minds, towards the insights and guidance of religion in order to ensure the appropriate application of the knowledge and skills generated by scientific inquiry. A fundamental principle of the Bahá'í Faith is the harmony of science and religion: "God has endowed man with intelligence and reason whereby he is required to determine the verity of questions and propositions. If religious beliefs and opinions are found contrary to the standards of science, they are mere superstitions and imaginations; for the antithesis of knowledge is ignorance, and the child of ignorance is superstition. Unquestionably, there must be agreement between true religion and science. If a question be found contrary to reason, faith and belief in it are impossible, and there is no outcome but wavering and vacillation" ('Abdu'l-Bahá, *Promulgation of Universal Peace*, p. 181).

[13] Fostering freedom of conscience includes allowing all individuals to investigate reality, to study and to appreciate other religions, and to change their religion if they so choose. The Bahá'í writings stress that force and coercion in matters of religion and belief are violations of the divine command: "the conscience of man is sacred and to be respected" ['Abdu'l-Bahá, *A Traveler's Narrative* (Wilmette, IL: Bahá'í Publishing Trust, 1980), p. 91]. Surely, the hallmark of what it means to be human is for the individual to investigate reality for herself, to freely choose her religion, and to worship God in the manner she believes is right.

[14] To move beyond such dogmas will require embracing the notion that all of the world's great religions are equally valid in nature and origin and are aspects of one divine, progressive, civilizing process, refining humanity's capacity to know, to love, and to serve. Bahá'u'lláh states, "There can be no doubt whatever that the peoples of the world, of whatever race or religion, derive their inspiration from one heavenly Source, and are the subjects of one God" [*Gleanings from the Writings of Bahá'u'lláh* (Wilmette, IL: Bahá'í Publishing Trust, 1994), p. 217]. The future of civilization ultimately rests on acceptance or rejection of this understanding of the nature and source of the world's great religions.

Religion and the United Nations
Possible Next Steps

For its part, the United Nations might begin the process of substantively involving religion in deliberations on humankind's future by hosting an initial gathering of religious leaders convoked, perhaps, by the Secretary-General. As a first priority, the leaders might call for a convention on freedom of religion and belief to be drafted and ratified, as expeditiously as possible, by the governments of the world, with the assistance of religious communities.[15] Such an action by the world's religious leaders, which would signal their willingness to accept freedom of conscience for all peoples, would significantly reduce tensions in the world. The gathering might also discuss the foundation within the United Nations system of a permanent religious forum, patterned initially perhaps on the UN's recently founded Permanent Forum on Indigenous Issues. The creation of this body would be an important initial step towards fully integrating religion into the UN's work of establishing a peaceful world order.[16]

For their part, religious leaders will need to show that they are worthy of participation in such a forum. Only those religious

---

[15] Other initial efforts might include the creation and ratification of international conventions on education and on the media. Building on the Convention against Discrimination in Education, these conventions should unreservedly condemn and forcefully sanction those who, in the name of religion, use education and the media to oppress freedom of conscience and to promote division, hatred, terrorism, violence, and bloodshed. There should be no tolerance for educational institutions and initiatives, or media policies and programs—whether public or private—that promote such attitudes and behavior.

[16] The notion that the diversity of religions precludes the possibility of effective religious involvement at the United Nations is questionable. The world's religions hold many spiritual truths in common and are increasingly coming together, at all levels, to explore shared values and aspirations, to work to effect governmental policies and programs, and to carry out an array of initiatives. In fact, the common vision of a peaceable future, held by all of the world's great religions, indicates the immense dedication, energy, and resources that religious involvement in the United Nations could bring to the organization as it seeks to fulfill its global mandate.

leaders who make it clear to their followers that prejudice, bigotry, and violence have no place in the life of a religious person should be invited to participate in the work of this body.

The Promised Reign of Peace and Justice

It is evident that the longer the United Nations delays the meaningful involvement of religion in its work, the longer humanity will suffer the ravages of injustice and disunity.[17] It is equally clear that until the religions of the world renounce fanaticism and work wholeheartedly to eliminate it from within their own ranks, peace and prosperity will prove chimerical. Indeed, the responsibility for the plight of humanity rests, in large part, with the world's religious leaders. It is they who must raise their voices to end the hatred, exclusivity, oppression of conscience, violations of human rights, denial of equality, opposition to science, and glorification of materialism, violence, and terrorism, which are perpetrated in the name of religious truth. Moreover, it is the followers of all religions who must transform their own lives and take up the mantle of sacrifice for and service to the well-being of others, and thus contribute to the realization of the long-promised reign of peace and justice on earth.

---

[17] The growing danger of a religiously provoked global conflagration only highlights the need to hasten religious involvement in the work of the UN. However, "such a danger civil government, unaided, cannot overcome." Nor should it be imagined "that appeals for mutual tolerance can alone extinguish animosities that claim to possess divine sanction." The situation "calls on religious leadership for a break with the past as decisive as those that opened the way for society to address equally corrosive prejudices of race, gender and nation. Whatever justification exists for exercising influence in matters of conscience lies in serving the well-being of humankind. At this greatest turning point in the history of civilization, the demands of such service could not be clearer" (Universal House of Justice, letter to the world's religious leaders).

Women's Leadership in Peace-Building

Statement by the Bahá'í International Community to the Global Peace Initiative of Women Religious and Spiritual Leaders, Geneva, Switzerland, 6–10 October 2002.

One of the most significant shifts to take place during the twentieth century is that the peoples of the world have finally begun seeing themselves as the members of a single human race, sharing the earth as a common homeland. Although conflict and violence continue to darken the horizon, prejudices that once seemed inherent in the nature of the human species—prejudices of race, gender, nation, and class—have been eroded to such a degree as to suggest that the end of religious prejudice might also be within the realm of possibility.

Sadly, religion, which should be at the forefront of efforts to promote social harmony and peace, is frequently one of the most formidable obstacles in the path of understanding and mutual respect, inasmuch as it has too often lent its credibility to fanaticism. It is here that women who, all over the world, have been rising to take their proper and equal place in society, can, in the field of organized religion play a crucial role in the emancipation of the human race from conflict and violence.

When religions have been faithful to the transcendent example of their illumined Founders, faith "has awakened in whole populations the capacities to love, to forgive, to create, to dare greatly, to overcome prejudice, to sacrifice for the common good, and to discipline the impulses of animal instinct."[1] It is this positive and constructive power of religion that the United Nations has yet to grasp. It is inconceivable that a peaceful and prosperous global society can be established and sustained without directly and substantively involving the world's great religions in its design and support. At the same time, given the record of religious fanaticism and its resurgence in our own time, it is understandable that the United Nations has been hesitant to invite religions into its negotiations.

Women are not only an entire half of humankind that, in this past century, has been emerging as a force for change. They are, Bahá'ís believe, endowed with a special destiny for the establishment of world peace. The Bahá'í writings promise that "as woman advances toward the degree of man in power and privilege … most assuredly war will cease; for woman is naturally the most devoted and staunch advocate of international peace."[2] A unique twofold challenge and responsibility, therefore, lies before us, the participants in this conference, as women and as religious and spiritual leaders.

With peace-building as our goal; with unshakable confidence in the One God; no matter how our different religious traditions conceive of the Godhead; armed with the certainty that hatred, violence, and blind prejudice are contrary to the divine will; we can exert an influence on the vision of all peoples that can overcome every obstacle in the way of establishing the world of tranquility, prosperity, and freedom for which all humankind must surely yearn.

---

[1] Universal House of Justice, letter to the world's religious leaders, April 2002.

[2] 'Abdu'l-Bahá, *The Promulgation of Universal Peace: Talks Delivered by 'Abdu'l-Bahá during His Visit to the United States and Canada in 1912*, rev. ed. (Wilmette, IL: Bahá'í Publishing Trust, 1995), p. 375.

In Support of the Working Group on Minorities

Oral statement by the Bahá'í International Community to the 54th session of the United Nations Sub-Commission on the Promotion and Protection of Human Rights, Geneva, Switzerland, 8 August 2002.

The Bahá'í International Community welcomes the progress made by the Working Group on Minorities and reported to this year's session of the Sub-Commission on the Promotion and Protection of Human Rights. We wish to take this opportunity to congratulate the Working Group on its diligent efforts, to support, in general, its findings and recommendations, and to draw attention to what we see as particularly valuable contributions.

Nearly 10 years have passed since the 1992 Declaration on the Rights of Persons Belonging to National or Ethnic, Religious and Linguistic Minorities articulated international standards to protect minority groups from discrimination. At the same time, the declaration promoted the much wider goal of encouraging cultural, linguistic, and religious diversity within countries—a goal we, as Bahá'ís, see as essential to peace, prosperity, and stability in the world. Those who work to support the implementation of these standards have faced many obstacles; nevertheless, the Sub-Commission's Working Group has through its determined efforts managed to produce tangible results. We find particularly useful the Commentary to the UN Declaration prepared by its able Chair, Asbjørn Eide, and published in Part 1 of the "UN Guide for Minorities."

The position of the Bahá'í International Community on matters involving minority rights has not changed. We consider all human beings as members of one worldwide family, sharing the same fundamental needs and aspirations, yet infinitely varied in temperament, language, religion, and culture. We believe that diversity is a fact of life that should be embraced as a source of enrichment in the life of society. When differences collide, fair solutions need to be sought through consultation guided by mutual respect for the rights of others and a belief that harmonious resolution is possible.

Constructive consultation is possible, however, only when people renounce all attitudes of superiority, all ancient grievances (however justifiable), and all extreme parochial attachments, which are merely a perversion of the pride that groups rightfully feel in their own culture. We see creative solutions emerging from an expansive view of world society that considers all human beings as members of one family and seeks to create harmony based on mutual respect, not sameness.

As the component elements of the human family begin to see themselves inextricably linked to all others as part of a whole, which, like any living organism, benefits from the well-being of its constituent parts, enduring solutions become possible.

Based on these firm convictions, the Bahá'í International Community has always given importance to minority rights. It contributed to the studies prepared by Mr. Eide, wholeheartedly supported the creation of the Working Group, and shall continue to participate in this work.

We support, in particular, the recent practice of undertaking country visits, which was initiated by the members of the Working Group. On-site evaluation not only helps the Working Group to assess a particular situation, but also contributes to raising awareness of certain minority issues that tend to be left aside or considered peripheral. We urge all member states to extend invitations in this regard, and we hope that the Working Group develops a method through which it will approach governments to request such visits.

Finally, we would like to support the recommendations made by the Working Group at its eighth session, in particular, its call for the Commission on Human Rights to consider "establishing a special procedure mechanism on the rights of persons belonging to minorities, such as a special rapporteur or special representative." We urge the Sub-Commission to endorse these recommendations and forward them to the Commission on Human Rights.

Bahá'ís in Iran
CURRENT SITUATION

Written statement of the Bahá'í International
Community to the 59th session of the United
Nations Commission on Human Rights, held from
17 March to 25 April 2003 in Geneva, Switzerland.

S ince 1979, Bahá'ís in the Islamic Republic of Iran have been subjected to attack, harassment, and discrimination solely on account of their religious beliefs. The extent and systematic nature of this persecution have been well documented over the years in reports issued by the United Nations Special Representatives.

Officials of the Iranian government have often claimed that resolutions adopted by the UN Commission on Human Rights were not helpful to the process of promoting human rights in their country. They have had the opportunity to demonstrate their willingness to progress on their own since the commission suspended its monitoring in Iran last year. Unfortunately, however, we must report that the collective and individual rights of Bahá'ís—not just civil and political rights, but a wide range of social, economic, and cultural rights, as well—are still being systematically violated.

Iran's anti-Bahá'í actions are not random acts, but deliberate government policy. A secret government document, obtained and published by the Commission in 1993, serves as a blueprint for the slow strangulation of the Bahá'í community. Produced by Iran's Supreme Revolutionary Cultural Council and approved by the Islamic Republic's Supreme Leader, this document sets forth specific guidelines for dealing with "the Bahá'í question" so that Bahá'í "progress and development shall be blocked." There can be no doubt that the policy is still in effect today.

The Bahá'í community poses no threat of any kind to the authorities in Iran. It is not aligned with any other government, ideology, or opposition movement. The principles of the Faith require Bahá'ís to be obedient to their government and to avoid partisan political involvement, subversive activity, and all forms of violence. Moreover, Bahá'ís seek no special privileges. They desire only respect for their rights under the International Bill of Human Rights, of which Iran is a signatory.

Recent government initiatives to promote the rights of religious minorities were never intended to include the Bahá'ís. The Constitution of the Islamic Republic of Iran stipulates (in Article 13) that "Zoroastrian, Jewish, and Christian Iranians are the only recognized religious minorities." Thus some 300,000 Bahá'ís—who constitute the largest religious minority in the country—do not benefit from government initiatives such as the Iranian National Committee for the Promotion of the Rights of Religious Minorities, or the recent "blood money" legislation. Bahá'ís are not a *recognized* minority under the constitution, and the Islamic regime still refers to the Bahá'í Faith as a heresy and a conspiracy. Classified as "unprotected infidels," Bahá'ís have no legal rights or protection at all, even though Iran is a signatory of the International Covenant on Civil and Political Rights, which guarantees freedom of religious belief.

Executions, Death Sentences, and Imprisonment

Since 1979, more than 200 Bahá'ís have been killed, and 15 others have disappeared and are presumed dead. The last Bahá'í executed was hanged on 21 July 1998. During the past few years, all of the Bahá'ís sentenced to death have either been released or had their sentences reduced. The government has stopped sending members of the community to prison for apostasy. Instead, the authorities now use arrest, interrogation, and short-term imprisonment as a means of harassing and intimidating Bahá'ís. This practice is more difficult to monitor and report to the international community.

As of February 2003, four Bahá'ís are still being detained in Iranian prisons because of their religious beliefs; Mr. Bihnam Mithaqi and Mr. Kayvan Khalajabadi are currently serving 15-year sentences, and Mr. Musa Talibi and Mr. Dhabihu'llah Mahrami are sentenced to life imprisonment.

Denial of the Right to Organize as a Peaceful Religious Community

Since 1983, the Bahá'í community in Iran has been denied both the right to assemble officially and the right to maintain its administrative institutions. It should be pointed out that:

- in other countries, these democratically elected bodies organize and administer the religious activities of the community;

- these sacred institutions perform many of the functions reserved to clergy in other religions and are the foundational element of Bahá'í community life; and

- since the Bahá'í Faith has no clergy, the denial of the right to elect these institutions threatens the very existence of a viable religious community.

The Iranian Bahá'ís gradually developed makeshift arrangements to worship in small groups, conduct classes for children, and take care of other community needs. However, authorities continue to harass them by disrupting meetings, arresting teachers, and giving students and participants suspended sentences to be carried out should they again commit these "crimes." The use of suspended sentences is a threatening tactic devised by the Ministry of Information (Intelligence). Under recent government practice, the Bahá'ís receive no written documentation relating to their arrest or punishment.

Denial of Access to Education

An entire generation of Bahá'ís has been systematically barred from higher education in legally recognized public and private institutions of learning in Iran. After having been denied access to these institutions for many years, the Bahá'ís established their own higher education program in 1987. In 1998, however, intelligence officers arrested (and subsequently released) some 36 faculty members of the Bahá'í Institute of Higher Education (BIHE) and also seized textbooks, papers, records, computers, and furniture.

In 2001, three classrooms used by members of the community were seized, and in mid-2002 an instructor of Bahá'í youth was summoned to the Intelligence Agency. In July 2002, the authorities disrupted BIHE qualification examinations in eight different locations simultaneously, videotaping proceedings, interviewing students, confiscating examination papers and Bahá'í books—thus showing that the government is pursuing its established policy of intimidation.

The Bahá'í Faith places a high value on education. Bahá'ís have always been among the best-educated groups in Iran, and the erosion of their educational level is inevitably impoverishing the community.

Confiscation and Destruction of Community Property

Bahá'í cemeteries, holy places, historical sites, administrative centers, and other assets were seized shortly after the 1979 revolution. No properties have been returned, and many have been destroyed.

Seizure of cemeteries throughout Iran has created problems for Bahá'ís, who have difficulties burying their dead and identifying gravesites. They are permitted access only to areas of wasteland, designated by the government for their use, and are not permitted to mark the graves of their loved ones.

Confiscation of Properties Belonging to Individual Bahá'ís

The property rights of Bahá'ís are generally disregarded. Since 1979, large numbers of private and business properties belonging to Bahá'ís have been arbitrarily confiscated, including homes and farms.

In recent months, there has been an increase in confiscations. Sometimes when property is confiscated, a court decree is issued, stating that the owner is an "active member of the misguided Bahá'í sect."

Denial of Employment, Pensions, and Other Benefits

The government is also systematically weakening the economic base of the Bahá'í community by depriving many Bahá'ís of the means to earn a living.

In the early 1980s, more than 10,000 Bahá'ís were dismissed from positions in government and educational institutions. Many remain unemployed and receive no unemployment benefits; many others had their pensions terminated, and some were even required to return salaries or pensions paid before their dismissal.

Employment opportunities are still limited. Even when Bahá'ís find employment in the private sector, in many cases government authorities somehow intervene and force the owners of the companies concerned to fire them. When Bahá'ís start a private business, the authorities attempt to block their activities. Moreover, there have been what we believe to be attempts to scare Bahá'ís engaged in agriculture away from their land.

Denial of Civil Rights and Liberties

Under Iranian law, Bahá'ís have no legal protection and thus their rights can be ignored with impunity. Harassment continues unabated in a number of communities.

The application of some laws has been modified. During the year 2000, measures taken by the government made it possible for married Bahá'í couples to be registered as husband and wife and for the children of such couples to be registered. But the relevant law has not been changed; neither Bahá'í marriage nor Bahá'í divorce is legally recognized in Iran. The right of Bahá'ís to inherit is also denied.

The freedom of Bahá'ís to travel outside or inside Iran is often impeded by Iranian authorities and sometimes denied. Although recent years have witnessed an increase in the number of Iranian Bahá'ís given passports, it is not clear that there has been a change of government policy on this issue.

Recent Official Statements

Iranian representatives have made several encouraging statements in
international fora during the past two years. In the June 2000 Session
of the ILO [International Labour Organization], the representative of
Iran reportedly stated: "Although the members of the Baha'i faith do
not belong to a recognized religious minority, under the terms of the
legislation approved by the Expediency Council in 1999, all Iranians
enjoy the rights of citizenship irrespective of their belief." At the
meeting of the Committee on the Rights of the Child held in May
2000, the Iranian representative reportedly said that the adoption
of this new law had improved the situation of those who followed
"non-recognized religions and beliefs such as the Baha'i faith."

We welcome these statements, but we have yet to see any evidence that the "right to citizenship" legislation is being implemented.
The patterns of persecution detailed above persist to this day.

Claims by the Islamic Human Rights Commission (IHRC) to have
achieved some success in investigating a number of cases involving
Bahá'ís also appear to be unfounded. Bahá'ís in Iran did submit some
cases to the IHRC when it was first established, and representatives of
the Bahá'í International Community spoke with the IHRC delegation
to the Commission on Human Rights last year. But no steps have
been taken by the IHRC to resolve any of the cases or to defend the
rights of the Bahá'í religious minority in Iran. On the contrary, the
situations of some Bahá'ís concerned in the cases submitted to the
IHRC have actually worsened.

Summary Conclusion

Overall, we must report that persecution of the Bahá'ís in the Islamic
Republic of Iran has intensified since the Commission on Human
Rights decided to suspend formal monitoring in this country. Arrest
and short-term detention of Bahá'ís has increased; teachers and students continue to be harassed; more properties have been confiscated;
and attempts have been made to scare Bahá'ís off their land.

The Iranian government is now declaring—especially to the
European Union, with whom it has started a Human Rights Dialogue—that it is committed to improving the human rights situation

within its borders. We would like to be hopeful, but we have yet to see the government take even one clear step toward ending the persecution and discrimination faced by the Bahá'ís, let alone make any move in the direction of establishing full legal protection for the Bahá'í community.

Bahá'ís in Egypt
CURRENT SITUATION

Oral statement of the Bahá'í International Community to the 59th session of the United Nations Commission on Human Rights, held from 17 March to 25 April 2003 in Geneva, Switzerland.

The harassment and injustices targeting the Bahá'ís in Egypt are clear violations of freedom of religion or belief. Regrettably, we have not seen any measures taken by the government of Egypt to right these wrongs, and so we are compelled to request that the international community call upon the Egyptian authorities to resolve the issue.

Since 1960, when President Nasser issued Presidential Decree No. 263, the Bahá'ís have been subjected to active persecution in Egypt. This decree singled out the Bahá'í community, dissolved its religious institutions, banned all its religious activities, and suppressed its community life. The decree is still used today to instigate police investigations, arrests, domicile searches, and the destruction of Bahá'í religious literature, and it is restrictively interpreted by the courts in ways that reduce the status of the Bahá'ís to that of second-class citizens.

All members of the community are under strict and constant police surveillance. They have no access to any form of legal marriage, cannot obtain custody of children, child allowances, or alimony, and are often denied access to pensions and inheritance. Not being legally married, they cannot even obtain a family record—a document required by law in Egypt for many official purposes.

The Bahá'ís are not free to profess their faith in Egypt. Article 46 of the Egyptian Constitution says that "The State guarantees the freedom of belief and the freedom of the exercise of religious rites," and it makes no mention of recognized religions. But many Bahá'ís have been detained on charges that stemmed from talking to friends in the privacy of their homes about their beliefs, or from gathering in private, in small numbers, for devotional readings and prayers. The authorities consider these to be activities previously performed by Bahá'í Assemblies and thus outlawed, regardless of their peaceful, private, and devotional nature.

The Bahá'ís are regularly denounced as apostates, in the media or in widely publicized court decisions, which are generally accompanied by advocacy of hatred on religious grounds. The Mufti of Egypt and members of the Academy of Islamic Research of the Azhar, who are government appointees, have associated themselves on several occasions with this incitement to hatred and violence, giving it an air of official approval. And the government does not take any action against those who cry out that Bahá'í apostates deserve to be killed. Published documents establishing these facts are easy to obtain. The Special Rapporteur on freedom of religion or belief has mentioned some of them in his reports.

The Bahá'í International Community expressed these concerns in a submission to the Human Rights Committee last year. In the Concluding Observations issued after its review of Egypt's periodic reports, the Committee deplored the ban on worship imposed on the Bahá'í community in this country. It also expressed concern about "the pressures applied to the judiciary by extremists claiming to represent Islam, who have even succeeded, in some cases, in imposing on courts their own interpretation of the religion."[1]

The Egyptian Bahá'ís are a law-abiding, peaceful community. Their only request is that the government remove all of the official obstructions and restrictions that target them, including Presidential Decree No. 263 of 1960. It is our sincere hope that the authorities will take all of the measures required, so that the Bahá'ís will soon be free to practice their faith in Egypt.

---

[1] See CCPR/CO/76/EGY, p. 5, para. 17.

Social Cohesion
DWELLING IN THE SAME LAND

*A statement by the National Spiritual Assembly of
the Bahá'ís of the United Kingdom, May 2002.*

Increased attention has been focused recently on the need to promote better intercommunity relationships between the various
elements of our society. Addressing this issue, a previous paper[1]
has already referred to the need for a society-wide change of moral
consciousness and understanding and a wider social vision. Poor
relationships between individuals and between groups are symptoms
of a dysfunctional and fragmented society. Particular attention has
been given to questions of race and color, but these are not the only
issues. Hostility and suspicion can develop not only across racial
boundaries, but also across those of ethnicity, culture, religion,
gender, generation, nationality, region, education, and class.

The stresses within our society can be seen as symptoms of
an unprecedented global restructuring of human society over the
past 150 years or so: the mingling of races, cultures, and creeds to
a previously unimagined degree, the reordering of long-cherished
institutions and a growing perception of our world as an increasingly interdependent "global village." The failure to respond fully to

---

[1] The National Spiritual Assembly of the Bahá'ís of the United Kingdom,
"Community Cohesion: A Bahá'í Perspective," February 2002, available at
http://www.bahai.org.uk/dp/s-cohesion.htm.

such change and what lies behind it is reflected not only in signs of social disintegration but also in an accompanying moral crisis and abdication of ethical and behavioral standards. These are all signs of a loss of understanding of our true nature as human beings.

There is a need to reappraise many accepted approaches and attitudes if this increased attention is actually to reduce the mistrust and antipathy that too often exist in our society.

The Bahá'í Vision

While association with all people of diverse beliefs, customs, and outlook is enjoined on His followers by Bahá'u'lláh, His vision of a truly cohesive society goes far beyond the limits of mere association or appreciation of cultural difference, important though these are. He sets out the building of a global society whose closely knit fabric shall be based on active cooperation, reciprocity, shared spiritual and moral values, and genuine concern for others. This society would go beyond a mere passive coexistence and would promote human dignity, stimulate the release of human potential, and actively cultivate the inherent nobility which Bahá'ís believe makes up the basis of human nature.

The foundation of this vision rests unambiguously on the principle of the oneness of the human race. Such a unifying vision should not be confused with uniformity:

> Far from aiming at the subversion of the existing foundations of society, it seeks to broaden its basis.... It can conflict with no legitimate allegiances, nor can it undermine essential loyalties. Its purpose is neither to stifle the flame of a sane and intelligent patriotism in men's hearts, nor to abolish the system of national autonomy so essential if the evils of excessive centralization are to be avoided. It does not ignore, nor does it attempt to suppress, the diversity of ethnical origins, of climate, of history, of language and tradition, of thought and habit, that differentiate the peoples and nations of the world.[2]

---

[2] Shoghi Effendi, *The World Order of Bahá'u'lláh: Selected Letters,* 2nd rev. ed. (Wilmette, IL: Bahá'í Publishing Trust, 1993), p. 41.

The global community thus envisioned will delight in the diversity of the secondary characteristics of every minority, race, and class within it, but will firmly uphold unity in fundamental principles. It calls for complete freedom from prejudice in dealings with peoples of a different race, class, creed, or color, and it imposes an inescapable obligation to nurture, encourage, and safeguard all, whatever their faith, race, class, or nation. A person's origins will no longer be seen as defining "who they really are," but will lend distinction and charm to such a society in demonstrating "unity in diversity."

Social change, in the Bahá'í view, begins not with the community but with the individual. A person's moral and ethical code and feelings of self-worth come from the basic forces of human nature, but they can be developed positively or distorted, even destroyed, depending on that individual's life experience. Social endeavors, from local group actions to changes in the structure of society's governing institutions, may be proposed or worked for, but no plan will have a lasting effect unless it is built upon an inner revolution, a dramatic change in the attitudes of the individual. It follows that establishing an agreed set of core values which all individuals, and hence society, are prepared to embrace is absolutely essential for any program of social cohesion.

A Reappraisal

Policies and attitudes concerned with diversity but which regard the human race as unalterably divided and which see society as a virtually impermeable "community of communities" need to be reassessed. They may all too easily be understood to reinforce old barriers and insularities, whether of culture, race, religion, or gender, be seen to protect groups from legitimate criticism and justify human rights abuses as "cultural differences," and they may unwittingly confirm the prejudices of those with no interest in integration.

And while anti-racist initiatives are clearly essential, and regulating behavior by legislation has a place, they are uncertain modifiers of basic attitudes and beliefs. Unless these latter are changed, it is doubtful if a truly cohesive society can ever be more than an unachievable ideal.

Racial discrimination is undoubtedly a major cause of division, and a force for harm in society, but it is not the only one. At the root of this and all forms of discrimination is the erroneous idea that humankind is somehow composed of separate and distinct races, peoples, or castes, and that those subgroups innately possess varying intellectual, moral, and/or other capacities, which in turn justify different forms of treatment. The reality is that there is only the one human race, a single people inhabiting the planet Earth, one human family bound together in a common destiny.

While a basic recognition of this reality is the antidote to societal division in all its forms, racial and ethnic prejudices are often reinforced by, or are manifestations of, other corrosive agencies: cultural, economic, and educational prejudice; religious fundamentalism; the impersonal nature of modern industrial society; or the influence of international events. Failure to recognize these influences will inhibit attempts to redress racial injustice and intolerance.

Much antagonism and confusion can be attributed to those who have appropriated religion for their own selfish purposes—fostering animosity, suspicion, and the condemnation of other creeds. Fanaticism, notions of superiority, and conflict poison the wells of tolerance and represent corrupt expressions of true religious values. As a result, the transforming power of religion is weakened or cancelled out and the positive contribution it can make reduced or eliminated. While the right to freedom of thought, conscience, and expression of belief is now codified in international human rights instruments, the irresponsible exercise of such freedom to promote hatred and disunity should be curtailed.

Changing Attitudes

Some intergroup prejudice expresses less a specific dislike so much as a kind of generalized timidity and feeling of awkwardness in coping with unfamiliar situations, unknown people, and misunderstood cultural practices.

If human beings were purely rational then the way to change attitudes and make them appropriate would be merely by the dissemination of facts. This has been tried time and time again but has been shown to have little effect. Information alone, when it differs from preexisting, currently held points of view, seldom if ever causes attitude change. It is more likely to be rejected as propagandist and one-sided.

Genuine personal and social contact between members of different ethnic groups can be more effective. However, even this has its limitations. It is most effective when contact is between people of approximately equal social status, when the individuals involved have other things in common. Thus education, class, generation, and socioeconomic circumstances have a role to play in social cohesion or lack of it. These factors deserve attention, but programs that exaggerate their importance or see things purely in sociological terms are bound to have limited results.

While such social distinctions are unavoidable indications of human diversity, it is a great mistake to believe that because people are less well-educated or live different lives they are lacking in either intelligence or sensibility. Discrimination against anyone on whatever grounds, whether social, cultural, or ethnic, is a violation of human dignity, is perverse, and must be repudiated. Prejudice and pretension are, in effect, failures to recognize, however the thought may be expressed, that we are all children of one loving God. At the same time, we should not be blind to the distinctiveness and sensitivities of people who come from different backgrounds.

Education is essential to increasing knowledge and understanding of the great diversity of the human race, but it must be more than the ingestion of facts. It must emphasize the oneness of humanity, inculcate moral and spiritual values, and promote those personal qualities needed for a proper understanding of human diversity: "courtesy, reverence, dignity, respect for the rank and achievements of others are virtues which contribute to the harmony and well-being of every community."[3] In cultivating these qualities, example is one of the best educators. Those who today act or are seen as role models may take note.

However, while the Bahá'í writings elevate respect, dignity, and reverence to a high station and describe courtesy as "the prince of virtues," they contrast them with frivolity and facetiousness, ribaldry,

---

[3] Universal House of Justice, letter to an individual, 22 February 1999.

and effrontery. These last all-too-prevalent qualities—finding expression in studied confrontation, intemperate abuse, and aspects of the adversarial system—have fomented mistrust and disdain for society rather than promoting harmony and well-being.

A Pattern for the Future

Greater social cohesion requires a commonly shared vision of community life. This vision should recognize both a sense of individual and community purpose and the worth that each individual and each group contributes to the wider community. The success of such a pattern of society depends upon the attitudes and perceptions, and the personal integrity and moral responsibility of the individuals who compose it. While misplaced loyalty to one particular creed or another has at times provoked division, the rejection by many of attachment to any creed or faith has not led to a marked increase in tolerance or brotherly love. We may deduce, therefore, there is still a place for the spiritual impulse to encourage human virtue and elevate human nature above the crudely material.

Inseparable from the elevation of human nature is an appreciation of what is meant by diversity and the oneness of humankind. Oneness and diversity are complementary and inseparable. That human consciousness operates through an infinite diversity of individual minds and motivations detracts in no way from its essential unity. Indeed, it is this diversity that distinguishes unity from homogeneity or uniformity. The notion of diversity without the concept of unity becomes merely a euphemism for division.

With an approach that is neither solely pragmatic nor solely spiritual, Bahá'ís suggest their own experience can offer a useful pattern of social cohesion. Their success in building a unified community stems solely from the inspiration of the spiritual teachings of Bahá'u'lláh, writing extensively, more than a century ago, about the importance of unity, the reality of oneness, and the imperative need for creating a peaceful world civilization. His words stand at once as a cornerstone of Bahá'í belief and as a challenge to all humankind:

> Know ye not why We created you all from the same dust? That
> no one should exalt himself over the other. Ponder at all times in

your hearts how ye were created. Since We have created you all from one same substance it is incumbent on you to be even as one soul, to walk with the same feet, eat with the same mouth, and dwell in the same land, that from your inmost being, by your deeds and actions, the signs of oneness and the essence of detachment may be made manifest.[4]

---

[4] Bahá'u'lláh, *The Hidden Words* (Wilmette, IL: Bahá'í Publishing Trust, 1994), Arabic no. 68, p. 20.

INFORMATION
AND RESOURCES

Obituaries

THOMAS R. BAUMGARTNER JR.

On 15 February 2003, in McMinnville, Oregon, the United States.

Thomas Baumgartner was born on 12 April 1922 in Kansas City, Kansas. He first learned of the Faith in his teens in Miami, Florida, and after becoming a Bahá'í in 1940, at the age of 18, he went on to live a life of distinguished service. He was initially active in the Miami Bahá'í community, was elected to the first Local Spiritual Assembly of Dade County, Florida, and later to the first Assembly in North Dade County. In 1958, he departed with his wife Dorothy and their five sons for Alaska, one of the goal regions of the Ten Year Crusade. Undeterred by the harsh conditions, they made their first home in the North Pole region. The family ultimately lived in some 14 different locales, including native villages, where they taught the Bahá'í Faith to members of the Inupiat, Athabascan, and Tlingit peoples. Mr. Baumgartner and his wife also adopted a daughter while living in Alaska. He worked for a time at the Geophysical Institute at the University of Alaska Fairbanks, and also in telecommunications, spending 26 years in the development and installation of satellite-based telephone service in many remote regions of Alaska. Some of his other efforts for the Faith included undertaking numerous trips to assist in the growth and development of Bahá'í communities in Alaska, Canada, the United States, and Dominica. The family moved back to the United States in the early 1970s and he continued to serve the Faith there until his death.

JOAN CAMRASS

On 17 September 2002, in Henderson, Auckland, New Zealand.
Joan Cynthia Heslop was born on 27 April 1926 in Harrogate, Yorkshire, England. After graduating from the University of Oxford in England, she worked as a teacher, occupying the post of head of the Geography Department at Roundhay High School for Girls in Leeds until 1960. She was elected a fellow of the Royal Geographic Society in 1953. During the 1960s and 70s, she wrote textbooks for secondary schools. In 1961 she married Rex Camrass. Mrs. Camrass became a Bahá'í in 1974 in Samoa and soon dedicated her efforts to serving the Bahá'í community in New Zealand. She served on the Auckland City Local Spiritual Assembly from 1975 to 1978 and on the Manukau Assembly from 1979 to 1983. She was widowed in 1978 and from that year until 1992 worked in New Zealand's national Bahá'í archives. There, she was devoted to caring for and cataloging the history and archives of the country's Bahá'í community. She initiated the filing system of the National Spiritual Assembly and wrote an instructional booklet on keeping archives. In 2001, her book *Resolute Advance*, a history of the development of the Faith in New Zealand, was published by Viking Press. To honor her memory and her efforts, the National Spiritual Assembly renamed its national library the Joan Camrass Reference Library.

ARAMIS COSTAS

On 18 September 2002, in Burzaco, Buenos Aires, Argentina.
Aramis Orlando Costas was born on 31 January 1932, in José Mármol, Buenos Aires. His parents became Bahá'ís in 1941 and from that point raised their children in the Faith. Mr. Costas affirmed his belief in 1945 and later took the Faith to new regions of Argentina. He worked as a designer and sign maker and was able to travel widely in pursuit of the needs of the Argentinean Bahá'í community. He married Lydia Barsellini in 1958 and they traveled together, accompanied by their only son, to carry out an intensive program of expansion of Bahá'í communities in the Mapuche area in General Roca. They established the first Local Assembly in General Roca in 1969, and during the family's four years there Mr. Costas had a regular radio program about the Faith, with listeners as far away as Chile. He was also instrumental, with his wife, in developing Argentina's first national bulletin in 1962. He served on the Local Assembly of Almirante Brown from 1976 until 1999 and, in 1967, Mr. Costas was elected to the Spiritual Assembly of Argentina.

LACEY CRAWFORD

On 21 July 2002, in Columbia, South Carolina, the United States.

Lacey Crawford was born on 12 December 1920 in Toledo, Ohio, and became a Bahá'í in 1964, after a tour of duty in the US Army. A graduate in photography from the Illinois Institute of Technology, he worked for Johnson Publishing Co., the world's largest black-owned publisher. His work as the lead photographer for a groundbreaking article on the Bahá'í Faith in *Ebony* magazine was used in Bahá'í teaching materials. During the 1960s, he moved with his wife, Ethel, to South Carolina to teach the Bahá'í Faith in the rural areas of the American South. In 1968 he abandoned a promising career as a highly regarded photographer to serve at the Bahá'í World Centre in Haifa, Israel, where he was the head of the Audio-Visual Department for more than 20 years. Returning to South Carolina in 1993, he and Ethel served the Cause with distinction. In its letter after his death, the Universal House of Justice particularly recalled his "steadfast faith and resolute devotion that shone through a gentle but enthusiastic spirit."

UNA DEAN

On 8 March 2003, in Edmonton, Alberta, Canada.

Daughter of Hand of the Cause of God George Townshend and his wife Nancy, Una Townshend was born in Ireland on 20 April 1921. She attended a women's college in Cheltenham, England, and was active as a Bahá'í from early on in her life, first in Ireland and later in Italy, serving there as a member of the British armed forces during World War II. In 1946 she became the first Bahá'í to settle in Dublin and was later a member of that city's first Local Spiritual Assembly. She also helped establish the first Local Spiritual Assembly in Liverpool. In October 1953, to fulfill a goal of the Ten Year Crusade, she became the first Bahá'í in Malta, an act for which Shoghi Effendi named her a Knight of Bahá'u'lláh. In a letter to her father, Shoghi Effendi wrote: "The work so splendidly initiated by your dear daughter is unique, historic, and of vital importance. I admire her courage, zeal, devotion, and perseverance." She returned to Ireland in 1954 to aid her ailing father and assist him in writing *Christ and Bahá'u'lláh*, which Shoghi Effendi called Mr. Townshend's "crowning achievement." After her father's death in March 1957, she moved to Canada. On a trip to Seattle she met and later married Richard (Dick) Dean and the couple settled in Edmonton, where she served on the Local Spiritual Assembly until 1987. The Deans' daughter, Farah, has a severe mental disability, and the family was among the founding members of the Alberta Association of Families in Action for the Dependent Handicapped. In a message after her passing, the Universal House of Justice wrote of her "exemplary courage" in taking the message of Baha'u'llah to the people of Malta and requested that the Bahá'ís of Ireland hold a memorial service to celebrate her life and services to the Bahá'í community.

FRANCES B. EDELSTEIN

On 22 February 2003, in Medford, Oregon, the United States.
Frances Bradford Jones was born on 8 April 1910 in Mattituck, New York, and embraced the Bahá'í Faith in 1938. During the 1930s and 40s her work for the Bahá'í community included efforts to improve race relations. In 1943, she assisted in forming the first Local Spiritual Assembly in Sioux Falls, South Dakota. Other services included working as secretary of the New York Bahá'í Center and the Green Acre Bahá'í School in Maine; she also served on Local Spiritual Assemblies in New Jersey and California. In 1954, she pioneered to Famagusta, Cyprus, at the request of Shoghi Effendi and stayed for two years before returning to the United States. Later she helped to form the first Local Spiritual Assembly in Lucerne, Switzerland, where she lived from 1960 to 1963. She married Ephraim "Frank" Edelstein in 1969; he died in 1973. Her last few years were spent in a care facility. Though blind, she still taught the Faith actively to all with whom she came in contact.

DAWN EDWARDS

On 24 December 2002, in Bellingham, Washington, the United States.
Dawn Edwards was born around 1916. Her services to the Bahá'í Faith included pioneering to Nepal from 1972 to 1975, to Turkey in 1975, and to Thailand from 1976 to 1978. She also undertook a trip to Romania in May and June 1991. Her published works about the Bahá'í Faith include *Pocket Thoughts*, *Bahá'í Basics*, and *Petals of Poetry*. In its message after her passing, the Universal House of Justice wrote that her "selfless services" as a pioneer were a "testament to her devotion" to the Faith.

ELAINE EILERS

On 3 November 2002, in Harare, Zimbabwe.
Elaine Snider was born in Champaign, Illinois, the United States, on 15 December 1917. Her father, Howard J. Snider, was a Knight of Bahá'u'lláh, and they served together on the first Local Spiritual Assembly of Smyrna, Georgia. She was also a member of the District Teaching Committee in Northern Georgia during the 1960s and '70s. She studied interior decoration, was an artist by profession, and was a contributor to the *Brilliant Star* children's magazine. She married William Eilers and the couple had three sons. Though she was partially paralyzed in her left leg from polio in 1949, it did not stop her travels for the Faith. A pioneer to Malawi in the early 1970s, she was only

able to stay for a year and a half before returning to the United States due to visa problems. In 1976, she returned to Africa, this time settling in the area of Rhodesia that would later become Zimbabwe, and remained there until the end of her life. Her services to the Bahá'í community in Zimbabwe included membership on various national and local committees, and work in the office of the Continental Board of Counsellors. She also offered financial assistance to many Zimbabweans for their education and contributed to the construction of seminar facilities and the national center in Harare.

KHOJASTEH KIYANI

On 11 November 2002, in Begnins, Vaud, Switzerland.
Khojasteh Khorshand was born in 1917 in Tehran, Persia (Iran), to a Bahá'í family. In Tehran, she served on the Committee for the Advancement of Women and the Committee for Liaison with Authorities, as well as financing and establishing a free school for village children in S̲h̲aríf-Ábád, Qazvín. Around 1956, she left Iran for Europe, settling first in Italy, where she helped to establish the first Local Spiritual Assembly of Padova. She later moved to Paris, where she married Hossein-Gholi Kiyani, who died in 1993. Together with her husband, she donated a building in Paris for use as the national Bahá'í center and also participated in the acquisition of a historic building where 'Abdu'l-Bahá had stayed during His visit to Paris in 1913.

KHODARAHM PAYMAN

On 2 August 2002, in Jakarta, Indonesia.
Khodarahm Hormozdyar Payman was born in November 1921 in Yazd, Persia (Iran), to a Bahá'í family. He moved to Bombay, India, in 1942 to start a career in business and during his time in the country was elected to the Regional Spiritual Assembly of India, Pakistan, and Burma. He married Parvin Siroosi in 1947, and the couple had three children. In 1950, they pioneered to Indonesia (then known as the Dutch East Indies) and remained in that country until the end his life. His business career continued in Indonesia, where he worked as an exporter of tea and later as a representative of a foreign telecommunications company. When he arrived, the country was engaged in a war for independence. There was only one other Bahá'í in Indonesia at the time, and during the majority of his time there, the Faith's activities were heavily restricted by the government, but he was nonetheless able to do much in support of the Bahá'í community. He was a founding member of the Local Spiritual Assembly of Jakarta and a member of the first Regional Spiritual Assembly of Southeast Asia when it formed in 1957. He also became fluent in the Indonesian language and was able to translate Bahá'í writings. He served as an Auxiliary Board member and in 1968 was appointed by the Universal

House of Justice to the Continental Board of Counsellors for Asia. He served
as a Continental Counsellor for 22 years and traveled extensively, undertaking
teachings trips to Malaysia, Burma, Laos, and the Philippines. Among his other
services was his membership on the Regional Board of Trustees of Ḥuqúqu'lláh
in Southeast Asia. After his death, the Universal House of Justice asked that
memorial gatherings be held in his honor in Indonesia and at the House of
Worship in New Delhi, India.

PAPALI'ITELE STEVEN PERCIVAL

On 17 December 2002, in Apia, Samoa.
Susuga Papali'itele Stephen Charles Percival was born on 13 February 1929 in
Nuku'alofa, Tonga. He became a Bahá'í in July 1957 and was elected to the
Regional Spiritual Assembly of the Bahá'ís of the South Pacific in 1959, also
serving on the first Local Spiritual Assembly of Apia. Despite having little
formal education, he established a successful business in Samoa and served
on several governmental advisory boards to assist in developing the country's
economy. In 1962, he established one of the first manufacturing plants in
Samoa, mass producing men's shirts with traditional design prints. Among
his many services to the Faith were his frequent travels to rural villages in
Samoa to teach the Faith. He also donated land for the first Bahá'í center
in Samoa, was instrumental in securing the property to serve as the site for
the House of Worship at Tiapapata, and negotiated with the government to
secure recognition of Bahá'í holy days as religious observances. He had five
children with his wife, Greta Gurau, whom he married in 1953. He was also
a close friend of His Highness Susuga Malietoa Tanumafili II, who bestowed
the title "Papali'itele" on him, a designation meaning "high chief."

JOYCE HONEYMAN PERDU

On 11 December 2002, in Cardiff, Wales.
Joyce Eileen Honeyman was born on 27 November 1922 in London. She
married Joseph Perdu in Cairo in 1951 and the couple had three children.
Although her husband taught her the Faith, she did not formally embrace it
until 1961, after separating from him. She lived in several countries in Africa,
including Sudan, Madagascar, and South Africa and worked for the British
Foreign Office in London and Beirut. For most of her life, she was an English
teacher. In 1961, after having formally declared herself as a Bahá'í in the UK,
she pioneered to the Canary Islands, initiating more than 40 years of traveling
in service to the Faith. She was a member of the Local Spiritual Assembly of
Las Palmas until she moved to Spain in 1964, where she served on the first
Local Assembly of Malaga and other Local Assemblies in Jaén, Córdoba, and
Almería through the 1970s and '80s. She also lived in Honduras from 1984 to

1996, assisting nascent Bahá'í communities and traveling extensively through the country before finally returning to the UK, where she passed away.

FUAD RIZAI

On 10 December 2002, in Tunbridge Wells, Kent, England.
Born in Tehran, Iran, on 5 January 1944, Fuad Rizai was a third generation Bahá'í. He moved to England in the early '70s and was first elected as a member of the Local Spiritual Assembly of Tunbridge Wells in 1975, serving on that body until 2001. In 1979, Mr. Rizai began working on the Bahá'í Advisory Service, a committee set up by the National Spiritual Assembly of the United Kingdom to assist Iranian Bahá'ís arriving in the UK in the wake of the Iranian revolution, during which time the Bahá'í community in Iran was heavily persecuted. He continued this valuable service for the rest of his life and was always available to help people with difficulties. In February 1991, he commenced work at the Bahá'í national center in London as office manager, and he remained in the National Assembly's service until shortly before his passing. He also served on the National Properties Committee, carrying out work on the various Bahá'í properties in the UK. In its message after his passing, the Universal House of Justice wrote of his "exceptional devotion and dedication," particularly in his assistance of the Bahá'í refugees. Mr. Rizai had three children with his wife, Jill Dinnings.

HESHMAT'U'LLAH SABET SHARGHI

On 27 May 2002, in Kampala, Uganda.
Heshmat'u'llah Sabet Sharghi was born in a small village in Kashan, Persia (Iran), on 20 March 1933. His family members were persecuted for their religion, as their father was a well-known Muslim teacher who became a Bahá'í. In 1953 he left Iran for the Persian Gulf region to spread the Bahá'í teachings. He resided in several different countries, serving on a variety of Local and National Spiritual Assemblies for more than 30 years. He was with the Hand of the Cause of God 'Amatu'l-Bahá Rúḥíyyih Khánum on her visit to Kenya and Ethiopia in 1968. She later advised him to go to Sudan, and in 1975 he pioneered to that country with his family, living and serving there until 1997. That year, the Universal House of Justice recommended that he and his wife Minou go to Uganda to serve as custodians of the House of Worship in Kampala. They served there for five years before his death. He was buried on the grounds of the House of Worship.

FADL'ULLÁH ÁSTÁNÍ SH<u>Í</u>SH<u>V</u>ÁN

On 2 January 2003, in Bukittinggi, Indonesia.
Fadl'ulláh Ástání was born to a Bahá'í family on 21 March 1917, in <u>Sh</u>í<u>sh</u>ván, Azerbaijan. In 1944 he married Lamieh Ahmadpour-Milani, and together the couple raised four daughters. Active as a Bahá'í while pursuing a career in medicine, he served on the Local Spiritual Assembly of Márá<u>gh</u>ih, Iran, from 1949 to 1955 and also founded a hospital in the city. In 1955, he pioneered to Indonesia with his wife and their four children. After two years in the country, he was elected to the Regional Spiritual Assembly of the Bahá'ís of Southeast Asia. His Bahá'í services and his work as a physician developed concurrently. He helped to establish a number of Bahá'í study classes, children's classes, and summer schools in both Padang and Bukittinggi and was instrumental in forming the Local Assemblies in Sigli, Padang, and Bukittinggi. He was also appointed director of the city health services and director of the public hospital in Sigli. Dr. Ástání was in charge of surgery in both the military and the public hospitals in Sigli, Padang, and Bukittingi and was decorated with medals of appreciation and certificates of achievement from the directors of the hospital in Padang. He received other commendations for his services to the people of Indonesia, including those from the Commander-in-Chief of the military and the Deputy Minister of Defense; he was also appointed as Professor Emeritus for anatomy at Universitas Andalas. Because of his reputation in the medical profession, he developed a good relationship with government authorities that aided the Bahá'í community when its members were harassed or censured during the 37-year period when the Faith's activities were restricted. After his death, the Universal House of Justice recalled his "magnificent example of unswerving conviction to the service of humanity."

BARBARA RUTLEDGE SIMS

On 24 April 2002, in Tokyo, Japan.
Barbara Helen Rutledge was born on 17 April 1918, in San Francisco, California, the United States. She was a third generation Bahá'í and lived in several communities in Southern California in her early years, but felt a strong desire to travel to another country. She married Charles A. (Sandy) Sims, who was not a Bahá'í but had been born and raised in Japan. This, combined with encouragement from Hand of the Cause of God Agnes Alexander, led her in December 1953 to pioneer to Japan, the country where she would dedicate the rest of her life to advancing the Bahá'í community. Although she found work with the US government, life was difficult in a country still recovering from the ravages of war. She was elected to the Local Spiritual Assembly of Tokyo in 1954, and in 1957 to the first National Spiritual Assembly of North

East Asia. In 1974, she was elected to the first National Spiritual Assembly of Japan, serving on that body until 1993. Her other services to the community included volunteering in the national Bahá'í office and the Bahá'í Publishing Trust, and helping to develop the national archives of Japan. She also authored books about the history and development of the Faith in Japan, Macau, South Korea, and Taiwan, and published her memoirs. In its message after her death, the Universal House of Justice advised Bahá'ís in Japan to hold memorial gatherings in her honor.

GERD STRAND

On 16 December 2002, in Oslo, Norway.
Gerd Osmundsen was born on 12 March 1910 in Oslo and became a Bahá'í in 1951. She raised one son with her husband, Oscar Strand. Besides her responsibilities as a wife and mother, her dedication to the Faith was her primary vocation. She served for more than 15 years on the Local Spiritual Assembly of the Bahá'ís of Oslo, on the Regional Spiritual Assembly of the Bahá'ís of Scandinavia and Finland from 1957 to 1962, and later on the National Spiritual Assembly of the Bahá'ís of Norway from 1962 to 1968. She also traveled extensively throughout Norway to teach the Faith, particularly after her appointment as an Auxiliary Board member, a position she occupied from 1968 to 1986. Mrs. Strand was a distinguished public speaker and translator of Bahá'í literature. In 1967, she was granted an audience with King Olav V to present *The Proclamation of Bahá'u'lláh* along with a letter to His Majesty from the Universal House of Justice.

MARIE LOUISE SUHM

On 20 August 2002, in Princeton, New Jersey, the United States.
Born 30 July 1925, Mary Louise Kelsey was raised in a Bahá'í family. With her husband, Richard T. Suhm, she moved to Whitefish Bay, Wisconsin, where they helped to form a Local Spiritual Assembly. Later, she, her husband, and their three-month-old son, the first of their three children, were the first Bahá'ís in Morocco (International Zone). Arriving in Tangier in 1954, they were soon able to form the first Local Spiritual Assembly there. Both Mrs. Suhm and her husband were named Knights of Bahá'u'lláh for their services in Morocco, one of the goal areas of the Ten Year Crusade. They stayed until 1956, when Mrs. Suhm contracted polio. The couple divorced in 1976 and she began working at the national Bahá'í center in the US, including a stint as manager of the Office of Pioneering from 1977 until 1987. She also went to Taiwan in 1988–89 to teach the Faith there. After her death, the message of the Universal House of Justice stated that her "sacrificial service will be long remembered."

URSULA VON BRUNN

On 6 April 2003, in Bolivia.

Ursula Klauss was born 21 October 1917 in Bell, Germany. In January 1943 she married Eberhard von Brunn, an army surgeon, who went missing in action in 1944. The couple had one daughter. Though Mrs. von Brunn had been raised by a Christian minister, she was impressed by the Faith in her encounter with it at public talks by Hands of the Cause of God Dr. Adelbert Mühlschlegel and Dr. Hermann Grossmann. She declared her belief in April 1952. In June 1953, she attended an international Bahá'í conference in Stockholm, where Shoghi Effendi's call for pioneers to virgin territories was read, and after seeking advice from Dr. Grossmann she decided to go to Wyk in the North Frisian Islands. There, she lived a simple life dedicated entirely to spreading the teachings of the Faith. As the first Bahá'í to settle in Wyk, she was appointed as a Knight of Bahá'u'lláh by Shoghi Effendi. She eventually had to return to the mainland, where she worked as chief secretary in a public library. She served on the Local Spiritual Assembly of Tübingen and on Bahá'í committees, particularly the Committee of the German Bahá'í Publishing Trust. In 1967, she was able to join her daughter and son-in-law in Bolivia, where they had pioneered some years earlier. There, she learned Spanish and worked as a secretary while spending much of her time teaching the Bahá'í Faith and assisting the community. In its message after her passing, the Universal House of Justice wrote of her "exemplary courage" and "devoted and selfless services."

SEYMOUR WEINBERG

On 6 February 2003, in Denver, Colorado, the United States.

Seymour Weinberg became a Bahá'í in the 1940s as a young soldier and served the Bahá'í Faith through his writings, public presentations, and other outreach efforts. With his wife, Cynthia, he pioneered to Thun, Switzerland, in 1960 for two years. The couple later relocated to Colorado, where he rendered services to both the Bahá'í community and the wider public. He worked as an auditor for the state of Colorado and was credited with developing and instituting accounting policies and practices that helped restore major government programs affecting the elderly. Although he suffered from many physical ailments during the last months of his life, he shared hundreds of copies of his articles on the Faith, as well as the US National Spiritual Assembly's statement on the destiny of America, with the medical personnel who assisted him. In its message after his passing, the Universal House of Justice wrote of the "adamantine faith and irrepressible zeal [that] characterized his deeds in the teaching and administrative fields."

FIROOZEH YAGANEGI

On 27 April 2002, in Vientiane, Laos.
Firoozeh Mehraban Bidenjeri was born on 14 February 1919 in Yazd, Persia (Iran). She embraced the Faith as a child, after attending Bahá'í moral education classes. She married Soroosh Forood Yaganegi in April 1935, in Pune, India, in the first Bahá'í marriage in the city. In 1941, she left with her husband and children as pioneers to the south of India, where they were the first Bahá'ís in Bangalore. Together with Lakshminarayan Reddy and her husband, Mrs. Yaganegi was one of the first Bahá'ís to start mass teaching of the Faith in that region of the country. She was elected to first Local Spiritual Assembly of the Bahá'ís of Bangalore in 1942. She later moved to the village of Sait Palyam and Karianapalya, where she served on the Local Spiritual Assembly until 2001. As the chairperson of the village council, she was instrumental in starting the village school and took special interest in promoting women's education, encouraging parents in the village to send their daughters to school. She had an excellent command of the Kannada language and traveled regularly to teach the Faith. Her home was open to every Bahá'í who visited the area and was used for many Bahá'í activities, including her moral education classes for children and youth. She and her husband eventually donated their property to the Bahá'í community, and it was used as a site for Bahá'í educational institutions. With her husband, who died in 1991, she had eight children, all of whom she actively encouraged to spread the Faith in other countries. In 2001, she moved to Laos, and passed away there a year later.

Statistics

GENERAL STATISTICS	
Worldwide Bahá'í population	More than five million
Countries/dependent territories where the Bahá'í Faith is established	191 countries/ 46 territories
Continental Counsellors	81
Auxiliary Board members	990
National/Regional Spiritual Assemblies	182
Local Spiritual Assemblies	10,344
Localities where Bahá'ís reside	More than 100,000
Indigenous tribes, races, and ethnic groups represented in the Bahá'í community	2,112
Languages into which Bahá'u'lláh's writings have been translated	802
Publishing Trusts	33

Geographic Distribution of Local Spiritual Assemblies by Continent

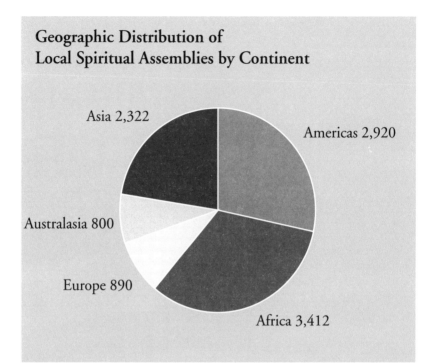

Asia 2,322

Americas 2,920

Australasia 800

Europe 890

Africa 3,412

Number of National and Regional Spiritual Assemblies

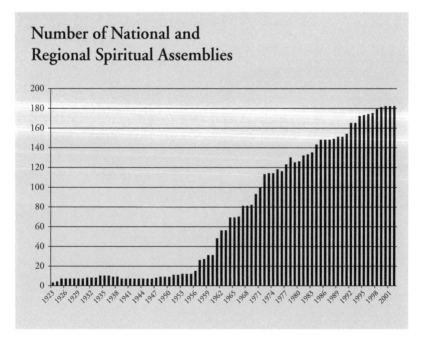

Social and Economic Development

Bahá'í development activities fall into three general categories. Whether initiated by Bahá'í institutions, individuals, or groups, these projects contribute to a global process of learning about a Bahá'í approach to social and economic development.

ACTIVITIES OF FIXED DURATION

Most Bahá'í social and economic development efforts are fairly simple activities of fixed duration in which Bahá'ís in villages and towns around the world address, through the application of spiritual principles, the problems and challenges faced by their localities. Activities either originate in the Bahá'í communities themselves or are responses to invitations from other organizations. It is estimated that in 2002–03 there were more than 2,500 endeavors of this kind, including tree-planting and clean-up projects, health camps, workshops and seminars on such themes as race unity and the advancement of women, and short-term training courses.

SUSTAINED PROJECTS

The second category of Bahá'í social and economic development consists of approximately 500 ongoing projects. The vast majority are academic schools, while others focus on areas such as literacy, basic health care, immunization, substance abuse, child care, agriculture, the environment, or microenterprise. Some of these projects are administered by nascent development organizations which have the potential to grow in complexity and in their range of influence.

ORGANIZATIONS WITH CAPACITY
TO UNDERTAKE COMPLEX ACTION

Certain Bahá'í development efforts have achieved the stature of development organizations with relatively complex programmatic structures and significant spheres of influence. They train human resources and address problems of local communities and regions in a coordinated, interdisciplinary manner. Also included in this category are several institutions—especially large schools—which, although focusing only on one field, have the potential to make a significant impact. In this category there are currently 45 such organizations.

Directory

Associations for Bahá'í Studies

Argentina
Centro de Estudios Bahá'ís
Otamendi 215
1405 Buenos Aires
Argentina

Australia
Association for Bahá'í Studies
173 Mona Vale Road
Ingleside NSW 2101
Australia
E-mail:
  secretariat@bnc.bahai.org.au

Brazil
Association for Bahá'í Studies
Rua Dom Pedro II, 1641
CP 233
90,000 Pôrto Alegre
Brazil

Chile
Asociación de Estudios Bahá'ís
Casilla 3731
Santiago 1
Chile

Colombia
Asociación de Estudios Bahá'ís
Apartado Aéreo 51387
Santa Fé de Bogotá DC
Colombia
E-mail: bahaicol@colombianet.net

East, Central, and Southern Africa
Bahá'í Studies Association
PO Box 42846
Nairobi
Kenya

Ecuador
Asociación de Estudios Bahá'ís
c/o Peter Newton
Apartado 1142
Cuenca
Ecuador

English-Speaking Europe
Association for Bahá'í Studies
27 Rutland Gate
London SW7 1PD
United Kingdom
E-mail: nsa@bahai.org.uk

Francophone Europe
Association d'Études bahá'íes
45 rue Pergolèse
F-75116 Paris
France

German-Speaking Europe
Gesellschaft für Bahá'í Studien
c/o Markus Mediger
Wirichsbongardstr. 40
52062 Aachen
Germany
E-mail: medi@gi.rwth-aachen.de

Ghana
Association for Bahá'í Studies
PO Box AN 7098
Accra-North
Ghana

Honduras
Association for Bahá'í Studies
Apartado 71 c/o Stover
La Ceiba
Honduras

India
Association for Bahá'í Studies
c/o Professor M.D. Teli
Flat 16, New Building
Mumbai University's UDCT Campus
Matunga-400 019
India
E-mail: absindia@bom5.vsnl.net.in

Japan
Association for Bahá'í Studies
c/o Jane Nishi Goldstone
Banberu 603
2-8-4 Momijigaoka
Fuchu-shi, Tokyo
Japan

Malaysia
Association for Bahá'í Studies
4 Lorong Titiwangsa 5
Setapak 53000
Kuala Lumpur
Malaysia
E-mail: nsa-sec@nsam.po.my

New Zealand
Association for Bahá'í Studies
PO Box 21-551
Henderson
Auckland 1231
New Zealand
E-mail: natsec@nsa.org.nz

North America
Association for Bahá'í Studies
34 Copernicus Street
Ottawa, Ontario KIN 7K4
Canada
E-mail: abs-na@bahai-studies.ca

Persian
Association for Bahá'í Studies in
    Persian
596 Upper Sherman
Hamilton, Ontario L8V 3M2
Canada

Puerto Rico
Asociación de Estudios Bahá'ís
c/o Dr. Cesar Reyes
Chemistry Dept.
University of Puerto Rico
Mayaguez 00680
Puerto Rico

Spain
Asociación de Estudios Bahá'ís
Matias Turrión 32
ES-28043 Madrid
Spain
E-mail:
    aen.secretaria@com-bahai.es

Trinidad and Tobago
Association for Bahá'í Studies
PO Box 755
Port of Spain
Trinidad, West Indies
E-mail: nsabahaitt@wow.net

Venezuela
Association for Bahá'í Studies
Apartado 934
Barquisimeto, Edo. Lara, 3001-A
Venezuela
E-mail: dwitzel@sa.omnes.net

West Africa
Association for Bahá'í Studies
c/o Farhang Tahzib, Secretary
PO Box 2029
Marina-Lagos
Nigeria
E-mail: ngrbahai@hotmail.com

Zambia
Association for Bahá'í Studies
c/o Mr. Vahdat Alavian
Box 51170
Lusaka
Zambia

Bahá'í Publishing Trusts

Argentina
Editorial Bahá'í
  Indolatinoamericana (EBILA)
Otamendi 215
1405 Buenos Aires
Argentina
E-mail: ebila@ciudad.com.ar

Australia
Bahá'í Publications Australia
173 Mona Vale Road
Ingleside NSW 2101
Australia
E-mail: bpa@bahai.org.au

Belgium
Maison d'Editions Bahá'íes
205 rue du Trône
B-1050 Brussels
Belgium
E-mail: meb@swing.be

Brazil
Editora Bahá'í do Brasil
Caixa Postal 198
Mogi Mirim, SP
13800-970
Brazil
E-mail: editbahai@mogi.com.br

Cameroon
Bahá'í Publishing Agency of
  Cameroon
PO Box 145
Limbe
Cameroon
E-mail:
  niazbushrui@globalnet2.net

Côte d'Ivoire
Maison d'Editions Núr
08 BP 879
Abidjan 08
Côte d'Ivoire
E-mail: asnci@aviso.ci

Fiji Islands
Bahá'í Publishing Trust
PO Box 639
Suva
Fiji Islands
South Pacific
E-mail: nsafiji@connect.com.fj

Germany
Bahá'í-Verlag
Eppsteiner Strasse 89
D-65719 Hofheim
Germany
E-mail: office@bahai-verlag.de

Hong Kong
Bahá'í Publishing Trust
c-6, 11th Floor, Hankow Center
1c Middle Road, Tsim Sha Tsui
Kowloon
Hong Kong
E-mail:
    execsec@hkbahais.ecofiz.com

India
Bahá'í Publishing Trust
f-3/6, Okhla Industrial Area
Phase-1
New Delhi 110 020
India
E-mail: bptindia@del3.vsnl.net.in

Italy
Casa Editrice Bahá'í
Via Filippo Turati, 9
1-00040 Ariccia (Rome)
Italy
E-mail: ceb.italia@pcg.it

Japan
Bahá'í Publishing Trust
7-2-13 Shinjuku
Shinjuku-ku
Tokyo 160-0022
Japan
E-mail: nsajpn@tka.att.ne.jp

Kenya
Bahá'í Publishing Agency
po Box 47562-00100
Nairobi
Kenya
E-mail: bpakenya@alphanet.co.ke

Lebanon*

Malaysia*

Netherlands
Stichting Bahá'í Literatuur
Riouwstraat 27
NL-2585 GR
The Hague
The Netherlands
E-mail: nsa@bahai.nl

Niger
Maison d'Editions Fadá'il
BP 12858
Niamey
Niger
E-mail: mef@intnet.ne

Nigeria
Bahá'í Publishing Trust
po Box 2029
Marina 101001
Lagos
Nigeria
E-mail: bptnigeria@yahoo.com

Norway
Bahá'í Forlag
Drammensveien 110-A
N-0273 Oslo
Norway
E-mail: bahaiforlag@c2i.net

Pakistan*

Philippines
Bahá'í Publishing Trust
po Box 4323
1099 Manila
Philippines
E-mail: nsaphil@skyinet.net

---

* Address communication to Bahá'í World Centre, po Box 155, Haifa
31 001, Israel.

Poland
Bahá'í Publishing Trust
ul. Nowogrodzka 18A/4
PO-00-511
Warsaw
Poland
E-mail: nsa@bahai.org.pl

Portugal
Editora Bahá'í de Portugal
Avenida Ventura Terra, No. 1
1600-780 Lisboa
Portugal
E-mail: aen@bahai.pt

Romania
Casa de Editurá și Tipografia
  Bahá'í
CP 124 OP 1
3400 Cluj-Napoca
Romania
E-mail: bahai@mail.soroscj.ro

Russian Federation
Unity Bahá'í Publishing Trust
PO Box 288
198 013 St. Petersburg
Russia
E-mail: unitybpt@mail.wplus.net

South Africa
Bahá'í Publishing Trust
PO Box 288
Worcester 6849
South Africa
E-mail: bpt@bahai.org.za

South Korea
Bahá'í Publishing Trust
249-36 Huam-Dong
Yongsan-gu
Seoul 140-190
Korea
E-mail: nsakorea@nuri.net

Spain
Arca Editorial
Joan d'Austria, 95-97, 5ª 1°
ES-08018 Barcelona
Spain
E-mail: edibahai@arrakis.es

Sweden
Bahá'íförlaget AB
Solhagavägen 11
SE-163 52
Spånga
Sweden
E-mail: forlaget@bahai.se

Taiwan
Bahá'í Publishing Trust
3/F, #149-13 Hsin Sheng South
  Road
Section 1, Taipei 106
Taiwan
ROC
E-mail: bpt@ms38.hinet.net

Uganda
Bahá'í Publishing Trust
PO Box 2662
Kampala
Uganda
E-mail:
  bahai@spacenetuganda.com

United Kingdom
Bahá'í Publishing Trust
4 Station Approach
Oakham
Leicestershire LE15 6QW
England
E-mail: bpt.enquiries@bahai.org.uk

United States
Bahá'í Publishing Trust
415 Linden Avenue
Wilmette, IL 60091
USA
E-mail: bpt@usbnc.org

Miscellaneous Addresses

Association médicale bahá'íe
c/o Mirabelle Weck
26 rue de Paris
F-78560 Paris
France

Bahaa Esperanto-Ligo (BEL)
Eppsteiner Strasse 89
D-65719 Hofheim
Germany
E-mail: bahaaeligo@bahai.de

**Bahá'í Association
for the Arts**
Dintel 20
7333 MC
Apeldoorn
The Netherlands
E-mail: bafa@bahai-library.org
Web: http://bahai-library.org/bafa

**Bahá'í Computer and
Communications Association**
c/o New Era Communications
Attn: Don Davis
5 Ravenscroft Drive
Asheville, NC 28801
USA
E-mail: bcca-cc@bcca.org
Web: http://www.bcca.org/

Bahá'í Health Agency
27 Rutland Gate
London
SW7 1PD
United Kingdom

**Bahá'í International Community,
Haifa Offices:**
• Secretariat
• Office of Public Information
  PO Box 155
  31 001 Haifa
  Israel

E-mail: opi@bwc.org
Web: http://www.bahai.org/,
http://www.onecountry.org/, and
http://www.bahaiworldnews.org/

**Bahá'í International Community,
New York Offices:**
• United Nations Office
• Office for the Advancement of
  Women
• Office of the Environment
  866 United Nations Plaza
  Suite 120
  New York, NY 10017-1822
  USA
  E-mail: bic-nyc@bic.org
  Web:
  http://www.bic-un.bahai.org/

**Bahá'í International Community,
Geneva Office:**
• United Nations Office
  Route des Morillons 15
  CH-1218 Grand-Saconnex
  Geneva
  Switzerland
  E-mail: bic@geneva.bic.org

**Bahá'í International Community,
Paris Office:**
• Office of Public Information
  45 rue Pergolèse
  F-75116 Paris
  France
  E-mail: opiparis@club-internet.fr

Bahá'í Justice Society
PO Box 79684
Houston, TX 77279
USA
E-mail:
info@bahaijusticesociety.org
Web: http://www.bahaijustice.org/

Bahá'í Medical Association of Canada
931 Beaufort Avenue
Halifax, Nova Scotia B3H 3X8
Canada

Bahá'í Office of the Environment for Taiwan
149-13 Hsin Sheng South Road
Section 1, Taipei 10626
Taiwan
E-mail: tranboet@asiaonline.net.tw

European Bahá'í Business Forum
c/o George Starcher, Secretary
35 avenue Jean-Jaurès
F-73000 Chambéry
France
E-mail: ebbf@ebbf.org
Web: http://www.ebbf.org/

European Bahá'í Youth Council
45 rue Pergolèse
F-75116 Paris
France
Web: http://new.ebyc.org/

Health for Humanity
415 Linden Avenue, Suite B
Wilmette, IL 60091-2886
USA
E-mail: health@usbnc.org

International Environment Forum
c/o Sylvia Karlsson
Sigmund Freudstrasse 36
D-53127 Bonn
Germany
E-mail: ief@bcca.org
Web: http://www.bcca.org/ief

Hong Kong Bahá'í Professional Forum
C-6, 11th Floor, Hankow Center
Middle Road, Tsim Sha Tsui
Kowloon
Hong Kong

Institute for Studies in Global Prosperity
866 United Nations Plaza
Suite 120
New York, NY 10017-1822
USA
E-mail: info@globalprosperity.org
Web:
    http://www.globalprosperity.org/

Mottahedeh Development Services
Bahá'í Unity Center
2370 Wesley Chapel Road
Decatur, GA 30035
USA
E-mail: mdssed@msn.com
Web: http://www.mdssed.org/

World Community Foundation
315 West 70th Street
Suite 14C
New York, NY 10023
USA

Selected New Publications
in English

The Devotional Meeting

Wendi Momen. Oxford: George Ronald, 2003. 224 pp.

Examines hosting of devotional meetings as a means to spiritualize the life of an individual and a community. It includes sections on an individual's devotional life, Bahá'í Houses of Worship, how to plan devotional meetings, use of music and the arts, and provides more than 50 examples of devotional meetings from around the world.

Earth Circles: Bahá'í Perspectives on Global Issues

Michael Fitzgerald, ed. Los Angeles: Kalimat Press, 2003. 187 pp.

A collection of spiritual perspectives on current social issues such as globalization, poverty, spiritual search, and the role of women. The book is the fifth in a series that includes *Circle of Unity*, *Circle of Peace*, and *Equal Circles*.

The Emergence of a Bahá'í Consciousness in World Literature: The Poetry of Roger White

Ron Price. Hong Kong: Juxta Publishing, 2003 (e-book). 290 pp.

Discusses Canadian poet Roger White's contribution to literature and his innovations in Bahá'í-inspired art.

Gems of Divine Mysteries

Bahá'u'lláh. Haifa: World Centre Publications, 2002. 82 pp.

The English translation of Bahá'u'lláh's Javáhiru'l-Asrár. (More information about this publication can be found on pp. 103–04 of this volume.)

Human Rights, the UN, and the Bahá'ís in Iran

Nazila Ghanea. Oxford: George Ronald, 2003. 640 pp.

A comprehensive account of the human rights situation of the Bahá'ís in Iran, with documentation from governmental representatives at the United Nations, nongovernmental organizations, the Special Representative appointed to monitor Iran's human rights situation, and the Special Rapporteur on religious intolerance.

Jesus and Early Christianity in the Gospels: A New Dialogue

Daniel Grolin. Oxford: George Ronald, 2002. 560 pp.

A historic look at the time when the Gospels were written and how their traditions were transmitted before they came into the hands of the Evangelists. The book considers major themes of Christianity such as baptism, the Last Supper, the Crucifixion, the Resurrection, and the life of Jesus.

A Journey of Courage: From Disability to Spiritual Ability

Compiled by Linda Bishop, Beverley Davis, Frances Mezei, and Shirlee Smith. Toronto, ON: Nine Pines Publishing, 2002. 160 pp.

A compilation of passages from the Bahá'í writings as well as stories and biographies about people coping with disabilities and transforming adversity into strength. The book is designed to serve as a source of insight and comfort to individuals, families, and health care providers. Includes "A Bahá'í Perspective on Disability," a statement by the National Spiritual Assembly of the United Kingdom.

Minimalism: A Bridge between Classical Philosophy and the Bahá'í Revelation

William S. Hatcher. Hong Kong: Juxta Publishing, 2003. 128 pp.

An application of modern logic to problems in classical philosophy, such as the existence and nature of God, and an attempt to form an empirical/logical approach parallel and complementary to the exegetical study of the Bahá'í writings.

Processes of the Lesser Peace

Babak Bahador and Nazila Ghanea, eds. Oxford: George Ronald, 2003. 288 pp.

A collection of eight essays highlighting developments that are transforming our world into the one envisioned by Bahá'u'lláh. The essays were originally presented at conferences of the Bahá'í Politics and International Law Special Interest Group of the Association of Bahá'í Studies for English–Speaking Europe by academics and practitioners in the fields of international law, the environment, government, and economics.

Overcoming Difficulties

Ginny Tod. Oxford: George Ronald, 2003. 80 pp.

A collection of verses from the Bahá'í writings, with commentary, about the challenges of spiritual growth.

Reason and Revelation: New Directions in Bahá'í Thought

Seena Fazel and John Danesh, eds. Los Angeles: Kalimat Press, 2002. 243 pp.

A collection of essays that explore issues in Bahá'í history and in Bahá'í thought. Volume 13 in the series Studies in the Bábí and Bahá'í Religions.

Sarah Ann Ridgway, First Bahá'í in the North of England

Madeline Hellaby. Oxford: George Ronald, 2003. 112 pp.

The story of a working-class woman, born in the middle of the nineteenth century into a family of cotton weavers, who was the first in her region to embrace the Bahá'í Faith, at that time little known in the West. Part of the Bahá'í Heritage Series.

This Decisive Hour: Messages from Shoghi Effendi to the North American Bahá'ís, 1932–1946

Shoghi Effendi. Wilmette, IL: Bahá'í Publishing Trust, 2002. 192 pp.

Correspondence from the Guardian of the Bahá'í Faith to the American Bahá'ís during the closing years of the first Bahá'í century. It is a revised and updated edition of *Messages to America* and contains letters not included in the previous edition.

To Build Anew: Creating Bahá'í-inspired Enterprises

Don Brown. Sooke, Canada: Paragon-Quest Enterprises, 2003. 207 pp.

Examines the principles, models, and processes essential to launching enterprises that continually improve the quality of human life, nurture the human spirit, and create prosperity through service and virtue.

A Basic Bahá'í Reading List

The following list has been prepared to provide a sampling of works conveying the spiritual truths, social principles, and history of the Bahá'í Faith. It is by no means exhaustive. For a more complete record of Bahá'í literature, see Bibliography of English-language Works on the Bábí and Bahá'í Faiths, 1844–1985, *compiled by William P. Collins (Oxford: George Ronald, 1990).*

Selected Writings of Bahá'u'lláh

The Kitáb-i-Aqdas
The Most Holy Book, Bahá'u'lláh's charter for a new world civilization. Written in Arabic in 1873, the volume's first authorized English translation was released in 1993.

The Kitáb-i-Íqán
The Book of Certitude was written prior to Bahá'u'lláh's declaration of His mission as an explanation of progressive revelation and a proof of the station of the Báb.

The Hidden Words
Written in the form of a compilation of moral aphorisms, these brief verses distill the spiritual guidance of all the divine revelations of the past.

Tablets of Bahá'u'lláh revealed after the Kitáb-i-Aqdas

A compilation of Tablets revealed between 1873 and 1892 which enunciate important principles of Bahá'u'lláh's revelation, reaffirm truths He previously proclaimed, elaborate on some of His laws, reveal further prophecies, and establish subsidiary ordinances to supplement the provisions of the Kitáb-i-Aqdas.

Gleanings from the Writings of Bahá'u'lláh

A selection of Bahá'u'lláh's sacred writings translated and compiled by the Guardian of the Bahá'í Faith to convey the spirit of Bahá'u'lláh's life and teachings.

Writings of the Báb

Selections from the Writings of the Báb

The first compilation of the Báb's writings to be translated into English.

Selected Writings of 'Abdu'l-Bahá

Paris Talks: Addresses given by 'Abdu'l-Bahá in Paris in 1911–1912

Addresses given by 'Abdu'l-Bahá to a wide variety of audiences, in which He explains the basic principles of the Bahá'í Faith.

The Secret of Divine Civilization

A message addressed to the rulers and people of Persia in 1875 illuminating the causes of the fall and rise of civilization and elucidating the spiritual character of true civilization.

Selections from the Writings of 'Abdu'l-Bahá

A compilation of selected letters from 'Abdu'l-Bahá's extensive correspondence on a wide variety of topics, including the purpose of life, the nature of love, and the development of character.

Some Answered Questions

A translation of 'Abdu'l-Bahá's answers to a series of questions posed to Him during interviews with Laura Clifford Barney between 1904 and 1906. The topics covered include the influence of the Prophets on the evolution of humanity, the Bahá'í perspective on Christian doctrine, and the powers and conditions of the Manifestations of God.

Selected Writings of Shoghi Effendi

God Passes By
A detailed history of the first 100 years of the Bahá'í Faith.

The Promised Day Is Come
A commentary on Bahá'u'lláh's letters to the kings and rulers of the world.

The World Order of Bahá'u'lláh: Selected Letters
An exposition on the relation between the Bahá'í community and the entire process of social evolution under the dispensation of Bahá'u'lláh, in the form of a series of letters from the Guardian of the Bahá'í Faith to the Bahá'ís of the West between 1929 and 1936.

Introductory Works

Bahá'u'lláh
Bahá'í International Community, Office of Public Information, 1991.
A brief statement detailing Bahá'u'lláh's life and work issued on the occasion of the centenary of His passing.

Bahá'u'lláh and the New Era
John Esslemont. 5th rev. paper ed. Wilmette: Bahá'í Publishing Trust, 1980.
The first comprehensive account of the Bahá'í Faith, written in 1923 and updated for subsequent editions.

The Bahá'í Faith: The Emerging Global Religion
William S. Hatcher and J. Douglas Martin. Rev. ed. Wilmette: Bahá'í Publishing Trust, 1998.
Textbook providing an overview of Bahá'í history, teachings, administrative structure, and community life.

All Things Made New
John Ferraby. 2nd rev. ed. London: Bahá'í Publishing Trust, 1987.
A comprehensive outline of the Bahá'í Faith.

Most of the books listed above have been published by various Bahá'í Publishing Trusts and are available in bookshops, libraries, or from the Trusts. Please see the Directory on pp. 285–87 for addresses.

Glossary

'Abdu'l-Bahá: (1844–1921) Son of Bahá'u'lláh, designated as His successor and authorized interpreter of His writings. Named 'Abbás after His grandfather, 'Abdu'l-Bahá was known to the general public as 'Abbás Effendi. Bahá'u'lláh gave Him such titles as "the Most Great Branch," "the Mystery of God," and "the Master." After Bahá'u'lláh's passing, He chose the name 'Abdu'l-Bahá, meaning "Servant of Bahá'u'lláh."

Administrative Order: The system of administration as conceived by Bahá'u'lláh, formally established by 'Abdu'l-Bahá, and realized during the Guardianship of Shoghi Effendi. It consists, on the one hand, of a series of elected councils, international, national, and local, in which are invested legislative, executive, and judicial powers over the Bahá'í community, and, on the other hand, of eminent and devoted Bahá'ís appointed for the specific purposes of the propagation and protection of the Faith under the guidance of the head of that Faith, the Universal House of Justice.

'Amatu'l-Bahá Rúḥíyyih Khánum: (1910–2000) Mary Sutherland Maxwell, an eminent North American Bahá'í who became the wife of Shoghi Effendi Rabbání, Guardian of the Bahá'í Faith, in 1937, after which she became known as Rúḥíyyih Khánum Rabbání. ('Amatu'l-Bahá is a title meaning "Handmaiden of Bahá'u'lláh.") She served as the Guardian's secretary during his lifetime and was appointed a Hand of the Cause of God in 1952. After Shoghi Effendi's passing in 1957, she traveled extensively to teach the Bahá'í Faith, consolidate Bahá'í communities, and serve as a representative of the Universal House of Justice at major events.

Arc, the: An arc cut into Mount Carmel in Haifa, Israel, along which the international administrative buildings of the Bahá'í Faith have been built.

Auxiliary Boards: An institution created by Shoghi Effendi in 1954 to assist the Hands of the Cause of God. When the institution of the Continental Boards of Counsellors was established in 1968 by the Universal House of Justice, the Auxiliary Boards were placed under its direction.

Báb, the: The title, meaning "Gate," assumed by Siyyid 'Alí-Muḥammad, Who was the Prophet-Founder of the Bábí Faith and the Forerunner of Bahá'u'lláh. Born on 20 October 1819, the Báb proclaimed Himself to be the Promised One of Islam and announced that His mission was to alert the people to the imminent advent of "Him Whom God shall make manifest," namely, Bahá'u'lláh. Because of these claims, the Báb was executed by order of Náṣiri'd-Dín S͟háh on 9 July 1850.

Bahá'í Era (BE): The period of the Bahá'í calendar beginning with the Declaration of the Báb on 23 May 1844 and expected to last until the next appearance of a Manifestation (Prophet) of God after the expiration of at least 1,000 years.

Bahá'í International Community: A name used generally in reference to the worldwide Bahá'í community and officially in that community's external relations. In the latter context, the Bahá'í International Community is an association of the National Spiritual Assemblies throughout the world and functions as an international nongovernmental organization. Its offices include its Secretariat at the Bahá'í World Centre, a United Nations Office in New York with a branch in Geneva, an Office of Public Information, an Office of the Environment, and an Office for the Advancement of Women.

Bahá'í World Centre: The spiritual and administrative center of the Bahá'í Faith, comprising the holy places in the Haifa-Acre area and the Arc of administrative buildings on Mount Carmel in Haifa, Israel.

Bahá'u'lláh: The title, meaning "Glory of God," assumed by Mírzá Ḥusayn-'Alí, Founder of the Bahá'í Faith. Born on 12 November 1817, He declared His mission as the Promised One of All Ages in April 1863 and passed away in Acre, Palestine, on 29 May 1892 after 40 years of imprisonment, banishment, and house arrest. Bahá'u'lláh's writings are considered by Bahá'ís to be direct revelation from God.

Bahjí: Arabic for "delight." Located near Acre, it is a place of pilgrimage for Bahá'ís which comprises the Shrine of Bahá'u'lláh, the mansion which was His last residence, and the surrounding gardens that serve to beautify the site.

Calendar, Bahá'í: Year consisting of 19 months of 19 days each, with the addition of certain "intercalary days" (four in ordinary and five in leap years) between the 18th and 19th months in order to adjust the calendar to the solar year. Naw-Rúz, the Bahá'í new year, is astronomically fixed, commencing at the vernal equinox (21 March). The Bahá'í era (BE) begins with the year of the Báb's declaration (1844 CE).

Consultation: A form of discussion between individuals and within groups which requires the subjugation of egotism so that all ideas can be shared and evaluated with frankness, courtesy, and openness of mind, and decisions arrived at can be wholeheartedly supported. Its guiding principles were elaborated by 'Abdu'l-Bahá.

Continental Boards of Counsellors: An institution created in 1968 by the Universal House of Justice to extend into the future the work of the institution of the Hands of the Cause of God, particularly its appointed functions of protection and propagation. With the passing of Shoghi Effendi, the Guardian of the Bahá'í Faith, there was no way for additional Hands of the Cause to be appointed. The duties of the Counsellors include directing the Auxiliary Boards in their respective areas, advising and collaborating with National Spiritual Assemblies, and keeping the Universal House of Justice informed concerning the conditions of the Faith in their areas. Counsellors are appointed for terms of five years.

Convention: A gathering called at a regional, national, or international level for consultation on matters affecting the welfare of the Bahá'í community and for the purpose, respectively, of electing delegates to a National Convention, electing members of a National Spiritual Assembly, or electing members of the Universal House of Justice.

Hands of the Cause of God: Individuals appointed by Bahá'u'lláh, and later by Shoghi Effendi, who were charged with the specific duties of protecting and propagating the Faith. (Four individuals were recognized posthumously as Hands of the Cause by 'Abdu'l-Bahá.) With the passing of Shoghi Effendi, there was no further possibility for appointing Hands of the Cause; hence, in order to extend into the future the important functions of propagation and protection, the Universal House of Justice in 1968 created Continental Boards of Counsellors and in 1973 established the International Teaching Centre, which coordinates their work.

Holy Days: Eleven days commemorating significant Bahá'í anniversaries, on nine of which work is suspended.

Ḥuqúqu'lláh: Arabic for "the Right of God." As instituted in the Kitáb-i-Aqdas, payment to "the Authority in the Cause to whom all must turn" (at present, the Universal House of Justice) of 19 percent of what remains of one's personal income after one's essential expenses have been covered. Funds generated by the payment of Ḥuqúqu'lláh are used for the promotion of the Faith and for the welfare of society.

International Teaching Centre: An institution established in 1973 by the Universal House of Justice to bring to fruition the work of the Hands of the Cause of God in the Holy Land and to provide for its extension into the future. The duties of the International Teaching Centre include co-ordinating, stimulating, and directing the activities of the Continental Boards of Counsellors and acting as liaison between them and the Universal House of Justice. The membership of the Teaching Centre comprises the surviving Hands of the Cause and also nine Counsellors appointed by the Universal House of Justice. The seat of the International Teaching Centre is located at the Bahá'í World Centre in Haifa, Israel.

Knight of Bahá'u'lláh: Title initially given by Shoghi Effendi to those Bahá'ís who arose to open specified new territories to the Faith during the first year of the Ten Year Crusade (1953–1963) and subsequently applied to those who first reached the remaining unopened territories on the list at a later date.

Lesser Peace: A political peace to be established by the nations of the world in order to bring about an end to war. Its establishment will prepare the way for the Most Great Peace, a condition of permanent peace and world unity to be founded on the spiritual principles and institutions of the World Order of Bahá'u'lláh and signalizing humanity's coming of age.

Local Spiritual Assembly: The local administrative body in the Bahá'í Faith, ordained in the Kitáb-i-Aqdas. The nine members are directly elected by secret ballot each year at Riḍván from among the adult believers in a community.

Monument Gardens: Beautifully landscaped gardens at the heart of the Arc on Mount Carmel where befitting monuments have been erected over the graves of the daughter and the wife of Bahá'u'lláh, His son who died in prison in Acre, and the wife of 'Abdu'l-Bahá.

Mount Carmel: The mountain spoken of by Isaiah as the "mountain of the Lord." Site of the Bahá'í World Centre including several Bahá'í holy places, the most important of which are the Shrine of the Báb and the Monument Gardens.

National Spiritual Assembly: The national administrative body in the Bahá'í Faith, ordained in the Bahá'í sacred writings, with authority over all activities and affairs of the Bahá'í Faith throughout its area. Among its duties are to stimulate, unify, and coordinate the manifold activities of Local Spiritual Assemblies and of individual Bahá'ís within its jurisdiction. The members of National Spiritual Assemblies throughout the world constitute the electoral college for the Universal House of Justice. At Riḍván 2003, there were 182 National or Regional Spiritual Assemblies. See also *Regional Spiritual Assembly*.

Nineteen Day Feast: The principal gathering in each local Bahá'í community, every Bahá'í month, for the threefold purpose of worship, consultation, and fellowship.

Pioneer: Any Bahá'í who arises and leaves his or her home to journey to another country for the purpose of teaching the Bahá'í Faith. "Homefront pioneer" describes those who move to areas within their own country that have yet to be exposed to the Bahá'í Faith or where the Bahá'í community needs strengthening.

Regional Bahá'í Council: An element of Bahá'í administration between the local and national levels, established at the discretion of the Universal House of Justice in countries where the condition and size of the Bahá'í community warrant. A means of decentralizing the work of the National Spiritual Assembly, a Regional Council may be formed either by election or by appointment, depending on local requirements and the condition of the Bahá'í community. It provides for a level of autonomous decision making on both teaching and administrative matters. In some countries, State Bahá'í Councils perform these tasks within specific civic jurisdictions.

Regional Spiritual Assembly: An institution identical in function to the National Spiritual Assembly but including a number of countries or regions in its jurisdiction, often established as a precursor to the formation of a National Spiritual Assembly in each of the countries it encompasses.

Riḍván: Arabic for "Paradise." Twelve-day festival (from 21 April through 2 May) commemorating Bahá'u'lláh's declaration of His mission to His companions in 1863 in the Garden of Riḍván in Baghdad.

Shoghi Effendi Rabbání: (1897–1957) The Guardian of the Bahá'í Faith after the passing of 'Abdu'l-Bahá in 1921, designated in His Will and Testament as His successor in interpreting the Bahá'í writings and as Head of the Faith.

Shrine of Bahá'u'lláh: The resting place of Bahá'u'lláh's mortal remains, located near the city of Acre, Israel. The Shrine is the holiest spot on earth to Bahá'ís and a place of pilgrimage.

Shrine of the Báb: The resting place of the Báb's mortal remains, located on Mount Carmel in Haifa, Israel, a sacred site to Bahá'ís, and a place of pilgrimage.

State Bahá'í Council: *See* Regional Bahá'í Council.

Tablet: Divinely revealed scripture. In Bahá'í scripture, the term is used to denote writings revealed by Bahá'u'lláh, the Báb, and 'Abdu'l-Bahá.

Ten Year Crusade: (1953–1963) Ten Year Plan initiated by Shoghi Effendi for teaching the Bahá'í Faith, which culminated with the election of the Universal House of Justice during the centenary of the Declaration of Bahá'u'lláh. The objectives of the Crusade were the development of the institutions at the World Centre, the consolidation of the communities of the participating National Spiritual Assemblies, and the spread of the Faith to new regions. See also *Knight of Bahá'u'lláh.*

Universal House of Justice: Head of the Bahá'í Faith after the passing of Shoghi Effendi, and the supreme administrative body ordained by Bahá'u'lláh in the Kitáb-i-Aqdas, His book of laws. The Universal House of Justice is elected every five years by the members of all National Spiritual Assemblies, who gather at an International Convention. The House of Justice was elected for the first time in 1963. It occupied its permanent seat on Mount Carmel in 1983.

Some entries adapted from *A Basic Bahá'í Dictionary*, ed. Wendi Momen (Oxford: George Ronald, 1989).

Index